T0208530

UBERING:
THE "RIDESHARE" STORY

UBERING:
THE "RIDESHARE" STORY

Rafael Fermoselle

iUniverse®

UBERING: THE "RIDESHARE" STORY

iUniverse books may be ordered through booksellers or by contacting:

iUniverse
1663 Liberty Drive
Bloomington, IN 47403
www.iuniverse.com
1-800-Authors (1-800-288-4677)

ISBN: 978-1-5320-9127-8 (sc)
ISBN: 978-1-5320-9128-5 (e)

Print information available on the last page.

iUniverse rev. date: 12/20/2019

Driving UBER in the Washington, D. C. Metro
Rafael Fermoselle, Ph.D.

Dr. Fermoselle is a retired U. S. Foreign Service Officer and author of several books. He has worked in one capacity of another for Uncle Sam for 51 years, including twenty+ years as a contractor for the U.S. Department of Defense. Dr. Fermoselle was a System of Systems Analyst (SOSA) instructor at the Standing Joint Forces Headquarters (SJFHQ-CET/S), at the U.S. Joint Forces Command (USJFCOM), which was tasked with development of Effects Based Operations (EBO). He participated in TASK FORCE IV (Reconstruction of Iraq), in support of the U.S. Central Command (USCENTCOM), in advance of the invasion in 2003, and in the training to stand up SOSA cells at the U.S. Pacific Command (PACOM), U.S. Southern Command (SOUTHCOM), U.S. European Command (EUCOM) and U.S. Northern Command (NORTHCOM) during 2003 and 2004. From 2004 to 2007, he worked at the US European Command (USEUCOM) in Stuttgart, Germany, where he was a member of the SOSA team, and the Strategy, Policy and Assessments Directorate, Effects Assessment Cell. In 2007 he worked at DIA's CNT-4 (counternarcotics), and deployed to Iraq in 2008 as a Senior Social Scientist with the U.S. Army Human Terrain program. In 2009-2010 he authored a book-length paper on *Methodology for Analyzing Insurgency: lessons learned 2002-2008,* for DIA and ODNI. Dr. Fermoselle has taught Intelligence Analysis as an Adjunct Professor in the Criminology Department of George Mason University. He works as a contractor at INSCOM. Dr. Fermoselle's experience in counterterrorism includes several years of experience in clandestine operations in support of national security and law enforcement. His assessment of rideshare in general, and Uber in particular, is a departure from his regular work, but his experience came in handy to truly understand and describe "Ubering" from the inside.

> *Uber**
>
> *Rafael, since your first trip on September 12, 2015, the commitment and service you've provided mean that there's always a quality, reliable ride...*
>
> *You've changed the way the world moves with every trip*
>
> *You've shared over 3 years with us*
>
> *You started on September 12, 2015*
>
> *You've shared over 7,800 trips*
>
> *With riders from 51 countries*
>
> *You've driven through 339 sunrises And 1,708 sunsets*
>
> *You've has 4,055 5-star trips*
>
> *And your longest 5-star streak lasted 40 trips*
>
> **And while we can't count all of the things you do**
>
> **The world can always count on you**
>
> *E-mail from Uber, dated 10 May 2019 – 12:45 PM
>
> Note: As of November 2019, I had driven over 9,000 passengers to their destinations.

Contents

Acknowledgements

This tour d 'horizon is based on extensive research and experience *Ubering* for over three years. It involved *"working from the inside"* to get an understanding of the Uber phenomenon. Special thanks to all the people who contributed to my findings and conclusions, including other Uber drivers, who shared their own experiences with me. In one way or another all my passengers contributed to this publication. This book would not exist if it were not for young entrepreneurs like Trevor Cordell Kalanick, Garret Camp, and Dr. Oscar Salazar-Gaitan, who created Uber, as well as company managers who helped to introduce technological advances, and CEO Dara Khosrowshahi and his team, who have continued to make improvements to the Uber app. And they have done it while fighting people and organizations defending the status quo, and hell-bent on blocking a significant contribution to transportation. Uber has expanded transportation for the masses beyond traditional taxi service, with multiple special features, in addition to expanding services to previously underserved areas. The grand vision is not perfect, ride-sharing is affected by multiple challenges in the operational environment, from criminal activity, to unfortunate mishaps that happen unintentionally, unexpectedly, and fortuitously. Uber's future is not assured, but if it fails, it will not be for lack of trying. Special thanks to my cousin Joaquin Fermoselle for helping me edit the manuscript.

BLUF. There are a few creations that have become *"products,"* because they became dominant in the market, and synonymous with an entire product category. Genericized names include Frigidaire, which became synonymous with "refrigerator," Xerox, which became synonymous with "photocopying," and Kleenex, which became synonymous with "tissues." That has been the case with Uber, which has become identical with "rideshare." Despite rapid growth since 2010, Uber has not become profitable, is carrying a cumulative loss of over $15 billion, as of November 2019, and it is doubtful if it will ever become profitable. Despite becoming an "eponym," a key component of the gig economy, and inspiring numerous copycats, there is no guarantee that Uber will be able to generate an adequate return on investment, and remain in business. The concept has fatal flaws that impair its legal soundness. In the end, consumers and society determine if any business succeeds or fails. Government regulations are largely non-partisan, and exist to protect society, the general welfare, and the free enterprise system. Uber and the ride-share concept may be plowed under by regulations that exist to protect the public interest. However, regulations sometimes backfire and cause unintended consequences.

Introduction

It is easy to talk about what you have earned the right to talk about.

Dale Carnegie

Uber is a *"ride-hailing service"* company, headquartered in San Francisco, California. The concept is technically referred to as a *Transportation Network Company* (TNC). *Ubering* is pervasive, and its influence is felt by everyone. The Uber story starts in March 2009, when young entrepreneurs Trevor Cordell Kalanick, Garret Camp, and Dr. Oscar Salazar-Gaitan, created a technology company in San Francisco.[1] Within three years it revolutionized public transportation. The technology, when applied to public transportation, allows people to use their cell telephones to request they be picked up at their location and driven to their destination at reduced fees when compared to traditional taxi service.

The technology allowed for people to share rides (pool) along the way to their destination, thus reducing costs by introducing efficiencies that had not been previously available, because the technology did not exist. After about nine years, Uber has about 73 percent of the market in the United States, is operating in about 66 countries, in about 785 metropolitan areas, and has over 12,000 employees not counting drivers. In London alone, about 45,000 drivers worked for Uber as of November 2019. Nevertheless, it is

---

[1] Dr. Salazar holds a B.S. in Telematics (University of Colima, Mexico), a M.Sc. in Electrical and Computer Engineering (University of Calgary, Canada), and a Ph.D. in Telecommunications from the *Institut des sciences et technologies de Paris* (Paris Institute of Technology). He was the Chief Technology Officer for Uber.

challenging to define the company, and the multiple copycats that have emerged since 2010. In California there are about 14 companies that fall within the definition of a "ride-share" company. Based on published information, as of July 2019, Uber handled between 14 and 17 million rides daily, and about 100 million people are frequent users.

Is Uber a technology company, as company executives claim, *or a transportation company,* as the people affected, and government regulators claim? As has happened throughout history, when new technology is introduced that addresses a need, transcendental changes occur, and the world changes from that point on. Affected parties can fight and complain all they want, but eventually it is impossible to stop *"progress,"* however defined. New technology has always taken a life of its own, and morphed to a point where not even the original creator can recognize the original idea and purpose. Nothing ever stays the same.[2]

Over the years, Uber changed numerous rules. For example, both, drivers and ride requesters can decide to cancel a ride. One of the most annoying things for Uber drivers was to click the app accepting a ride, and after driving for miles to pick up a passenger, the trip was cancelled by the requester, thus wasting gas and time, plus unnecessary wear and tear of the vehicle. Another annoying thing was to arrive at a location to pick up a rider, but they were not ready. Uber partially corrected the problem by charging a nominal

---

[2] As happened in the French Revolution (1793-1794), leaders of the so-called *"Reign of Terror"* executed by guillotine thousands of people suspected of treason to protect the revolution from domestic enemies, but eventually the leaders of the movement ended up going to the guillotine themselves. Among them, George Danton and Maximillian Robespierre. In mid-2017 the Uber Board of Directors removed Trevor Kalanick of the CEO position, due to complaints of mismanagement. Dara Khosrowshahi, the former CEO of Expedia was named to replace Kalanick.

fee after one minute of waiting. (Waiting for a rider to show up in a busy traffic area does not have an easy solution. Cancelling rides impacts driver's income.) Volumes could be written about the imprecise information generated by GPS, which further complicates ride-share, but at the same time GPS is an essential component of the concept.

A driver never knew where he was going until after a passenger had entered the car and the app revealed the destination. Trips can be short with minimal compensation, or as long as over an hour, with substantial compensation.[3] As of December, 2018, some of the rules had changed to overcome driver objections in some of these areas. Nevertheless, there are multiple problems with directions provided by the GPS apps that Uber uses. The level of accuracy is not anywhere close to the degree of accuracy that would be necessary for driverless vehicles to be safe. Based on the multiple mistakes made by GPS applications, driverless vehicles are very far in the future. They could never receive an operating license from any jurisdiction in the United States, with the state of the technology in mid-2019. It would take time for passengers to accept being driven by a computer.[4]

Rarely, a passenger decides to give verbal instructions to the driver about how to reach a destination. In the meantime, the Uber GPS app is blasting away redundant instructions to the driver. When it happens, it is very annoying. Sometimes, the rider does have a better idea about how to reach a destination more efficiently, and drivers need to pay attention. Drivers very often override GPS instructions using their own

---

[3] I experienced an almost five-hour drive one way, with a similar return drive home.

[4] In farming in the U.S. driverless tractors are now in wide use. They are driven through a combination of satellites, GPS, and programming to obtain optimal crop yields while reducing farm labor. But one thing is to operate a tractor in an open field with no one around, and another to operate a driverless vehicle in congested roads with people inside.

knowledge and experience. GPS provides suggestions, while drivers make decisions about the best course of action.

An overwhelming percentage of the riders do not tip, but in some rare occasions the riders that one would least expect hand over a tip, usually about $5, but I received tips of $10 to $20 on a few occasions. In mid-2017 Uber introduced a new feature to the app, which allows riders to add a tip. Afro-American riders, particularly women, tend to tip more often than other riders. In general, Uber clients tend to be well educated and polite. I only recall a few times when teenagers from a wealthy area left behind in the car some trash. Some teenagers can be a royal pain to deal with, but most are well behaved. Considering that I drove thousands to their destinations, these instances of having to deal with spoiled brats did not even reach one quarter of one percent.

The principal problem encountered by drivers are technical in nature, normally associated with the Uber app and GPS instructions. Considering that the company calls itself a "technology" company instead of a "transportation" company, it is significant that technology failures are one of the principal challenges experienced by drivers. However, it does not happen every day that the app suffers some kind of failure. But it happens often enough to figure that driverless vehicles are not about to appear any time soon.

Calling Uber to discuss a problem can turn into a wild frustrating experience. The company uses a phone bank located somewhere in India. The operators tend to be overly nice and super polite, as compared to Americans. *Then the problems start!* They have a heavy accent, do not have a good command of English, most have never visited the United States, and have no idea of what a driver is calling about. For example, explain *"dynamic tolls"* during rush hour in the D.C. Metro on I-66, the Washington Beltway (I-495), or I-95 between D.C. and Quantico, Virginia, to someone who has never been to the U.S. If one has not ever experienced these highways, it is futile to try to explain the issues to a person in India. Technology does not have all the answers. Uber can design an app that can register tolls that are fixed, but I do not see how dynamic tools can be recognized in real time and factored in to Uber rates. The first step to fix these challenges would be to set up a call center in the United States, and that would add additional costs to a company that is yet to make a profit as of November, 2019.

As of 16 September 2019, a new threat to ride-sharing emerged in California, with the enactment of legislation that will force the ride-share sector to put all drivers on a regular payroll and abandon the concept that was started by Uber in 2010. As a result, the cost of a huge payroll, with all the applicable taxes and benefits, operating costs would go up by an estimated 25 to 30 percent. Ride-share companies that have been losing huge amounts of money stand to go out of business. Other states will follow California and enact similar legislation. Over two million people stand to lose the way they have been making a living for several years. The public, particularly the elderly, people with physical handicaps, young people on their way to school and back to their homes, people who have been partying and drinking and want to return home safely, will lose their preferred mode of transportation.

Is Uber a modern-day Unicorn?
**Library of Congress collection, published circa 1607 LC-USZ62-95208
(No known restrictions on publication)**

UBER (As of April 2019)

Chairman: Ronald Sugar
CEO: Dara Khosrowshahi –
Motto: "*We do the right thing*"

Employees: ~12,000 (Not counting drivers, who are self-employed)

Gross Revenue 2017: ~$37 billion
Net Revenue in 2017: ~$7.5 billion
Loss: ~ $4.5 billion

Gross Revenue 2018: ~ $50 billion
Note: Revenue slowed compared to previous years
Net Revenue 2018: ~$11.3 billion (~43% increase)
Loss: ~$1.8 billion (Significant reduction)

Uber operates in over 500 cities in about 60 countries

Source: Based on Uber's release to Bloomberg

> However beautiful the strategy,
> You should occasionally look at the results.
>
> **Winston Churchill**

Uber in The American Milieu[5]

The United States of America has been incredibly resilient, but American society has created such a heavy burden of illogical nonsense that it can no longer handle all the contradictions. The situation resembles the old paradox: *The omnipotent Being that created a stone so heavy that not even the omnipotent Being*

Sisyphus
No known restrictions
on publication.

could lift.[6] While suffering from a superiority complex (We are #1), Americans no longer know what is right or wrong, and cannot meaningfully address the critical challenges associated with the managing the government, the economy, national defense, education, health care, immigration, what goes on in the bedroom, or what goes on in a rideshare vehicle.

The rules have changed under a bizarre *"new normal."* Americans have to redefine how the justice system deals with polymorphous predators, psychopaths, anti-social behavior, violence, and mental disorders. A society has been created in which everything is relative. Everything seems to be the same: right and wrong, ugly and pretty, real and false. Criminals have more rights than their victims, and the actions of some law enforcement officials often resemble those of criminals. The intoxicating atmosphere of *"relativism"* is nothing but

---

[5] Milieu by William-Webster: *The physical or social setting in which people live or in which something happens or develops.*

[6] In Greek mythology, Sisyphus (Σίσυφος), was sent to Hell where he was forced to push a Boulder up a hill, but before he could reach the top of the hill, the boulder would always roll back down, and he had to start all over again.

another excuse to disregard right and wrong. Rideshare drivers have to deal with these conditions every day.

A large segment of society suffers from nihilism. Leftists reject established social conventions, especially morality and religion. Others question objective truth, or believe that there is no objective basis for truth. Right-wingers tell great stories, but most of their "talking heads" never were in the military or worked in law enforcement, or intelligence, and many have never even been overseas as tourists. Yet, they pontificate constantly with absurd extremist views without ever personally doing any of the things they want others to do, as for example, going to war. Too many people make statements without having any idea of what they are talking about. It's best for ride-share drivers to keep their mouth shut during rides.

All of these changes and lack of direction, one could argue, led to the election of Donald John Trump as President of the United States in November 2016. Promising radical changes, starting with: *Making America Great again.* Restoring economic prosperity, returning honesty to government (*Draining the Swamp in Washington*), reducing the size of government, renegotiation of trade deals, controlling illegal immigration, making America energy independent, renovating American infrastructure, removing criminal aliens from the country, reducing taxes, creating incentives for companies to invest in America, thereby creating jobs, establishing tariffs to discourage companies from taking jobs overseas, reducing government regulations, and restoring community safety, to mention the key areas for change. Obviously, not everyone was happy, particularly left-wingers, including key components of the *"Uber generation,"* and the so-called *Uber intellectuals,* and the *annoyingly entitled.*

Uber drivers try to scrape a living while catering to the entitled, and serving investors hoping to make tremendous wealth on the promise that there would be huge profits in the future, while the company has failed to make a cent in profit since it was created. *Nine years without a single cent in profit!* Uber has gone through melodramatic management incidents of mismanagement, sexual harassment of employees, and hiding from the public hacks that have exposed personal information of thousands of riders, and who knows what else. Most people in the country, well over 80%, have never used Uber, and the majority do not even have any idea of what it is all about. Management tells drivers not to complain because they are fortunate that Uber is keeping them from the unemployment line.

Driver Profile

Recruiting qualified drivers is a gigantic challenge. Both, Uber and Lyft, are constantly offering incentives to drivers to help recruit more drivers by offering them monetary rewards. Based on both, my own personal observations, plus conversations with many passengers about their experiences with other drivers, many drivers are unqualified for multiple reasons. For example, an article in *The Washington Post* pointed out that a study conducted by the State of Maryland which started in September 2015, resulted in the dismissal of about 6 percent of Uber drivers for various reasons, including operating with driver's licenses illegally issued by the state to illegal immigrants in violation of Federal legislation.[7]

I visited Uber offices in the D.C. Metro Area multiple times. During each visit, which lasted about one hour, I saw employees dealing with a never-ending flow of drivers or people wanting to drive for Uber. About half of the employees were female, of which only three were white. One was female

---

[7] Faiz Siddiqui, Maryland has booted more than 4,000 UBER drivers for failing the state's screening requirements, *The Washington Post*, 10 April 2017.

and the other two were male. The people at the Uber office were representative of the population of the D.C. Metro Area, where there are a large numbers of ethnic minorities population. The experience resembled a visit to the bizarre Mos Eisley Cantina in the first Star Wars movie... with a down-on-their-luck set of Uber drivers.

The staff resembled the drivers and applicants to become drivers. I did not see a single White driver or applicant, but they do exist. There were two Spanish-surnamed visitors, and three Arab or Middle Eastern visitors.[8] All the rest were Afro-Americans or African immigrants. The information presented here is based on personal experience visiting the D.C. Metro Area office, formerly located by the intersection of 21st and M Streets, N. W. in the heart of the District of Columbia. It then moved to a location outside the city in the Forest Heights area of Maryland, fairly close to Andrews Air Force Base. That area is basically a Black American community, with pockets of immigrant households, for the most part *Hispanics* (Whatever that means... The U.S. Bureau of the Census, originator of the term. Spain is "whiter" than the United States any day of the week, and people with Spanish surnames come in all shades of color, ethnicities, and mixes of ethnicities.) Under this stupid classification, a Dominican of exclusively African ancestors, but with a Spanish surname is a *"Hispanic."* So is a Chinese Cuban, or a

---

[8] Please note that a Spanish surname does not indicate that the individual is necessarily non-white. Spain, Argentina, and Uruguay, for example, are "whiter" than the United States. There are native Americans, people of African descent, Arabs, Chinese, and all kind of people with different degrees of ethnic mixing that are Spanish surnamed. While Mexicans and Central Americans have populations with a heavy presence of "native Americans," Argentina is for the most part composed of Italians, Spaniards, German, Hungarian, British, Irish and other European ethnicities, as well as a larger percentage than the United States of Jewish people, whose families originated in Germany, Eastern European countries, and Russia.

blond Cuban with Spanish grandparents from Northwestern Spain with Irish and German ancestors. The same applies to a Native Americans born in Mexico of exclusively Western Hemisphere/American ancestors without a drop of Spanish blood. They are also "Hispanics."

I visited the Uber office for the DC Metro Area on Minnesota Avenue, in North East Washington in November 2018, after it moved from Forest Heights, Maryland. The drivers and would-be drivers were all Black, and several were African immigrants. I did not see a single White person (whatever that means). A couple seemed to be Middle Easterners. Several spoke with heavily accented English. The staff, as in the past was almost all Black, with the exception of a couple of White males in their twenties. I was helped by a smart and well-educated Black male about thirty years old. He helped me to update my Uber App on my dedicated cell phone, and took notes about a recent nightmare trying to get proper compensation for a ride that included driving on toll roads with EZPass and with dynamic tolls. Two weeks later, nothing happened to correct the problem, but I cannot blame the lack of corrective action on that employee. *How can Uber deal with "dynamic tools" to properly compensate drivers?*

According to published driver profiles, about 37% are White/Caucasian, 18% of drivers are Black/African Americans, 16% are Hispanic/Latino, 15% are Asian or Pacific Islander and about 14% have some other ethnic background or do not want to self-classify. About 24% are over 50 years old. But the bulk of the drivers, or about 30% are between 30 and 39 years old, and an estimated 26% are between 40 and 49 years old. About 48% have college degrees, with an unknown percentage having graduate education. Roughly 28% do not have a college degree. I do not believe these statistics, because they do not match what I have witnessed at Uber offices. This sample of the names of the visitors says a lot:

FIRST NAME OF APPLICANTS
TO DRIVE FOR UBER
(16 December 2016)

Abenet (Ethiopian name)	Fuad (Arabic)	Luis (Spanish)	William
Clovis	Gilberto (Spanish)	Mamadu (West African)	Zakria
Daniel	Girmay	Mohammad (Arabic)	
Diedi	Haily	Monroe	
Earlene	Harrache	Randolph	
Fauntroy	Kathy	Victor	

Most of the drivers I have seen visiting the Uber offices in the D.C. Metro Area are members of a minority group, namely Afro-American males, or immigrants, mostly from Muslim countries in the Middle East and Africa. Most are males. According to published articles, only about 14 percent of the drivers are female. Although published articles claim that drivers tend to be younger than the average taxi driver, the fact is that there are many drivers visiting Uber offices that are older than 50 years of age. Based on conversations with passengers, a large percentage of drivers that they have interacted with in the past claimed to have college degrees. Comparing them to regular taxi drivers, they seem to be better educated. Most of them claim to hold a regular full-time job and only drive Uber part time, namely about 15 hours per week. Only about 20% drive over 35 hours weekly, but some drive as many as 60 hours per week, and Uber is their principal source of income.

There were more than 160,000 active Uber drivers by the end of 2014. ("Active" means that a driver gives at least four rides per month.) Some 120,000 of those drivers had signed up with Uber in the previous 12 months. There are somewhere between 200,000 and 300,000 drivers associated with Uber, but there are indications that there is a very high rate of turnover, which is very costly for any type of business. There are estimates that there may as many as four million drivers. Can this be measured in dollars? Even if there are no formal interviews, it takes time to recruit and process people into the company. Retention is always a high priority for any type for business, including Uber, otherwise the company would not be constantly offering incentive pay to drivers to help recruit new drivers. Yes, Uber drivers are *"outside contractors,"* not direct employees, but that is a scheme to save on payroll taxes and reduce company responsibilities. Any way you look at it, turnover is expensive.[9]

One of the challenges associated with recruiting large numbers of people for unusual employment arrangements is that the system to check on *bona fides* can fail easily. Very often there are no signs to clearly identify a person as a potential troublemaker. For example, Sayfullo Saipov, a legal immigrant from Uzbekistan, was driving for Uber in New Jersey in 2016 and 2017. He shocked Uber and numerous people who knew him when he mowed down eight people on the West Side Highway in New York City. Nobody seemed to have noticed that he had links to Islamic terrorism. This terrorist was described as *"very friendly."*

The laws of probability and *hamartia*[10]

The U.S. population was estimated to total 328,253,956 million as of 5 January 2019. An infinitesimal percentage of

---

[9] I learned on 22 November 2019 that Uber was no longer paying drivers in the DC Metro Area for recruiting other drivers. If the company is no longer paying for referrals, either there is an effort to cut costs, or there is overstaffing in some markets.

[10] Tragic flaw and ironic consequences…leading to catharsis (cleansing).

people are touched by tragedies, but tragedies occur daily, and any of them can become a catalyst for conflict. *A tragedy is: an event causing great suffering, destruction, and distress, such as a serious accident, crime, or natural catastrophe.* Perpetual recidivists, including criminals with some form of mental illness, are allowed to roam freely in the U.S. to continue victimizing innocent people. Uber drivers are exposed to the population, including criminals, the mentally-challenged, and people impaired by alcohol and narcotics. It comes with the job. Everyone in the country is exposed to dangers, but rideshare and taxi drivers suffer a greater exposure due to the very nature of the job dealing with the public. When a driver answers a call on the Uber app, he/she has no idea of what they may encounter.

It only takes a relatively small number of mentally unfit people to produce episodic tragedies. Anybody can make the wrong judgement, misinterpret or misapprehend facts, act based on inadequate knowledge, or simply make a mistake. There is a chain of cause-and-effect tragedies that unfortunately are part of the compass of daily life for over 328 million people. Sometimes the culprit is obvious, unmistakable, and undeniable, but other times it is unclear, obscure, and practically impossible to easily identify who did what to whom, or why. Regardless of the facts, there are demoniacal people who take delight in upsetting the peaceful course of life. Apocalyptic predictions are not justified, but without a doubt something has to be done to stop the tragic never-ending chain of events that are leading to catastrophe. The situation is not just the product of *happenstance* or *happenchance,* or part of a complex plot. It is a large country, and when discipline is not <u>enforced</u>, the possibility of something going wrong happens.

LEADING CAUSES OF DEATH IN THE U.S.

- Heart disease: 635,260
- Cancer: 598,038
- **Accidents (unintentional injuries) 161,374**
- Stroke: 142,142
- Alzheimer's disease: 116,103
- Diabetes: 80,058
- Influenza and Pneumonia: 51,537
- Nephritis, nephrotic syndrome and nephrosis: 50,046
- Intentional self-harm (suicide): 44,965
- **In 2016, there were 15,696 murders, or 43 murders daily**
- As of 2013, the top cities with violent crime were, Flint, Detroit, Oakland, Bridgeport, New Orleans, Cleveland, St. Louis, Jackson, Baltimore. The DC murder rate was back up in 2018 and 2019.

Source: Center for Disease Control and Prevention, Federal Bureau of Investigation

These facts of life affect Uber, as an American entity. But where is the balance between finding an increasing number of people to drive for Uber, and performing a reasonable background check? Uber is hostage to government systems in place to assist the private sector with background checks, but these systems are not infallible. It is practically impossible to have these systems updated in real time. Geography is a factor. One thing is to perform a serious background check on an applicant in the New York City Metropolitan area, or the Miami Metro area in Florida, and anther completely different situation in Richmond, Virginia, or Kansas City, Missouri. There are 50 states and eight territories, and they may resemble each other, but they are not alike.

The same luck-of-the draw applies to riders. It all depends on chance. Once a rider contacts Uber through the app to request a ride, and provides a credit card for billing purposes the emphasis is on credit worthiness. It is a bridge-too-far to expect Uber to be able to verify in seconds the bona fides of every rider beyond the ability to pay. A good number of them are foreign tourists who speak another language other than

English during their ride. How can a driver know if they are talking a foreign language about their visit to a museum or planning a terrorist attack? What are the chances that a driver may speak the language of the passengers and be able to tell what they are up to?

Ride-sharing and politics

Both, Conservatives and Liberals, find certain aspects of ride-share in general, and Uber in particular, to be representative of their views.[11] For example, Senator Marco Rubio (R-FL) in March 2014, remarked that overburdensome regulations that impede companies like Uber from deploying their innovative business ideas throughout the country without having to fight thousands of battles should be reduced or eliminated. He pointed out that Republicans generally are opposed to unnecessary government red tape. Additionally, he spoke in favor of free-market creative ideas that allow for companies like Uber and Airbnb, to come about.[12]

Uber has been regarded as an example of free market Conservatism, and admired by young Conservatives. They embraced Uber and other ride-share companies and supported them in their battles with left-of-center taxi unions, and local governments controlled by Democrats who support regulations to block the new ride-share companies. RNC Chairman Reince Priebus commented that when legislators over-regulate, they impede new companies from creating innovations, such as Uber. Governor John Kasich of Ohio, a Republican, supports ride-share and has gone as far as

---

[11] Emily Greenhouse. Is Uber Democratic or Republican? *Bloomberg*. 14 January 2015.

[12] David Catanese. Why Marco Rubio's Embracing Uber. *U.S. News and World Report*. 24 March 2014. AP, Sen. Marco Rubio Says Critics of Uber and Airbnb are 'Out of Touch', *Associated Press*. 6 October 2015.

calling policy makers to *"Uberize"* government, as equivalent to bringing private-sector efficiency to the public sector.[13]

Hillary Clinton complained about companies like Uber that rely on contract workers, and the "gig" economy or "on-demand economy" as committing wage theft. She seemed to side with court rulings in California and Florida that ruled that Uber drivers are company employees, not independent contractors.[14] However, not all Democrats agree. New York Democratic Governor Andrew Cuomo publicly supported Uber as one of the great inventions of the "gig" economy, but Democratic New York City Mayor Bill de Blasio has taken the opposite view, and has been openly opposed to ride-share services in the city, sharing the views of the Brotherhood of Teamsters, who are decidedly against the "gig" economy, as a trick to strip workers of their rights.[15]

Travis Kalanick, co-founder of Uber, spoke in favor of President Obama's *Affordable Care Act*, claiming that *"ObamaCare"* helped Uber drivers, adding that the legislation was a boon for entrepreneurs who can start a new business with all the worries linked to lack of access to medical care for themselves and their families.[16] However, he agreed to join President Trump's Business Advisory Council, but was forced to quit by a well-orchestrated social media leftist campaign after President Donald J. Trump on 27 January 2017 put into effect for 90-days an order to suspend immigration and visitor travel to the U.S. from Iran, Iraq, Libya, Somalia,

---

[13] Douglas Ernst. Young Republicans say Uber driver kicked them out of car, taunted 'welcome to the resistance.' *The Washington Times*. 17 July 2018.

[14] Robert W. Wood. Hillary Clinton Disses Uber and On-Demand Economy. *Forbes*. 14 July 2015.

[15] Jared Meyer. Why Hillary Hates Uber: Democrats think attacking the "gig economy" is a winning strategy. *Reason.com*. July 2016.

[16] Steve Benen. Republicans get ready to break up with Uber. *MSNBC*. 17 November 2014.

Sudan, Syria, and Yemen, all majority Muslim countries.[17] The campaign urged people to *#deleteUber*. The anti-Trump campaign included Uber drivers; this happens to include an undetermined number of Muslim immigrants. The council was initially composed of business leaders from Apple, Blackstone, IBM, Disney, GE, GM, Pepsi, Tesla, Uber and Wall-Mart.[18] [19]

Ride-share companies, like Uber and Lyft, have taken actions that show that they are not biased, even though they have taken actions allegedly for the purpose of correcting biases. Drivers – who are independent contractors, and not direct employees of the companies- have shown significant biases. By their actions, they show that management and drivers both suffer from a leftist bias. Some Uber drivers have decided on their own to join the so-called "resistance" to the Trump Administration, and are refusing to provide service to Republican riders. When riders engaged in conversation and it became evident to the driver that the passengers were Republican, they have proceeded to dump them after telling them that Republicans are not welcome. Politically-oriented discrimination is being tolerated by Uber management.[20] Examples:

- Uber and Lyft banned far-right activist Laura Loomer from using their services because she complained about a large number of Muslim drivers. In a string of tweets, she complained that she was late to an

[17] CBS News. Uber CEO slammed for Trump connection after immigrant ban. *CBS News.* 29 January 2017.

[18] Leslie Hook. Uber chief Travis Kalanick quits Trump business Council. *Financial Times.* 2 February 2017.

[19] Max Kutner. A Taxi Union takes on Trump Ban, and Uber suffers. *Newsweek.* 31 January 2017

[20] Kelli Ballard. Uber's Message to Republicans: Welcome to the resistance.Libertynation.com. 18 July 2018.

appointment in New York City because she could not find a driver who she did not believe was a Muslim. She complained *This is insanity!*[21]

(Laura Loomer is a journalist, political commentator and alt-right event speaker, who has been censored by Twitter and other organizations for her views.)

- An Uber driver refused to pick up a couple of Black supporters of President Trump when they requested a ride from the Capitol to the Trump International Hotel in Washington, D.C. The Uber driver spotted their MAGA hats and refused them a ride. No information has been published about any punishment by Uber for the driver, who should have been immediately terminated. Since when is political discrimination legal? *Both would-be riders were Black Americans!* Since when is racial discrimination tolerated by Uber? Is it legal for a driver in the District of Columbia to discriminate Afro-American Conservatives? Can they do it to Afro-American Liberals?[22]

  Uber has issued guidelines about what the company will not tolerate from drivers and riders. There are things that can get you banned from Uber:[23]

- Carrying firearms
- Carrying alcoholic drinks in open containers
- Drugs, human trafficking, or the sexual exploitation of children

---

[21] Chelsea Bailey. Laura Loomer Banned from Uber and Lyft after Anti-Muslim Tweetstorm. NBC. 2 November 2017.

[22] Sean Adl-Tabatabai. Black Trump Supporters Are Now Banned from Using Uber. News Punch. 25 July 2018.

[23] Blake Montgomery. 7 things that'll get you Banned from Uber. BuzzFeed news. 8 December 2016.

- Damage to the driver's property, or another rider's property
- Discriminatory comments against religion, national origin, disability, sexual orientation, sex, marital status, gender identity, the age of a driver, or another rider
- Physical attacks- hurting a driver or a rider

Nevertheless, apparently Uber drivers can refuse service to Trump supporters and people with Conservative views without retribution. People are supposed to be sheltered in the U.S. from discrimination, but apparently the left only remembers that when it applies to them, but refuse to grant similar rights to people with opposite political views. Sooner or later, Uber will be hit with a law suit by a Conservative organization or a Conservative individual who is denied service for whatever reason, such as wearing a MAGA hat. *What goes around comes around!*

The curse of the unapologetic autocrat

In June 2017, the Uber Board of Directors decided that Travis Kalanick had to go, and forced him to resign as CEO. Based on published reports, the principal investors (venture capitalists) presented him with an ultimatum: *he had to resign.* They included principal investors in Uber, including the mutual funds company Fidelity Investments, and Benchmark. The details of what went down may never be known, as the participants each have their own personal view of what happened and why. The outcome is what is important.

After taking a brilliant idea from creation to making it a reality allegedly worth billions of dollars, the prime mover failed to properly manage the company. What happened is not unique. Many inventors have come up with brilliant ideas, but later, fail to deliver proper management, and other people have to step in to make needed corrections before the whole thing comes crashing down. The investors accused Kalanick of concealing numerous misdeeds, in what could be summarized as *"the curse of the unfettered autocrat."* [24] [25]

Many brilliant inventors are confident, ruthless manipulators, who never bridle their tongue, because they fear no one. They are *the boss*! However, investors in a company that has never produced a single cent in profit, place their hopes in an eventual initial public offering (I.P.O.) that will generate the highest possible valuation for the company, so that they can recoup their investment and make a profit. Kalanick and Uber had been the subject of a very negative campaign, mostly from Liberals. They never appreciated his alleged links to President Trump. But there were multiple other issues. For example, illegal and improper tactics to undermine Lyft, buying influence by hiring members of the press to counteract critics, and wasting lots of investor's money in self-driving technologies, expansion without proper planning, and

MAJOR UBER NVESTORS*
Axel Springer
Black Rock
Bechtel Ventures
Benchman Capital
Jeff Bezos
Fidelity Investments
First Round Capital
Goldman Sachs
Lowercase Capital
Menlo Ventures
Morgan Stanley
New Enterprise Associates
Qatar Investment Authority
Softbank
Tencent
Venture Hacks
NOTE: This is not a complete list, and it is possible that some of these entities may have backed out.

---

[24] Mike Isaac. Inside Travis Kalanick's Resignation as Uber's C.E.O. *The New York Times.* 21 June 2017

[25] Reuters. Uber investor sues to force former CEO Kalanick off board: Reuters. 11 August 2017.

mistreatment of drivers.[26] [27] Upon Kalanick's demise, Iranian-American Dara Khosrowshahi, the former CEO of Expedia, took over the reins of Uber.

But what is an autocrat? Typically, abrasive leaders have a curse that leads them to transgress their limits of power. That is their principal vulnerability. They lead with a sense of purpose and strength, but these traits do not legitimize authoritarianism. There are people who have never been trained to determine if a leader is an autocrat, and do not have any university degrees that qualify them to categorize someone like Travis Kalanick as one. They may have never met the man, yet, they feel qualified to pass judgement.

I, personally, never met Mr. Kalanick, and do not feel qualified to pass judgement. Keep in mind that some of the wrongdoing and misconduct allegations did not involve him personally, but were linked to other people who worked under him. Perhaps, he employed poor judgement selecting people to work for him. Sexual harassment, racial bias, and bullying, should not be tolerated, and he should have predicted the outcome.[28] [29]

Sometimes things do not go as planned

At its initial public offering (IPO) on 10 May 2019,) Uber management planned to sell about 180 million shares, for between $44 and $50, based on an estimated value of about

---

[26] Sam Levin. Uber's scandals, blunders and PR disasters: The full list. *The Guardian*. 27 June 2017.

[27] Sophie Roberts. Uber Rich – Who is Travis Kalanick and why has he quit as Uber CEO? *The Sun* (UK),3 October 2017.

[28] Reuters. Uber's controversial CEO, Travis Kalanick, could face leave of absence. *Reuters*. 6 November 2017.

[29] Rebecca Blumenstein. Uber CEO Kalanick on Resistance to Uber Around the World. *The Wall Street Journal*. 21 October 2015.

$80 billion.[30] Finally, shares went out at $45, and dropped immediately upon going into the market. About 20 days later the company disclosed that it had lost $1 billion ($1.84 per share) in the first quarter of 2019, although revenue had gone up to $3.1 billion.[31] The market reacted positively and shares went up by 2.6 percent, but continued trading below the IPO price.

Prior estimates of Uber's valuation had fluctuated wildly from about $60 billion to as high $120 billion. Uber management's goal was to raise about $9 billion, based on multiple articles published about the IPO. However, as the performance disclosure at the end of May 2019 indicated, while revenue continued to increase, so were costs. As time passes, it is becoming more difficult to add new riders, and the conflicts with drivers and regulators continue in practically all markets, domestic and international.[32] [33]

Uber management has issued multiple excuses for not producing a profit, from investing in future growth, diversification, to spending on incentives and promotions to retain drivers. There continues to be an absence of a clear path to a profitable future, but not for lack of trying. Since 2009, Uber expanded operations practically all over the world, facing numerous obstacles, multiple legal brick walls, as for example, in Western Europe, and then having to pull back. Uber sold its operations in Russia, and China. Add to the mix numerous internal scandals, which led to the removal of the company's founder in 2017. The search for new ways to earn

---

[30] Kate Gibson. Uber files for what could be the biggest IPO in years. CBS News. Updated 11 April 2019.

[31] Alexandria Sage and Arjun Panchadar. Uber loses $1 billion in quarter as costs grow for drivers, food delivery. *Reuters*. 30 May 2019.

[32] Cathy Bussewitz. Uber looks to raise up to $9B in initial public offering. *Associated Press*. 16 April 2019.

[33] Eric Newcomer. Uber's Self-Driving Arm Gets $1 Billion Investment Ahead of IPO. *Bloomberg*. 18 April 2019.

a profit is without a doubt linked to the inability to earn a profit due to the constant process of trial and error.

Reshuffling of Upper Management

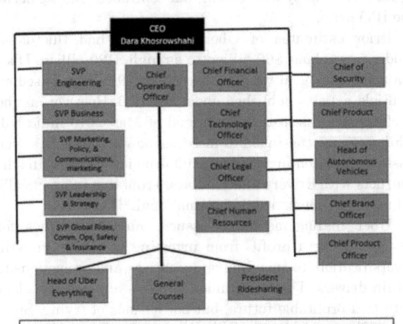

In April 2017, the Uber Board of Directors decided to reshape the company's management structure, after the removal or the former CEO Travis Kalanick, who was replaced by Dara Khosrowshahi. After the IPO in May 2019, the Board once again decided to carry out another shake-up in upper leadership. Marketing, Policy, and Communications were combined under one person. COO Barney Harford, and Chief Marketing Officer Rebecca Messina left the company, after a relatively short period. Andrew Macdonald was promoted to SVP Global Rides, Community Operations, Safety, Insurance, and Uber for Business.

Within a month of the IPO, Uber announced a shake-up in upper management, and a reshuffling of upper level managers. Among the departing managers was the top marketing manager. According to published reports, Uber CEO Khosrowshahi continued a process of "change management," that started as soon as he replaced Trevor Cordell Kalanick.[34] [35]

What Uber needs is someone who understands simple math. You spend $2 to produce something that sells for $1.... You will go out of business sooner or later when your assets run out. You spend $2 to produce something that you sell for $3.... You will continue to survive in the business world. *This is not rocket science!*

Example of "Dumb" ideas that lose money

Earning a "profit" is the basic goal of any business enterprise, including Uber. A profit is the financial gain after paying all costs, including the cost of money, and taxes, that are implicit in sustaining a business activity. It is the money that is gained after paying all the costs of producing and selling goods and/or services. There are some crappy ways to lose money in ride-share, and this story reveals some of them. Sometimes, remedies can be worse than the disease.[36] Uber management should incorporate this thought before they get "creative," and achieve the opposite effect that they had intended.

An example of a dumb idea:

On 12 June 2019, the demand for ride-sharing was very high towards the end of rush hour in downtown Washington,

---

[34] George Bradt. How the Uber Change Agent Survives His Own Change. *Forbes.* 8 June 2019.

[35] Eric Newcomer. Uber Operating, Marketing Chiefs Leaving in Leadership Shake-Up. Bloomberg. 7 June 2019.

[36] Quote from Francis Bacon (1561-1626), 1sr Viscount St. Alban, English philosopher, statesman, and member of the British Parliament from 1584 to 1617. Bacon is best known for his promotion of the empirical "scientific method," regarded as the foundation of modern scientific inquiry.

D.C. Uber was offering as much as \$4 extra to drivers if they accepted any new ride. To further entice drivers to continue working, Uber shut down temporarily a feature of the app that allows drivers to select a destination, as a way of searching for riders who are heading in that same general direction.

Unable to set a direction using the feature in the app, I had to turn off the system, and head home. I am sure that I was not the only driver who decided to turn off the system because the app feature was not available. Why did I do that?

I had started my work day at 6 a.m. in my regular work as a defense contractor, and turned on the Uber app after completing my 8-hour shift at about 2:00 p.m. By 7:30 p.m. I had completed several ride-sharing drives, and wanted to find a place to go to the bathroom, and go home for dinner and rest. It had been a long day. Normally, I would set my destination on the Uber app, and most of the time I could pick up a rider or two going in my same general direction: home.

However, Uber had turned off the app function in an apparent attempt to keep drivers working, as the demand for rides was unusually high, and in addition, Uber was paying an incentive of about \$4 dollars extra per ride accepted and completed. I had experienced the same issue about a couple of days before. I did not notice that when the "set destination" function was grayed out; the system would not work.

I accepted a ride near the intersection of 16th Street and Columbia Road, N.W., and to my surprise, the passenger was actually going about 14 miles to North East Washington, which was exactly in the opposite direction of my intended direction South West of the city, across the Potomac River to Virginia. I completed the ride, and thankfully, I found a McDonald's restaurant where I could go to the bathroom after I dropped off my passenger. I realized that the app was not working well. I turned it off, and went home.

Once again, I encountered the same problem on Wednesday, 12 June, after working a total of about 13 hours, between my two jobs. As a result, I reduced my potential income for the day, as I could not pick up a passenger going towards my home, and Uber actually lost a driver that would have been available at a point where there was a huge demand for ride-sharing services. Multiply that across the board, and the bottom line for both, drivers and Uber, were negatively affected. Passengers looking for a ride were affected, and they may have used another service provider.

Uber management apparently does not understand, as they should, that drivers have to go the bathroom, and sometimes they have to eat, or complete a long work day. The intended consequences of their strategic move turning off the app, had the opposite result. After about nine years without turning a cent in profit, Uber management should weight their actions to consider potential unintended consequences of their "brilliant" ideas.

I called the Uber hotline as I drove home, to alert them of the result of their actions, and without a doubt my experiences were not unique. First, after they answered my call, the choices given did not clearly show a link to the reason why I was calling, but I found a way to talk to a caseworker. She was very nice, polite, and interested in my comments, but she was obviously not a native speaker of English, and I had to explain my predicament about three times using a different approach before she understood the point I was trying to make. She took note, and told me that she would pass up my comments.

The following day, using my computer at home I went to the Uber site, and looked up my record for the week. I could see my results for Monday, Tuesday, and Thursday, in minute detail, trip by trip. However, the record for the Wednesday in question only showed that I had made about $44, and the details were missing... Obviously, someone was reviewing the record. Uber does follow up on calls and evaluates these situations reported by drivers. I don't know if they actually learn from the experience, or simply dismiss suggestions.

Rider profile

The D.C. Metro area has a large presence of foreign-born residents and visitors for multiple countries. First, there are 177 diplomatic missions represented in Washington, D. C. In addition, there are numerous international organizations. Among them, the Inter-American Defense Board, Inter-American Development Bank (IDB), International Monetary Fund (IMF), Organization of American States (OAS), Pan American Health Organization (PAHO), and the World Bank. These organizations, as one would expect, employ thousands of foreign diplomats, and employees of international organizations.

The city attracted an estimated 21.3 million visitors in 2015, of which an estimated two (2) million were foreigners, excluding Canadians and Mexicans.[37] It is estimated that every visitor (including foreign tourists) generates about $333 in expenditures, including about $65 in tax receipts, of which about $36 goes to local government. Each visitor generates about $183 in wages to people working in the tourism sector.

The U.S. Government, employs thousands of naturalized and cleared American citizens in national defense jobs. For example, the 16 intelligence agencies, commonly referred to as the Intelligence Community (IC), employs hundreds of interpreters and translators fluent in Arabic, Chinese, Farsi,

---

[37] D.K. Shifflet & Associates; *Travel Market Insights, National Travel & Tourism Office,* U.S. Department of Commerce. Data about foreign visitors is generated by the required I-94 Survey of International Air Travelers form that foreigners are required to file complete. The data is released annually by the U.S. Dept. of Commerce.

French, German, Italian, Portuguese, Russian, Spanish, Turkish, and multiple African languages, to mention only a few. Many of these naturalized American citizens are in uniform, as members of the U.S. Armed Forces. Others work as civilian contractors or as Civil Service employees.

It should not be unexpected that Uber drivers in the D.C. Metro would drive people of all ethnic groups and nationalities around town. Based on a visual observation of the hundreds of Uber drivers and applicants that visit company offices, a large percentage are themselves foreign born. It is impossible to tell how many of them may be illegally present and working in the United States, despite legislation that burdens employer with checking the status of all applicants and their eligibility to work.[38] I do not recall Uber asking me about my status in the country, and in multiple visits to the Uber regional office for the DC Metro Area, I always noticed that a large percentage of the visitors seeking employment or drivers already employed were foreign born. However, remember that Uber drivers are self-employed freelancers and do not

---

[38] As in many other areas, the U.S. government provides contradictory guidance to employers. The EEOC tells employers that they *"should not ask whether or not a job applicant is a United States citizen before making an offer of employment. The Immigration Reform and Control Act of 12986 (IRCA) makes it illegal for employers to discriminate with respect to hiring, firing, or recruitment or referral for a fee, based on an individual's citizenship or immigration status."* Employers, are required to *"verify the identity and employment eligibility of all employees hired after November 6, 1986, by completing the Employment Eligibility Verification (I-9) Form, and reviewing documents showing the employee's identity and employment authorization. The law prohibits employers from rejecting valid documents or insisting on additional documents beyond what is legally required for employment eligibility verification (or the Department of Homeland Security (DHS) Form I-9), based on an employee's citizenship status or national origin."* Obviously, these government directives are contradictory... Employers are told one thing by EEOC, and they are directed to do the opposite by IRCA!

work directly for the company. There is no employer-employee relationship.

The fact that many Uber drivers are foreign born and fluent in foreign languages presents an interesting situation. They can listen to passenger conversations and unless they disclose that they can understand what is being said, the passengers have no idea that their conversations are being monitored by the driver.

RIDERS FROM AT LEAST 40 COUNTRIES

Algeria	**El Salvador**	**Mexico**
Argentina	E. Guinea	Moldova
Armenia	Egypt	Mongolia
Australia	Ethiopia	Morocco
Austria	France	Nepal
Bangladesh	Georgia	Netherlands
Belarus	Germany	New Zeeland
Bolivia	Ghana	Nigeria
Brazil	Guinea	Pakistan
Bulgaria	**India**	Philippines
Burkina	Iran	Singapore
Faso	Ireland	Syria
Canada	Ivory Coast	S. Korea
Chile	Israel	Sudan
China	Japan	Thailand
Colombia	Kazakhstan	UK
Congo	Kuwait	
Egypt	Malta	

Countries highlighted indicate that significant numbers have been recorded using Uber by the author. Foreign passengers from all countries were not recorded due to language issues that prevented communications, or other circumstances that were not conducive to starting a conversation. According to

Uber records (May 2019), I drove people from 51 countries to their destination.

Tricksters or ingenious businesspeople?

Are Uber managers cunning tricksters or ingenious businessmen? Uber management tried to present the company as a "technology" provider, not as a "transportation" company. That theory was the basis for establishing a special relationship with drivers as independent businessmen, instead of as employees. However, Uber has expanded to provide other transportation services, including the rental or electronic scoters and bicycles, as well as delivery services. Creativity and daring may not necessarily turn Uber into a profitable company. How can Uber management continue to defend the notion of a "technology company," when in fact it is engaging increasingly in transportation? Rental of e-scooters, e-bikes, food delivery, helicopter rides from downtown in large cities like Sao Paulo and New York to airports, research on driverless vehicles.... *If it quacks like a duck, walks like a duck, has feathers like a duck.... Looks like a duck... It is bound to be a duck!*

Uber has made large investments in the development of an autonomous-car and related technologies. There is widespread competition in this area, with multiple companies trying to come up with the appropriate technology. After driving over 9,000 riders, and experiencing problems with the GPS apps used by Uber, I can attest that the technology is far from reaching a safe and reliable way of taking riders to their destinations without a driver. Driverless vehicles are a big con game, but Uber is not alone, and casualties are mounting, making it more difficult for regulators to authorize driverless vehicles on the road. It would be better to let vehicle manufacturers fight it out, and then purchase the best product. Using the purchasing power of buying a fleet to obtain a large discount from a successful manufacturer makes more sense than trying to produce a self-driving vehicle.[39]

Self-driving vehicles face considerable experiments, because it is a "number's game," as much as a technology challenge. There are 50 states and eight territories in the U.S. Each state has a state police, as well as county and municipal police departments, transportation administrations at the state and local levels. In the D.C. metropolitan area alone, there are about 35 police organizations, including the Park Police, FBI and Secret Service uniformed police departments, Capitol Police, Metro Transit Police, D.C. Metropolitan Police, plus the Maryland and Virginia State Police, and at least five county police organizations. They are all entering transportation related information into data bases which may or may not be integrated, and the information is not entered in real time, to be available to an app managing a self-driving vehicle. These vehicles would need to be equipped with cameras with an app similar to "facial recognition" technology, and programmed to recognize multiple perils, from pedestrians, to scooter and bicycle riders, dogs, deer, moose, bears, and even alligators! *The sky is the limit!* Let vehicle manufacturers deal with the challenge and concentrate on getting people to their destination in an efficient way at a reasonable cost.

Violation of company regulations

Company regulations are a basic component of management systems. They are tied to occupational health and safety, avoiding hazards, accident prevention, standardized employee

---

[39] Alistair Barr. One Theory why Lyft, Uber IPOs flopped: Special purpose vehicles. *Bloomberg*. 17 May 2019.

conduct, and established duties and responsibilities, not an abstract concept of self-regulation. Regulations of all kinds have existed for centuries. They imply a rationale to improve efficiency in a fragile environment that if left unchecked, would cause harm. The Uber "rules" cannot be compared with the *Code of Hammurabi*, the Babylonian code of law (c. 1754 BC), or Moses coming down from the mountain to deliver the Ten Commandments to the Israelites on the plains of Moab, as explained in Exodus 20:1-17 and the *Book of Deuteronomy* 5:6-21.

Let me be specific with clear examples of how Uber rules are violated all the time... because drivers have to exercise *"good judgement."*[40] That implies that one is able to weigh options accurately, and figure out all the intimate pros and cons of choices available. The situation could best be defined as *gamming the system:*

Situation A: According to the Uber rules, the person who makes a request for a ride has to be one of the passengers. On Sunday 13 July 2019, I answered a ping on the Uber app, and as I drove to the pickup location, I received a text message and a phone call. I was supposed to pick up a 93-year-old passenger who needs to use a "walker" to get around, and deliver her to St. Agnes Catholic Church, in Arlington, Va. Obviously, the Uber client making the request -*was not going to be in the car* – as I drove the lady to attend Sunday mass. Her son placed the request to Uber, but he let me know the situation. One of her daughters was with her when I arrived. I helped the passenger into the car, folded the walker and put it in the trunk. The daughter did not come for the ride. Once we arrived at our destination, I helped my passenger out, unfolded her walker, and helped her to her on her way.

---

[40] Meaning, the ability to weigh available options accurately. With it comes the ability to imagine all the possible consequences of the choices, both good and bad.

There was no one at the Church to render assistance when we arrived.

Analysis: Drivers violate the Uber rules all the time... Thousands of times daily, husbands and wives request rides for their spouses, and for elderly parents. *That is a clear violation of the Uber rules!* Tolerated violations of rules shape behavior. People are manipulative, and if they can get away with one violation, they will ignore other rules, and find ways to game the system. In addition to using *"good judgement,"* drivers have to accept these trips, or they would never be able to earn an acceptable income. Uber would suffer additional operating losses. Boundaries don't work when they are only enforced some of the time. There has to be consequences when rules are violated. Are there significant potential problems with these cases due to legal and insurance regulations? Possibly. Good judgement means being able to weigh your options accurately. *However, what is the purpose of having rules, if they are violated all the time?*

Situation B. Student credit cards are designed for college students who may have a limited or thin credit history, not for high school students who generally are under 18 years of age. On the same day that Uber had its IPO, I answered a ping, and went to pick up my rider. The pickup point was a multi-million-dollar mansion with its back to the Potomac River, along the Mount Vernon Parkway that goes to George Washington's home in Alexandria Virginia. My passenger was – Nicholas - a teenager, between 16 and 18 years old. He told me that he was a high school student at a prestigious private school nearby. I asked him if one of his parents requested the ride for him, and he told me that he did it himself, and that he had a student credit card linked to his own Uber account. His destination was the Belle Haven Country Club at 6023 Fort Hunt Rd in Alexandria, Virginia. My passenger was on his way to play golf. Was this ride within the "Uber rules?" I opted not to play cop and accepted the ride. During the ride we maintained a conversation, and the young man turned out to be smart and well-educated, but I doubted he was 18 years old. On that particular day the company was facing a strike by some drivers to complain about company practices, as the company staged its IPO. Turning down business would have been like participating in a process to undermine the company, as some drivers in New York City were trying to do!

Analysis. Every day subscribers, Uber management, and drivers engage in *"gaming the system."* This obviously has a negative connotation, while *"working the system,"* has a positive meaning. Both indicate *a significant conflict between theory and practice. According to the rules, parents are not allowed* to call for an Uber (or Lyft) driver to pick up a minor who will not be accompanied by an adult. Technically, the adult who calls for a pickup should be riding in the vehicle. Drivers violate the rules all the time, despite knowing that their accounts could be deactivated. (*Do they really know that?*) Can drivers and Uber afford to reject underage passengers? According to the Uber rules: *Account holders must be 18 or over and CANNOT request a ride for minors unless accompanied by the account holder making the request.* Should schools and school boards allow ride-sharing drivers to pick up minors from schools? Legally, schools are expected to exercise reasonable care for supervising students at dismissal. There is no way to stop all the shenanigans without a serious look by officials at the Federal level, leading to enactment of legislation that is applicable nationwide. That seems to be the only viable alternative, but depending on how it comes out, legislation could cripple rideshare and hurt a lot of people who do not have viable alternatives.

Uber has to either amend the rules, of enforce them as they are. If the rules of the road had been enforced, the company would have gone out of business long ago. That is the dilemma. *A difficult choice has to be made between two*

29

or more alternatives, especially equally undesirable ones. Are the rules as they are mandated by legislation or by insurance requirements, or both? If they are not, it is high time to change them. They should have been changed long ago because they are violated all the time. If they are required, then, the next one out please turn off the lights!

Current GPS technology is not perfect

These are some examples of what I have encountered:

- The app tells me to make a left turn at the next corner, but when I get there, I find that the crossing street is one way, going in the opposite direction.
- I get to the corner, but I find that there is a "No left turn" sign during rush hour between 4 and 7 P.M.
- In the Georgetown neighborhood in Wash. D.C. along the Potomac water front, there are two thoroughfares that are one on top of the other: The Whitehurst freeway on top, and the continuation of K. street N.W. down below. The GPS cannot handle the situation and provides the wrong information to the driver. This happens all the time! The app and the GPS cannot figure out where the client is...
- In Fairfax Virginia, Route 66 runs perpendicular to Gallows road, with a bridge over the highway. About a block from that intersection, there is a Metro rail station. The GPS cannot figure out if a rider wants to be picked up on the side of Route 66, down below, or at the Metro station above. The system runs wild and directs drivers into a convoluted series of instructions that fail to direct the driver to the correct location where a rider is waiting to be picked up. The only solution is to have experienced drivers who have

previously been faced with the problem and learned a lesson or two.

Both, Uber and Lyft, use outside vendors that provide them GPS service. Neither company has an internally-developed GPS system. Companies that are trying to develop driverless vehicles would need to create more advanced and constantly updated GPS systems to avoid challenges similar to the ones I list above. Without a doubt, they would run into the same problems, because in a rapidly changing environment, over huge geographical areas, it is practically impossible to have a data base constantly updated in real time.

Never ending conflicts with drivers

There is a permanent conflict between drivers and companies like Uber and Lyft. Rideshare companies need drivers; they are constantly short of them... and the situation forces them to be always recruiting. They offer considerable incentives to drivers if they recruit their friends to become drivers. The rate of turnover is huge. Conflicts between drivers and rideshare companies have been a fact of life all over the world over whether they are company employees or freelance self-employed contractors. Assuming that the development of an efficient driverless vehicle is successful, without a doubt there would be an explosion of conflicts with the drivers who would be facing replacement by machines.

The public would be concerned about safety, and insurance companies without a doubt would refuse to participate in something that would exponentially increase their exposure. How could they price their policies? For ride-sharing systems, insurance is without a doubt their *Achilles Heel*. It would take years for the public to accept driverless vehicles.

Based on published reports, over two million people have signed up to drive for Uber and Lyft worldwide.[41] If this gig is so bad, why do so many people sign up to be a rideshare driver? On the day before the IPO, a number of Uber drivers staged a heavily promoted strike, mostly in the New York City area. Although the strike did not receive much support from drivers, investors had another reminder that the Uber business model needs thousands of drivers, not a huge turnover rate. Study after study have pointed out that the average driver earns "less than the take-home pay of 90% of American workers.[42] [43] There is no way Uber can make a profit without finding a new and more productive relationship with drivers, leading to a reduction of the high rate of turnover.[44] Uber uses about three million drivers to service an estimated 14 to 17 million riders world-wide daily.

So what?

Are ride-sharing companies like Uber and Lyft selling magic illusions? Promises of future high returns are incredibly risky.[45] [46] Is it possible to carry out a real assessment of the

---

[41] Graham Rapier. Uber and Lyft drivers reveal what they wish they knew before signing up to work for the apps. Businessinsider.com. 3 July 2019.

[42] James Brumley. It's time for some honesty about the Uber stock IPO and why it flopped. Finance.Yahoo.com. 14 May 2019.

[43] Ellen Cranley. Uber and Lyft drivers are planning a massive strike this week over work conditions and pay rates. *Businessinsider.com.* 5 May 2019.

[44] Graham Rapier. A Texas congressman drove for Uber during a legislative recess. Here's what he learned.*Businessinsider.com.* 4 May 2019.

[45] Mike Isaac and Kate Conger. Uber, losing $1.8 Billion a Year, Reveals I.P.). Filing. The New York Times. 11 April 2019.

[46] Brad Stone. On-Demand Startups Are Hemorrhaging Tens of Billions a Year. Bloomberg. 1 April 2019.

value of a rideshare - and rapidly diversifying on-demand company? Can they cut costs to become profitable? The only way these questions can be answered is by collecting and analyzing real experiences of long-term drivers and company employees that can shed light on the real world.

Most of the on-demand companies, regardless of their business areas, have lost large amounts of money while building their name brand, and discovering additional lines of related business opportunities, such as Uber's expansion to food delivery, renting electronic scooters and bicycles, and investing in the development of driverless vehicles. However, rather than producing profits, they may only add serious new liabilities to the already complicated ride-share business.

Uber Chief Financial Officer, acknowledged in an interview with CNBC that they had a tough time. Based on the number of speculators engaging in short-selling, the expectation continues to be for a rough road ahead.[47] [48] But not all assessments are negative. A former GM executive expressed his views on the Uber IPO in a CNBC interview, and claimed that despite a dismal debut, the future is bright for Uber.[49] [50] On 3 July 2019, the NY stock market reached another historical high point. What happened to the Uber shares on that day? They actually went down to $44.11 at closing, on a historical day. After trading for about a month, Uber shares finally closed above the IPO price of $45, on 27 June at $45.13. However, by mid-September, share price was fluctuating between $32 and $34, due to the enactment of

---

[47] Alistair Barr. One Theory why Lyft, Uber IPOs flopped: Special purpose vehicles. *Bloomberg.* 17 May 2019.

[48] James Brumley. It's time for some honesty, op. cit. 14 May 2019.

[49] Berkeley Lovelace Jr. Uber's 'future is bright' despite dismal market debut, says former GM exec Bob Lutz. *CNBC.* 13 May 2019.

[50] Hamilton Nolan. The Stupid Idiot's Guide to the Future of Uber and Lyft. 2 April 2019. https://splinternews.com/the-stupid-idiots-guide-to-the-future-of-uber-and-lyft-1833741006

legislation in California that will force rideshare companies to convert drivers regular employees, the game could very well be over for rideshare companies. After results of 3rd quarter 2019 financial results, Uber shares went down to $27.01 on 8 November 2019. The following pages relate the story of working from the inside in rideshare as a driver.

Thank you for moving the world,

one trip at a time

$500 for you

Rafael, since your first trip on September 13, 2015, you've been there for the early morning pickups, late-night dropoffs, and everything in-between.

We're grateful for everything you've done to help get us where we are. As we move toward a new milestone, we want to thank you.

Right before the IPO, Uber sent bonus rewards to drivers who had been with the company for some time. By 11 April 2019, I had already completed over 7,000 rides. I received a bonus of $500.

Financial Analysis for Drivers

Is driving for Uber a worthwhile side gig? How much money can a driver make with UBER driving full time? It is practically impossible to accurately answer these questions for multiple reasons. There are some obvious costs, and some hidden costs. Gas is an obvious operating cost. Paying the employer and employee Social Security tax, which adds to a little over 15% of gross income is an unknown to unsophisticated and undereducated drivers. Wear and tear and depreciation on the vehicle used is another important cost that a large percentage of drivers are too unsophisticated to figure out. Vehicles depreciate at a much higher rate when they are new, and Uber requires drivers to use vehicles that are less than five years old, whereas taxi companies frequently use dinosaurs for their business. Property taxes are much higher for vehicles used for business rather than personal use. Let's explore some of these items.

Fuel costs

Every gas station is not the same. In the D.C. Metro area, the cost of a gallon of fuel differs widely from one jurisdiction to the next. In Northern Virginia, (Arlington, Alexandria, and Fairfax), the price of a gallon of regular gasoline in December 2016 sold from 2.05^9 at a Sunoco or Liberty gas station, to 2.39^9 at a Shell or Exxon gas station, depending on location. In nearby towns, such as Fredericksburg, Va. the price of gas at a WAWA gas station fluctuated between 2.09^9 and 2.15^9 per gallon. However, even the same brands post a different price at locations that are less than a mile from each other, and within the same local jurisdiction (municipality).

Within the District of Columbia, the price of gasoline sold from about $2.40 to $2.60 or more, due to local taxes and higher real estate costs. In the Maryland suburbs, the price of gasoline differs widely like in Northern Virginia, depending on location. Filling up a Honda Civic or Toyota Corolla with about 12 gallons of fuel costs about $4 to $5 more in D.C. than in Virginia. For the average Uber driver, that translates into about $5.00 more in operating costs daily (or about $35 for a week, and about $140 for a month, and $1,680.00 for a year).

Uber is promoting a Visa Debit Card for drivers that will give them discounts, with up to 4.5% cash back at Exxon and Mobil stations, as well as other discounts, including a 2% cash back at Walmart. What the company does not tell drivers is that Uber would get a small percentage of interests charged by Visa, as well as commissions for the issuance of new cards, without the company increasing its exposure to debts incurred by cardholders.

Vehicle Property Taxes

Every jurisdiction has its own vehicle property tax assessment rules. These are the rules for the Commonwealth of Virginia, as of January 2019. All cities and counties in the state have their own rules for assessing taxes on motor vehicles that are garaged within their jurisdiction. For example, the Arlington County Board set a tax rate for 2018 at $5 per $100 of assessed value of a vehicle, which is based on the *National Automobile Dealers Association Used Car Guide*. Based on the Personal Property Tax Relief Act of 1998 (PPTRA), residents are given a tax relief, but to qualify, vehicles cannot be used more than 50% of the time for business purposes. Uber and other ride-sharing drivers who use their vehicles over 50% of the time for business, are not entitled to tax relief. State and local governments can obtain information on how vehicles are used based on the mileage claimed as a business expense for Federal Income Tax purposes. If more than 50% is used for depreciation as a deduction as a business expense in Federal Income Taxes. This is another factor to consider to figure out the costs associated with driving for Uber.

Conventional fuel vehicles in Arlington, VA, normally receive a 100% tax relief on the first $3000 of the vehicle's value, and 28% relief on the next $17,000 of the vehicle's value, from $3,000 to $20,000. No exemption is granted for the portion of a vehicle's assessed value over $20,000. There are higher exemptions for vehicles equipped to transport physically disabled individuals, and qualifying clean-fuel vehicles. Uber and other ride-sharing vehicle owners who use their vehicle over 50% of the time for business do not qualify for these exemptions. Uber does not inform new drivers about these types of situations, which cuts down on their income.

Traffic fines

Another nightmare for Uber drivers is the proliferation of traffic cameras. For example, within the District of Columbia, cameras are increasing in numbers. Sooner or later everyone will get caught in one. The average cost of a traffic ticket may be around $150.00, which is more than the average Uber driver makes in one day in gross sales. For a large percentage of drivers who depend on Uber to cover basic necessities, such as food and shelter, traffic violations are a very serious issue. It takes time to learn about "camera trap's" that seem to be more designed to produce revenue for the local government than to lower the incidence of traffic accidents.

For example, there are traffic cameras under Washington Circle, in a tunnel on K Street, N.W. in Washington, D.C. There are no interceptions or pedestrians. There are no cross streets. A speed limit of only 25 miles per hour is hard to justify. Drivers who are not aware of the cameras during times when there is hardly any traffic may speed up to 35 or 40 mph or more, and get zapped. A love note will arrive in the mail within days with a traffic fine anywhere from $150 to $400. They sure deter drivers from making the same mistake again. Those in the know slowdown in future trips past that area, with the drivers who are not aware, getting bent out of shape because the car in front of them is not moving fast enough for their taste... when in fact that driver is doing them a big favor, forcing them to slow down and avoid a fine.

Video cameras everywhere

Since the Rodney King incident in 1991, video recordings have played a significant role in law enforcement. In the Ferguson, Dayton, and Staten Island cases, video recordings played a key role in the investigations. However, there are many more instances where recordings have become the detonator for follow-up incidents. For example, a man who appeared to be mentally challenged was handcuffed by police officers from the Antioch Police Department near San Francisco, CA. The detainee was tasered, hit with a baton, and then subjected to an attack by a police dog to the point that the man was left bleeding and in severe pain. Several witnesses began recording the incident with their cell phones. Police officers forced witnesses, to erase their recordings, and confiscated several cell phones. They even pulled a lady out of her car to force her to give up her phone.[51] Technically, police

[51] Alan Wang, Witnesses upset over Antioch arrest, police confiscating cellphones, *ABC 7 News (San Francisco, Oakland, and San Jose)*, 8

need to get a search warrant before they can view recordings from confiscated equipment. Incidents of overkill or brutality have resulted in firings and convictions of police officers, and for that reason, police officers do not want witnesses, particularly recordings that can be entered as evidence in court against them.

Have the cameras reduced police brutality? The issue has not been studied seriously, because it would be necessary to have data or evidence of cases of brutality before the advent of camcorders to answer the question, and such data is not available. It will take several more years before change-over-time assessments can be made.

Different states have different legislation about video recordings, and there are inconsistent interpretations of the Constitution. For example, in New York and Massachusetts, it is legal to record police officers while performing their duties. Nevertheless, numerous witnesses have been arrested for videotaping police in the performance of their duties in both states.[52] Federal courts have sided multiple times with the rights of citizen to record police incidents. The lack of a consistent way of handling these incidents across the country add to the increasing disunity in a country that is called the *"United"* States of America.

Civil Libertarians, the ACLU, left-wing and right-wing groups have objected to law enforcement use of surveillance for a very long time. Video surveillance is supposed to be governed by the Fourth Amendment to the Constitution, and, technically, intelligence and law enforcement agencies must show a court that they have probable cause that there

---

August 2014.

[52] For example, the U.S. Court of Appeals for the First Circuit in Boston ruled that police violated the First Amendment rights of Simon Glik by arresting him for making a cell-phone video of a police arrest, and Glik was awarded $170,000 in damages and legal fees. Adam Cohen, A New First Amendment Right: Videotaping the Police, *Time*, 21 May 2012.

is evidence of criminal activity that can be secured through video surveillance to obtain a search (recording) warrant. The hypocrisy of these groups is that the very technology that they object to has been instrumental in clarifying right and wrong in cases of police brutality. Subversives are always going to protest any means of identifying them before they have an opportunity to carry out their fantasies as revolutionaries through terrorism.

Fourth Amendment rights could be violated by increasing government surveillance, but not using these technologies could result in a repeat of the *big surprise* received on 11 September 2001. Is warrantless surveillance justified or a clear violation of the concept of unreasonable search and seizure? As long as terrorists are unable to carry out a successful attack the public debate will continue, but if they happen to "score big" the opposite public outcry will materialize overnight.

A legislative attempt to place limits on data collection was narrowly defeated in the House of Representatives by 217 to 205 on 23 July 2013.[53] In January, 2014, several Federal judges, members of the Foreign Intelligence Surveillance Court (FISA) unanimously objected to and rejected the notion of an *"independent advocate"* to the FISA court to increase transparency and oversight in reaction to allegations of excesses in domestic and foreign intelligence surveillance programs.[54] After the Ferguson incident and the decision of the grand jury not to indict the police officer who shot Michael Brown, President Obama announced a plan to use Federal funds to provide personal video cameras to police officers all over the country as a way of reducing police misconduct. This

---

[53] Spencer Ackerman, NSA surveillance: Narrow Defeat for Amendment to Restrict Data Collection, *The Guardian*, 24 July 2013.
[54] Ken Dilanian, Secret Surveillance Court Judges Oppose Reform Ideas, *Los Angeles Times*, 14 January 2014.

is typical of left-of-center American politics... *they want to have their cake and eat it too...*

There have been cases of Uber and Lyft drivers handed a suspension or being fired for video-recording their passengers.[55] Unsuspecting riders were recorded without their consent. Uber has banned drivers from broadcasting recordings of riders.[56] Depending on the jurisdiction, recording passengers may or may not be legal. Do riders have a reasonable expectation of privacy? In most states, notice has to be given to riders so that they are aware that anything they say or do can be recorded. In some jurisdictions – Los Angeles, for example – drivers must post a notice on the outside and in the inside of their cars regarding the presence of recording devices. In many jurisdictions all parties have to provide consent to record a private conversation.[57]

Rider scams

When a driver receives a request for a ride through the Uber App, the only information available is the location of the requester, and his or her name. In some cases, information on the number of people is made available, particularly for pool rides. When the driver arrives, the requester may or may not be already waiting, but very often it is necessary to wait until someone shows up. In the old days (two or three years ago), the driver was not compensated for the time wasted waiting for the rider to show up. Now, after a reasonable amount of time, the clock starts ticking and the rider is billed and the

---

[55] Stephanie Gosk. Uber driver suspended after recording, livestreaming passengers. MSN.con. 23 July 2018.

[56] Derrion Henderson. Uber bans drivers from broadcasting recordings of riders. Fox2- St. Louis. 9 November 2018.

[57] A partial list includes California, Connecticut, Florida, Illinois, Maryland, Massachusetts, Montana, New Hampshire, Pennsylvania, and Washington.

driver gets compensated. The passenger has the license plate number, as well as a picture of the driver. The driver has nothing other than the first name and location of the person requesting a ride.

There are scammers who will claim to be "the passenger," and jump into the car. It is entirely possible for a mistake to be made by both, rider and driver, and people do get into the wrong cars, but the mistake is normally sorted out within seconds. The problem are the "scammers" who try to get a ride for nothing, and there are associated safety risks. An exchange of names by drivers and passengers is critical to avoid potentially dangerous situations.

All teenagers are not necessarily "angels" in need of going somewhere. An Uber driver was physically attacked by two teenagers in Las Vegas after they were refused service by the driver. The driver was beaten up, but the incident was recorded by the driver's dashboard camera. Apparently, the reason for the refusal was that they had requested one seat through the UberPool, but there were two of them. The issue was not that they were underage. The driver cancelled the request. The two teenagers were arrested.[58] Drivers are not supposed to be recording passengers!

Minors as passengers

According to Uber policy, a customer must be at least 18 years old to open an Uber account and request rides. It is impossible to really apply this rule, as many minors carry a credit card that is registered to a parent, who provides a copy to their children. Do drivers ask to see the credit card and ID from young people to see if they are over 18 years of age? No. If they did, they could be accused of discrimination.

---

[58] Nicolas Rojas. Las Vegas Uber driver attacked by two teens after refusing their ride. Newsweek. 16 January 2019.

If they did, the incident could turn into an ugly confrontation with the rider and/or their parents. Are drivers going to forgo making some money for the sake of an obscure rule? No.

Parents very often request that their children be picked up at schools, for example. This happens thousands of time every day. Underage passengers use rideshare providers all the time – both Uber and Lyft. There is another Uber rule that is seldom followed. The person requesting a ride needs to be one of the riders. This rule is seldom, if ever, enforced. Neither the driver nor the rideshare company are willing to forego making a buck enforcing this rule – riders are not turned away because a parent asked that their child be picked up at a school and delivered to their home. Very often, a school kid and a couple of friends are picked up at a school and delivered to a home. Very often kids are picked up at their home and delivered to school. *That is reality!* Obviously, there are plenty of possible vulnerabilities with these situations.[59]

Every day parent requests an Uber ride for a child to be picked up by a driver at a school. The child shows up with a couple of friends, whose parents may not even be aware this is taking place. *This is a tricky situation that gets ignored every day!* Should Uber or Lyft drivers pick up and transport minors? There are potential liabilities and insurance problems associated with this situation, in addition to different legal issues depending on location. We have 50 states and eight territories, and they do not agree on multiple legal issues. In the D.C. Metro area, there are three jurisdictions within a few short miles, District of Columbia, Virginia, and Maryland. Technically, ride-sharing drivers

---

[59] Simon Kwok. Should Uber Drivers and Lyft Drivers Pick Up Minors and Underage Passengers? https://ridesharedashboard.com/2018/05/11/Uber-drivers-lyft-drivers-pick-minors-underage-passengers/. 11 May 2018.

should not pick up unaccompanied minors – but this rule is continually violated.

In many cases, minors are picked up as part of an Uber pool ride. What if a child predator happens to be one of the next riders that enters the vehicle? What is the driver's responsibility? What is the ride-sharing company's responsibility? Would they be considered accomplices if a child were to become a victim of a predator? On rejecting a ride through the Uber App, a driver can cancel a trip and note that the reason is that the passenger is underage. But this seldom happens, based on interviews with drivers. These situations are examples of why a dashcam could help to protect both, the driver, the ride-sharing company, and the passengers. *But is it worth a potential life-changing experience for four or five dollars to transport an unaccompanied minor?*

Ride-sharing companies should have a very clear protocol that has to be followed in situations where there is a request to transport an unaccompanied minor – *written and reviewed by attorneys*- and run by local authorities. Insurance companies should be consulted to figure out what kind of coverage, if any, would provide cover for everyone involved. The top vulnerability for drivers and Uber is insurance coverage, and the issue of unaccompanied minors is a particularly difficult subject.

Child restraint and booster seats

The issues related to the use of child restraint and booster seats on ride-sharing vehicles are complicated, and have produced some ugly incidents between drivers and passengers. Seldom does an Uber driver carry a car seat for babies or toddlers. In my experience, most parents bring along and strap their toddlers and babies to their own car seats. Based on published articles, in 34 of the fifty states taxis and rideshare vehicles are "exempted" from requirements to use child restraint seats.

What are the legal requirements? What does Federal Law say on the subject?

- Legislation covering the use of car seats is determined by state – A total of 34 states exempt taxis and ride-sharing vehicles from their child restraint laws, but the rules are not very clear.
- Apparently about 50% of parents use their own seats when they are taking children in an Uber, and the other 50 % do not use them, and take a chance that nothing will happen.
- In the D.C. Metro Area (D.C., Maryland, and Virginia) it is illegal to transport a child who is not in a child restrain seat – *but it happens all the time!*

Select bibliography on the subject of minors and the dangers of riding in an Uber vehicle:

Adam Tuss. Who is responsible for providing car seats in rideshare vehicles? *4Washintton NBC.* 19 November 2018

Adeline Tan. Exclusive: No Grab or Uber for those with young children. *The New Paper* (Singapore). 26 January 2017.

Again: Somali Uber Driver Sexually Assaulted 15-year-old passenger in Colorado. http://www.illegaliencrimereport.com/again-somali-Uber-driver-sexually-assaulted-15-year-old-passenger-in-colorado/14. November 2018.

Bringing Baby in a Lyft, Uber? Child Car Seats Are Rarely included. *Health Day News for Healthier Living.* 9 November 2018.

Darcy Spears. Las Vegas drivers say Uber, Lyft not addressing violations of picking up unaccompanied minors. *KTNV – Contact 13.* 30 October 2018.

Donna Harper. Kidnapping, Carjacking, Terrifying crimes against Uber and Lyft drivers. https://www.clickondetroit.com/news/defenders/kidnapping-carjacking-terrifying-crimes-against-Uber-and-lyft-drivers. 14 May 2018.

Gabriel Samuels. Uber drivers accused of 32 rapes and sex attacks on London passengers over the past year. *Independent*. 19 May 2016.

Neufeld, Kleinberg, & Pinkiert, PA. Uber Drivers and Car Seats. https://Ubercaraccidentlaw.com/Uber-drivers-car-seats/. (Last accessed on 20 January 2019.)

Susannah Bryan. Parents turn to Uber to shuttle kids, even though it is not allowed. *Sun Sentinel*. 23 August 2017.

University Transportation Centers Program, *U.S. Department of Transportation*. Child Safety Seat Usage in Ride-Sharing Services. February 2018.

Analysis of Operating Costs

Driving 35,000 miles may produce a gross income of ~ $35,000.00	The tax deductible of $0.54 pm will shelter about $18,000		COST PER MILE BASED ON 27 MILES PER GALON		Net income before payroll taxes
Annual mileage	Tax deductible $0.54 p/m in 2018 (Deduction went to $0.58 in 2019)	Gallons of gas per mile	Gas cost	Oil change every 5000 miles = 7 oil changes @ $40	Tires, depending on quality last about 35,000 miles
35,000	$18,000.00	1151 gallons x $2.15	$2,474	$280	$600
	Taxable income would be 35,000–18,000= **$17,000**		The fuel cost per year ~ $2472.00, thus $17,000 - $2472=$14,528	$14,528 - $280= **$14,248**	$14,248–4600= **$13,648**

Note: The $0.58 per mile deduction in 2019, is supposed to cover depreciation of the vehicle, gas, and maintenance. In the above case, the driver – who is operating a business – and IS NOT EMPLOYED – by Uber, has a cash flow that may look much better than it actually is, because the vehicle is being depreciated, and eventually it will have to be replaced, without a doubt by a similar car after about three or four years of intensive driving. The residual value will be much less that the initial cost, and due to inflation, a replacement vehicle will cost more.

A gross income of ~$35,000 I in fact be a net of ~$17,000. Uncle Sam is not stupid... allowed depreciation is based on actuarial analysis and the government is not going to lose money by miscalculating actual costs. After subtracting fuel costs and oil changes, the real net income may be closer to ~$13,648. A driver can earn that kind of income working for minimum wages at a fast food restaurant without all the risk associated with driving for a rideshare company.

Analysis of Driver Income (2016)

Period Ending	Hours on line	Number of Trips	Total Payout	Average Gross Income per hour	Average Income per trip
25 July 2016	12.67	27	$251.39	$19.84	$9.31
1 Aug 2016	27.23	55	$575.64	$21.13	$10.46
8 Aug 2016	24.92	38	$483.74	$19.41	$12.73
22 Aug 2016	23.62	38	$454.83	$19.25	$11.96
5 Sept 2016	10.18	21	$192.65	$18.92	$9.17
19 Sept 2016	17	37	$346.50	$20.38	$9.36
26 Sept 2016	7.36	18	$150.71	$20.47	$8.37
10 Oct 2016	19.47	38	$356.32	$18.30	$9.37
17 Oct 2016	14.07	33	$238.35	$16.94	$6.27
24 Oct 2016	10.62	18	$188.28	$17.72	$10.46
31 Oct 2016	10.19	21	$206.70	$20.28	$9.84
7 Nov 2016	6.58	13	$134.19	$20.39	$10.32
14 Nov 2016	26.74	63	$548.87	$20.52	$8.71
21 Nov 2016	21.12	51	$404.26	$19.14	$7.92
28 Nov 2016	6.22	10	$89.17	$14.33	$8.91
5 Dec 2016	19.46	30	$365.26	$18.76	$12.17
12 Dec 2016	9.71	22	$182.22	$18.76	$8.28
17 weeks	267.16	533	5,169.08	$19.34	$9.69

NOTE: To understand the real income per hour it would be necessary to factor in gross income received by the number of miles driven, and then factoring in the $0.54 per mile deductible from taxes, to cover maintenance, fuel cost, and depreciation on the vehicle. Not everyone drives the same type of vehicle, and for that reason all that can be assumed is the average income per mile driven, taking into account the legal tax deduction. The higher the cost of the vehicle the lower the net income to the driver. These calculations are based on the time a driver is actually driving a rider, not the time spent between rides, or the time returning home after the last trip of the day. The actual time working can be substantially higher than the recorded time because wait time between trips fluctuates depending on the time of day, whether conditions, and urban vs rural areas.

What about mileage?

Uber only reported in the *"Tax Summary"* at the end of the tax year the mileage from the point passengers were picked up to the point of delivery. However, that has changed. Uber now reports all deductible mileage from the point the app is turned off to the point it is turned off. Nevertheless, it is advisable for drivers to keep contemporaneous notes of all the mileage on a daily basis. In the event of an IRS audit, contemporaneous notes are the best way to support a tax-deductible claim. Drivers should discuss with a professional tax accountant without waiting for the time when tax returns have to be filed. By then it is too late to do anything about the previous year.

Drivers need to get a notebook and record every day their starting mileage, and their mileage at the end of their work day, and deducting one from the other they can obtain their actual mileage for the day. To do that properly, they need to set up their notebook with the following information:

Date: Starting mileage:

#	Trip	Day income	Weekly income	Mileage at the end of the trip	Time of start	Time at end
1						
2						
3						
4						
5						

Analysis of Driver Income 2017

2017 - Week of	# of hours	Income	Income per hour	# of trips
July 11 - July 17	40 h 15 m	966.32	24.06	89
July 4 - July 10	25 h 52 m	388.78	15.23	46
June 27 - July 3	27h 18 m	610.38	22.45	53
June 20 – June 26	43 h 45 m	1156.66	26.62	92
June 13 – June 19	48 h 3 m	788.83	16.33	92
June 6 – June 12	38 h 51 m	630.34	16.36	65
May 30 – June 5	36 h 9 m	650.53	17.62	67
May 22 – May 29	23 h 49 m	432.93	18.43	47
TOTAL		**$5,624.77**	**157.10**	**551 trips**
8 weeks	~34 trips per week	Average	$19.63 per hour	Average
		$703.09 per week		69 trips per week

NOTE: The averages for 2016 and 2017 did not change by much. Uber implemented some positive changes in 2017, such as charging passengers for excessive waiting time after a couple of minutes of waiting, and cancellation fees for passengers who practically wait until a driver is ready to arrive at their location to cancel a trip. Drivers used to be forced to absorb the cost, despite working with small profit margins.

Wage comparisons

My part time average gross income from Uber during 67 days between Monday and Friday during June, July and August 2017, was $83.02 ($5563 / 67: $83.02). To produce that income, a considerable amount of money had to be spent in the purchase of fuel and two oil changes. Even with a fuel-efficient car like the Honda Civic, mileage dropped to an average of 28 m/pg. from a higher average of at least 31.7 m/pg. I was driving from about 2 p.m. until about 7 p.m. during the afternoon rush hour. My average gross income was $16.60 per hour (83.2 / 5= $16.60).

The wear and tear on the vehicle reduced the value of my car. From the time I accepted a trip to the point where I delivered the rider to his/her final destination, I was totally exposed to insurance coverage provided by Uber, as personal insurance did not cover a driver while driving for business. Although I was surprised with the coverage provided when another Uber driver hit my car resulting in slight damage, I am not sure about liability coverage, and the $1000 deductible which was waived in my case to cover damage to my car for that incident.

There are other factors that affect income driving Uber. First, during summer thousands of tourists visiting the Nation's Capital Area increasing demand for taxi and rideshare service. Tourists are not present in large numbers at other times of the year, with the exception of the approximately three-week period when the *Cherry Blossom Festival* takes place in late March and Early April every year, depending on the peak flowering season, which is affected by weather. Another important factor is that daylight goes from about 6 a.m. to about 9:00 p.m. during the summer, resulting in optimum driving conditions. During winter months daylight is reduced to between 7:00 a.m. and 5:00 p.m. resulting in a negative impact on Uber drivers. People do not enjoy going out during dark winter evenings, and as a result, demand for taxi and drive-share services drops.

My gross income during the week of 1-7 October 2018, was $485.89 in 23hours and 18 minutes, or an average of **$20.96 per hour**. Two weeks earlier, during the week of 17 to 23 September, I earned $246.38 in 12 hours and 41 minutes, for an average income of **$19.85 per hour**. During the week of 20-26 August, I earned $303.38 in 15 hours and 40 minutes, for an average income of **$19.70 per hour**. My average per hour income increased during this two-month period. However, the average price of regular gas in the DC Metro Area went up by about $0.10 per gallon, and the prices were continuing to move up due to a spike in crude oil prices.

As previously explained, there is a big difference between gross and net income.

Other estimates of Uber driver compensation

Multiple estimates have been made of Uber driver compensation in the United States since the company opened for business in 2010. One estimate published in October 2018, claimed that after factoring in vehicle expenses, drivers make less than $10 an hour, which is barely equivalent to minimum wages at the time at the low end of geographic locations in the country.[60] According to this study Uber lures drivers with promises that they can become their own boss and make excellent income. The study estimates that the average driver makes about $14.73 hourly, after factoring in tips, which are seldom provided. They estimate that the average per hour cost of operating vehicles at about $5 per hour, which leaves drivers with about $9.73, and possibly less.

Based on these estimates, drivers working 40 hours weekly would make an estimated gross income of about $31,000. When operating expenses of about $20,000 are factored in, drivers live under the poverty line. In addition, drivers have to pay taxes. Although taxes could be waived because of the low income, other payroll taxes like Social Security and Medicare are levied, regardless of income. And drivers, as self-employed workers, have to pay both, the employee and the employer portion.

Both, my own study, as well as published studies reveal that Uber estimates of driver income of $70,000 to $90,000 annually are a farce. Thousands of drivers are working for

---

[60] Rani Molla. Half of U.S. UBER drivers make less than $10 an hour after vehicle expenses, according to a new study. Recode.net / Ridester. 2 October 2018

minimal net income and exposed to accidents, high insurance costs- provided they can actually get insurance, traffic fines, and crime. A study by the Economic Policy Institute, which apparently may have been sponsored by Uber, estimated average hourly expenses for drivers at about $4.78, which has to come out of the average $16.44 per hour that they estimated drivers make gross on average. The U.S. Bureau of Labor Statistics published its own estimate that taxi and ride-sharing drivers in 2017 made $11.96 per hour. In general, there is a lot of *heifer dust* in these estimates of Uber driver income. There are so many variables, that it is practically impossible to determine net hourly income.

Uber and payroll taxes

Comparing a part time office job that pays $20 per hour with driving Uber, just about any other job comes out ahead. First, as a self-employed person, Uber drivers pay both, the "employee" and "employer" payroll taxes, which otherwise are split in half. The Federal Insurance Contribution Act (FICA) covers Social Security retirement, is shared in equal amounts by both.

Self-employed workers pay both, the 6.2% tax deducted from employees, as well as the employer portion of 6.2%, for a total of 12.4%. To cover MEDICARE, employees pay 1.45% tax, and their employer pays another 1.45% tax, for a combined 2.9% tax on income. In other words, Uber drivers have to pay a total of 15.3% for these payroll taxes. In addition, they pay State and Federal Unemployment Taxes (SUTA and FUTA). The FUTA tax is 0.8%. The SUTA tax depends on each state's rate, as well as the number of employees that file for unemployment. Uber self-employed workers pay the minimum amount, because they obviously do not fire or RIF anybody. In 2017, the Social Security Wage Base was

$127,200. After reaching that income cap, any additional wages are not taxed. Uber drivers do not come even close to making that kind of income, and thus pay these taxes on the totally of their income.

In my case, I collect a Federal pension, as well as Social Security, and earn a full-time income of roughly twice the $57,617 median income in the United States. Regular rideshare drivers do not have that advantage. They end up paying 15.3% of their income in payroll taxes.[61]

$800 x 52 weeks= $41,600.00 Annual income
40,000 miles x $0.54 = **$20,000.00 tax credit**

$21,600.00 income after taxes x 15.2% = $3,283.00 FICA payroll tax= **$18,317 take home income...**

Gas 3 times per week at $20.00 per tank = $60.00 per week
52 weeks x $60.00 = $3120 annual cost of gas

The $0.54 tax deductible includes the cost of gas; In other words, the $20,000 credit for standard deduction includes the recovery of the cost of gas, or $16,880.00 are left to cover oil changes, and other maintenance, plus the actual depreciation of the vehicle. The U.S. Government is not stupid, all the relevant studies have been made to come up with a pretty good estimate that the $0.54 per mile deductible is fairly accurate. Drivers are not making extra money by getting any additional take home money from the deductible. It may look like additional income, but in reality, it is not additional income.

_____

[61] In other words, a person making over a base wage of $127,200 in 2017 pays $7,886.40, which is the cap for the year. A person making $127,200 pays the same as a person making a million dollars. Any income earned above the $127,200 base is not taxed. MEDICARE taxes of $1.45% are paid for the total amount of wage income, without any type of cap. Uber drivers pay both, the employee and employer MEDICARE tax for a combined total of 2.9%.

The challenge of recruiting and retaining drivers

January Unemployment	2011	2012	2013	2014	2015	2016	2017	2018	2019
Percent	9.1	8.2	7.9	6.6	5.7	4.9	4.8	4.1	3.9
Nat'l Average Wage Index In Dollars	42,321	44,321	44,888	46,481	48,098	48,642	50,321		

- The average taxi driver in the U.S. earns on average $17 hourly, as of 28 December 2018, but the range is estimated at about $14 to $21
- UBER claims that UBER drivers earn an average of $19.51 per hour as of 12 December 2018. UBER drivers in the DC Metro are estimated to earn more than 33% above the national average
- LYFT claims that drivers in the DC Metro earn between $15 and $20 per hour, estimated to be about 19% higher than the US national average
- Taxi drivers in the DC Metro are estimated to earn about $38,929 annually
- UBER and Lyft do not take into account that the drivers have to pay their costs from thei gross earnings. They also fail to mention that as self-employed workers, they have to pay both, the employer and employee Social Security Taxes.
- As the level of unemployment is reduced, the incentive to drive for a company like UBER and LYFT is reduced, as there are increasing alternatives for them to earn a living

Both, Uber and Lyft are in a constant recruitment mode, because both suffer from a high rate of turnover. When the compensation is compared to the level of exposure, it is not a surprise that both companies have to be constantly trying to attract new drivers. The riders are exposed to the high risk that their drivers have not been properly vetted or scrutinized to weed out potential nefarious actors who should not be driving around unsuspecting passengers. Although both companies try to carry out due diligence, the possibility that people who should not be driving are hired is relatively high. It is outstanding that with all the possibilities of something going wrong the actual number of nasty incidents is low, based on what gets reported in the news media.

The Concept of "Independent Contractors"

A "brilliant concept" introduced by Uber is a key vulnerability to the future of the company. Drivers, according to the Uber business plan, are independent contractors, freelancers, not company employees.[62] Not only are driveshare companies vulnerable, due to this concept, but the entire so-called "gig economy" is exposed. But what is the "gig economy?"

- *A labor market characterized by the prevalence of short-term contracts or freelance work as opposed to permanent jobs – working in the gig economy means constantly being subjected to last-minute scheduling...*
- *A gig economy is a free market system in which temporary positions are common and organizations contract with independent workers for short-term engagements...*
- *Gig economy definition: an economic sector consisting of part-time, temporary, and freelance jobs*
- *The gig economy gets its name from each piece of work being akin to an individual 'gig' – although, such work can fall under multiple names.*
- *Cambridge English Dictionary defines "gig economy" as:*

A way of working that is based on people having temporary jobs or doing separate pieces of work, each paid separately, rather than working for an employer...

According to an article by Bill Wilson, a business reporter at the BBC News:

Proponents of the gig economy claim that people can benefit from flexible hours, with control over how much time they can work as they juggle other priorities in their lives.[63]

---

[62] Irina Ivanova. Labor Department says gig workers aren't employees. CBS News. 30 April 2019.
[63] Bill Wilson. What is the 'gig' economy" BBC News, 10 February 2017.

A driver, who is an "independent contractor," enjoys a lot of flexibility. The concept is what provides a large number of drivers the possibility to work a full-time job, or go to school, or enjoy retirement while working only a few hours per week as a driver. On the other hand, as already explained in the previous sections, drivers have to pay the payroll taxes of an employer, as well as the taxes levied on employees. For drivers, the concept presents numerous vulnerabilities, as they are not covered by basic insurance, including coverage for accidents on the job, temporary or permanent disability, unemployment compensation, life insurance, or paid time off.

The companies are exposed. Uber is not alone dealing with this vulnerability, as it applies to Lyft and other ride-sharing companies, as well as multiple other business enterprises that apply a similar pattern. Some Uber and Lyft drivers, organized labor, and leftist politicians have fought against the concept everywhere that ride-share has opened for business.

The Supreme Court of California in May 2018, ruled that a test using specific criteria has to be used to determine if drivers are employees or independent contractors. The case, known as *Dynamex v. Superior Court of Los Angeles County.* Dynamex is a Washington State company engaged in courier and delivery services.[64] [65] [66] [67] A key component of the case has to do with the issue of "unfair competition" that companies that use the concept of independent contractors have over other companies that provide regular employment to their workers. They provide standard worker protection to their

---

[64] Andrew j. Hawkins. Uber and Lyft drivers could get employment status under California court ruling. *The Verge.* 1 May 2018.

[65] Cyrus Farivar. New court ruling could force Uber, Lyft to convert drivers to employees. *ARSTechnical.com.* 2 May 2018.

[66] Daniel Wiessner. Uber says recent 9th Circuit ruling undercuts drivers' Dynamex claims. *Reuters.* 20 September 2018.

[67] Noam Scheiber. Gig Economy Business Model Dealt a Blow in California Ruling. *The New York Times.* 30 April 2018.

employees, including minimum wages, and other benefits, and pay all due payroll taxes.[68] According to the California Supreme Court, the relationship between employers and workers can be determined by asking three key questions:

- Is the driver (person) free from employer's control and direction with regard to the performance of the work assigned?
- Is the driver performing work that is outside the usual course of business for the employer?
- Is the driver (person) engaged in an "independent established trade of the same nature of the work being performed for the company (Uber)?

This court decision in California is only valid within that state. Courts in other states, as for example, in New Jersey and Massachusetts, have not ruled in the same way as California. However, what happens in California will spread all over the country.

Another important court ruling came about in September 2018, when the 9th Federal Appeals Court in San Francisco, ruled that Uber can force its drivers into arbitration over pay and benefits disputes. Based on this ruling, Uber drivers are not allowed to join in class-action suits against the company, according to the unanimous ruling of the three-judge court. The decision overturned a prior December 2015 court ruling that had allowed a case to go forward against the company. This decision by the Federal Court of Appeals now prevents drivers to jointly fight in court against Uber, and forces each driver to seek resolutions of conflicts with the company through independent arbitration case by case.

Legal cases of this type are being decided in parallel in other countries where Uber operates. For example, on 18

---

[68] Molly Zilli. Can Uber and Lyft Drivers Get Employment Status Under New CA Ruling. *Findlaw.com.* 8 May 2018.

December 2018, a court in the UK determined that Uber drivers are "workers," in a case brought by a group of twenty-one London Uber drivers against Uber related to paid holidays and minimum wages regulated by law. The Employment Tribunal and the Employment Appeal Tribunal found that the drivers are "workers," not independent contractors, and should be treated as such, during all the time they have their Uber App turned on, and were ready and willing to accept a ride. In a dissenting vote, a judge stated that the drivers should only be treated as workers from the time they accepted a ride to the moment they delivered the passenger to the final destination. The Employment Tribunal granted Uber approval to appeal the ruling to the British Supreme Court, and the company has stated that it plans to appeal to the higher court. If the Supreme Court affirms the ruling of the lower court, Uber and competitors will be in a huge mess.[69]

> **The only advantage Uber might have achieved is taking advantage of its drivers' lack of financial acumen — that they don't understand the full cost of using their cars and thus are giving Uber a bargain.[70]**
>
> **Yves Smith**

---

[69] Karen Plumbley-Jones. Court of Appeal Says Uber Drivers are workers. TheHRDirector.com. 4 January 2019.

[70] Yves Smith. Uber is headed for a crash. *Intelligencer.* 4 December 2012. h

III

The Epiphany

In the first week of August 2019, I had a sudden revelation or insight about driving for Uber. I became conscious of key components of rideshare after conducting considerable research for about three years, and driving over 8,500 passengers to their destinations. The enlightening realization came about while testing ways to reduce costs by shifting to a hybrid vehicle, and acquiring comprehensive insurance coverage to reduce exposure to the unpredictable. It was not a scientific breakthrough, but the result of carrying out a process of innovation seeking profitability for the ridesharing concept. It was a flash of recognition that some of my previous analysis was wrong.

Testing a hybrid for ridesharing

On Saturday 3 August 2019, I purchased a 2019 Honda Insight Touring, a hybrid car. I had put over 155,000 miles on my 2015 Honda Civic Touring. Although the car could have been driven perhaps another 50,000 miles, I decided that I needed to have a more reliable car. I had several questions in mind:

- Do hybrid cars offer something beyond improved fuel economy?
- What are the real costs of operating a hybrid car in driveshare?

- The cost of my new 2019 Honda Insight was about $1000 more than a similar Civic Touring. Was it worth it?

There were some obvious benefits of driving a hybrid: I had fewer trips to a gas station, in addition to savings on fuel cost. I decided to use my new car during the week from Monday 5 August to Sunday 11 August, collecting meticulous records as part of my interest in finding answers to these questions, but several unexpected factors occurred.

It just happened that during that first week, fuel prices plummeted from $2.41 to $2.34 per gallon. As recently as a month before, fuel prices were in the $2.60 range. Because of the decline in fuel price during my test week, it complicated obtaining a clear picture of the savings by driving a hybrid vehicle. However, I keep all kinds of records, and I was able to reconstruct a picture of my experiences since the first of the year.

During the first 15 days of January 2019, I paid around $2.00 per gallon of fuel. During the second half of January, prices started to climb to about $2.15 per gallon. By the middle of February, prices had dropped again to about an average of $2.05 per gallon. However, by the end of February, prices had gone up to about $2.30. By the middle of March, prices had gone up to around $2.45 per gallon. I fueled by car 34 times between 1 January to 30 March, at an average of $2.37 per gallon. During the winter months my driving was somewhat limited due to weather conditions, including shorter daylight, and I prefer not to drive at night.

During the period from April to the end of July I fueled my car 49 times, and the average price had gone up to $2.55 per gallon. As the day light increased, and as Washington became packed with tourists to see the Cherry Blossoms, demand for ride-sharing support increased. By the middle of April, gas prices had climbed to about $2.75, and by the beginning of May they were fluctuating between $2.69 and $2.75.

By the middle of June, the price had declined to about $2.49, and remained at that level through the middle of July, when the price of a gallon went back up to a range between 2.56 and $2.60. During the first week of August, as I was testing my new Honda Insight Hybrid, the price of gas declined sharply to $2.34 by Sunday 11 August.

The price of gas at the pump is tied to the international spot price of crude oil. On 1 August, 2019, the spot market price of crude oil dropped by 8.1 percent in one day. According to analysts, trade tensions between China and the U.S. and other factors, as for example, currency manipulations, and a decline in demand for crude triggered the price drop. Crude oil prices had been steadily increasing since the first of the year, reaching a peak of $66.60 per barrel around the week of 22 April 2019, and then turned around. The price began trading between $53.59 and $60.94 since June. On 2 August, the price was at $55.75 per barrel.

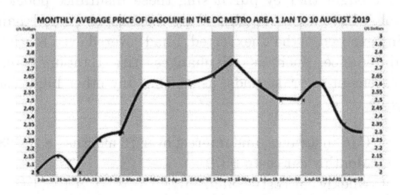

MONTHLY AVERAGE PRICE OF GASOLINE IN THE DC METRO AREA 1 JAN TO 10 AUGUST 2019

Insurance policies against all perils

In addition to purchasing a hybrid to reduce by about half my fuel costs, I decided to spend some more money to purchase extended warranty to protect me from mechanical failure for up to 10 years and/or 100,000 miles, in addition to coverage for all maintenance, including oil changes, tire rotations, and brake pad replacement through a car care service plan. I added "gap insurance" to cover the depreciation of the car in case of an accident. My total insurance package added to a hefty $6,460. I had been fortunate to purchase insurance to cover tire and rim damage for my previous Honda Civic. Twice I had to replace Michelin tires after they were damage in potholes. I would have had to pay around $500 each time had I not had insurance.

INSURANCE PLAN	COST
Platinum Mechanical failure service contract 10 years or 100,000 miles	$2,895.00
Road Hazard Tire and Wheel Coverage	$ 995.00
Total loss protection or gap insurance	$ 895.00
Car care service plan	$1,675.00
Total insurance cost	$6,460.00

I thought that by purchasing these insurance policies I would have a clearer idea of my fixed costs, rather than being exposed to the unexpected. I had covered even routine maintenance, such as oil changes, tire rotations, and replacement of brake pads, as well as any other high-cost repairs.

- Car, insurance, and interest over 72 months= $41,688
- Monthly car cost= $579
- Weekly car cost= ~$144
- Gross income for the week= $654 (Which covered my costs for a month- including when I am not driving Uber! – my regular job as a government contractor is about 20 miles from my home.)

Road Hazard insurance pays

Buying tire and wheel insurance when I bought my new car on 3 August turned out to be a wise move. On Monday 7 October, I turned on my Uber app around 3:00 P.M. I answered a ping and went to pick up a couple of HS students in Alexandria, Va. I delivered them to their homes. Within about five minutes, I answered another ping, but as I drove on US 1 (Richmond Highway) to pick up the passenger, I hit a bump on the road, and blew the back-passenger tire. I pulled to the side of the road and called Honda Road Assistance, which is delivered by AAA. The tow truck driver arrived about one and a half hours later. He confirmed that the back tire had blown as a result of hitting the pot hole, and gave me the bad news that the front tire on the same side had a nasty cut, and should be replaced. He towed my car to a nearby Honda dealership. I showed my insurance papers and both tires were replaced. They only had about 7,700 miles. As tire and auto manufacturers try to increase fuel efficiency by reducing weight, they apparently have reduced tire strength. This was the second time since 2015 in which I had a similar incident. In over 50 years of driving I never had any similar incident until 2015.

I took until 8:00 P.M. to get the tires replaced, too late to continue *Ubering* for the day. This experience points out that it is prudent to purchase this type of insurance. I did not have to pay a cent for towing or the replacement of the tires. Had I not bought insurance; I could have been out of pocket at least $600. Ride-share drivers have to control costs and be covered for unexpected surprises. But how many drivers can afford this type of insurance?

Mileage analysis Monday 5 to Sunday 11 August

My starting mileage for the week was 227 miles on Monday 5 August, and my ending mileage on Sunday 11 August was 1254. My gross mileage for the week was 1027. However, that mileage did not represent only the mileage while driving for Uber. For example, the distance between my home and my place of work at Ft. Belvoir is 22.7 miles. Between Monday and Friday, I drove to and from work for a total of 227 miles, which were included in the total mileage for the week. My estimated net mileage driving for Uber that week was approximately 792 miles.

My fuel costs for the week were considerably lower than with my previous 2015 Honda Civic, which averaged about 29 miles per gallon (MPG). My new hybrid averaged during the week 49.7 MPG.

Date	Amount paid	Odometer miles	Price paid per gallon of gas
Monday 5	$13.00	321	$2.47
Wed. 7	$11.40	545	$2.42
Sat. 10	$15.40	881	$2.36
Sun. 11	$17.00	1260	$2.34
Total cost Of fuel	$56.80	Starting mileage 262 Ending mileage 1254 Total miles driving Uber 800 miles	Average cost of fuel $2.40

Every day I recorded my starting and ending mileage for every Uber event. I did not record my mileage in between trips while I was trolling.

Day	Starting mileage	Ending mileage	Total miles
Monday	262	310	48
Tuesday	344	458	114
Wednesday	493	559	66
Thursday	587	678	91
Friday	712	794	82
Saturday	823	1018	195
Sunday	1058	1254	196
Total miles driving for Uber			792

- I used 16 gallons of fuel while *Ubering* ((792/49.5=16)
- My fuel cost for the week was= $2.40 x 16=$38.40
- My gross income for the week was $654, and my cost was $182. (Cost of fuel and prorated cost of car payment for the week)
- My Federal Tax credit / depreciation, maintenance, and fuel cost @ $0.58 p/mile= 792 x 0.58= $459.36

My gross income for the week derived from driving rideshare for Uber was $654. My allowed tax deduction at $0.58 per mile, for the 792 miles driven amounted to $459.36. Ride-sharing drivers may look at these figures and see an interesting cash flow, apparently sheltered by the tax deductions, but that is a big mistake.

The tax allowance of $0.58 per mile is a credit provided by the Internal Revenue Service (IRS), which is supposed to compensate for the fuel, maintenance, depreciation of the vehicle. The 2019 optional standard mileage rates used to calculate the deductible costs of operating an automobile for business, charitable, medical or moving expenses starting on 1 January 2019 was pegged at $0.58 per mile, up 3.5 cents from the rate for 2018.

The standard mileage rate for business use is based on an annual study of the fixed and variable costs of operating an automobile. (IRS Notice 2019-02)[71] In other words, from a gross income of $654, one subtracts the standard mileage rate according to IRS rules of $459.36, and the net income for the week drops to $194.64. Without a doubt the IRS has carried out considerable research on the actual costs of operating a vehicle for business. They are not in the business of giving money away. The $0.58 per mile represents the IRS's best estimate for the real costs, and if anything, it is a conservative figure. The real costs are bound to be higher.

Drivers can get confused and think that they have a nice positive cash flow from their income driving for Uber. The reality is that the standard mileage deduction allowed by the IRS represent real costs: fuel, maintenance, insurance, and depreciation.

Even if the $654 in gross income is divided by 41 hours of work, the earnings per hour come out to about $15.95. However, that is not real! From the $654 in gross income one should deduct the $459.36 from the IRS gross income, because that figure represents *the true cost of driving for the week*. The actual per hour wages was really $4.74. How is that?

Minimum wage legislation

According to the Fair Labor Standards Act (FLSA), the current minimum wage is set at $7.25 per hour. The minimum wage for federal contractors in 2019 is $10.60 per hour. New York City passed an ordinance requiring ride-sharing companies to pay drivers at least $17.86 per hour. The

---

[71] IRS issues standard mileage rates for 2019. https://www.irs.gov/newsroom/irs-issues-standard-mileage-rates-for-2019 (Last accessed on 13 August 2019)

District of Columbia was the first jurisdiction to cross the $10 threshold among states. The minimum wage was increased to $14 per hour beginning on 1 July 2019, which will be going up to $15 per hour in 2020. Maryland's minimum wage rose in 2019 to $8.25 per hour. Virginia's minimum wage is like the federal rate of $7.25. These figures are superior to the actual wages earned for the week of 5 to 11 August 2019, of only ~$4.74. *Is that a rip off or not?*

Drivers don't know what they don't know

All the Uber mobility options depend on drivers, from rideshare to food delivery, to freight. The drivers have to make a reasonable "profit," as they are not "employees," but independent business owners.

Rideshare drivers, in general, do not have any idea of what their real costs are. As a result, they cannot figure out how much they are really making. They do not have an accurate idea of how much they are making. Those who are leasing their cars are not aware or ignore that there are limitations of how much they can drive their cars. With limitations of no more than 12,000 miles per year, there is no way they can afford to use their car for driveshare. They are exposed to unpredictable vehicle maintenance beyond oil changes, tire rotations, and perhaps replacement of brake pads. They are exposed to damage beyond the normal wear and tear of a normal vehicle. The more miles they put on a car, the greater the damage they can potentially suffer. Insurance coverage is a critical concern for drivers. Generally, drivers are not aware that they have to cover a $1,000 deductible if their vehicles are damaged while their Uber app is turned on. They do not earn enough money to justify the exposure to accidents, which can cause catastrophic damage to their personal finances.

Based on my own experience, as well as published research findings, the median per hour income is somewhere between $14.00 and $16.00 per hour. Because they are paid weekly, and part of their income is sheltered from taxes by the $0.58 deductible per mile, they assume that they are getting a gift from Uncle Sam, but that is far from the truth. That deductible allowed by the IRS is a realistic estimate of what it costs to operate a vehicle for business. They are in fact incurring expenses beyond that amount. A lot of them are not confronted with the reality of having to pay employee and employer Social Security and Medicare taxes, until it is time to file their tax returns by mid-April every year, and by then it is too late. Real income may be closer to around $5 per hour, as I found, based on my own research. Driver earnings satisfaction is very poor, which leads to a high turnover, which in turn increases costs for Uber and competitors. It is estimated that between 25 percent and 50 percent of Uber drivers quit annually. Bottom line, the vast majority of Uber drivers – around 70 percent, are not happy with their earnings. And most drivers don't even know about all the hidden expenses.[72] [73]

So What?

Driveshare drivers do not earn minimum wages, have no benefits, are exposed to accidents which could result in some kind of disability for the rest of their lives, as well as huge financial liabilities. And for all of that, they have to bring along an expensive vehicle, which is something they do not have to do for any other type of low wage employment! And

[72] Ridester Staff. How Much Does an Uber Driver Make in 2019? [The Inside Scoop]. *Riderster.com*. 30 July 2019.
[73] Wylee Post. How long does an average Uber driver wait between fares? Quora 15 December 2018.

the ride-share companies do not have to invest a cent on the fleet of vehicles that the drivers bring to the relationship. All the bonuses offered to drivers are nothing but a gimmick to keep them confused. Local authorities in some jurisdictions, as for example, New York City, have enacted legislation to force ride-share companies to pay drivers minimum wages, and without a doubt, these requirements will spread to other jurisdictions.[74] [75] [76]

[74] New York Uber minimum wage: city passes first minimum wage rate for Uber and Lyft drivers. Vox.com. 5 December 2018.

[75] Peter Holley. New rules guarantee minimum wage for NYC Uber, Lyft drivers. The Washington Post. 4 December 2018. (The rule applies to Uber, Lyft, Via, and Juno)

[76] Nick Gillespie. New York Passes Minimum Wage Law for Uber, Lyft Drivers, Hikes Costs To Riders. Reason.com. 5 December 2018.

• IV •

Crime, Mental Illness, and Ride-Share

Homicides in the United States

When Uber was created in 2009, there were 16,799 homicides across the country, of which 11,493 were carried out with firearms. The murder rate, as well as the rate of violent crime has fallen since then, despite a considerable increase in the number of people who own firearms. There are many factors that come into play, from changes in demographics to more strict prosecution of people who commit violent crimes. There are over 320 million firearms in private hands, according to estimates made by the Bureau of Alcohol, Tobacco, and Firearms (ATF), independent research institutions, and the National Rifle Association (NRA). Regulation on firearm brokers and on private gun ownership are generally respected by law abiding citizens, but the problem arises when other people, including minors, mentally challenged people, and criminals, get hold of weapons. Uber functions with this background, and there is nothing the company can do about it. Drivers are more exposed to this problem than the average person, simply because they deal with more people from all walks of life. Several incidents in which Uber drivers have been killed in 2019 alone illustrates the problem. To make matters worse, ride-share drivers have very little if any insurance coverage at all.

Mental illness and weapons

The challenges associated with mental illness are not unique to the United States. Every country is affected by behavioral and emotional disorders. To start with, diagnosing a mental illness and the degree of impairment is complicated. Based on published statistics, somewhere between four and five percent of Americans are affected by some form of mental illness, with the highest concentration in the 18-to-25- year-old bracket. As of November 2015, there were about 326 million people living in the U.S. of which between 12 and 16 million suffer some form of mental illness. According to the *Diagnostic and Statistical Manual of Mental Disorders*, there could be around 11.4 million adults with serious mental illness.[77] Most of these people are not institutionalized, and many have not even been diagnosed as suffering from a mental illness. The "system" to take care of the mentally ill is broken, which compounds the problem of establishing and enforcing gun control legislation, because there is no complete database of people who should not have access to guns.

The issue of criminal insanity is highly controversial, as the legal profession uses "cognitive" insanity as a means to defend lawbreakers. Without a doubt, many people who commit crimes are not able to discern right and wrong, are mentally impaired, and are incompetent to stand trial. The issue is further complicated by mentally challenged criminals, who clearly are not mentally competent. Instead of ending in institutions that can provide needed care, they end up in jail

---

[77] 20 percent of Americans are mentally disturbed, 19 January 2012, http://rt.com/usa/disturbed-mental-illness-study-225/; U.S. Census Bureau, POPClock Projection, 29 December 2012; See National Institute of Mental Health's National Comorbidity Survey, and Substance Abuse and Mental Health Services Administration's National Survey of Drug Abuse and Health (NSDUH).

instead. Based on a study carried out in 2010, using 2004-2005 data, it was determined that there were three times more seriously mentally ill persons in jail than in hospitals. It was further determined that at least 16 percent of inmates in jails and prisons (about 319,918 individuals) have a serious mental illness.[78] In 1955 there was one psychiatric bed for every 300 Americans. In 2005 there was one psychiatric bed for every 3,000 Americans, of which the majority were filled with court-ordered "forensic cases," and not really available.[79] What happens when the large population of criminally insane individuals complete their sentences? They are released without any kind of follow up or treatment, which leads to a high rate of recidivism.

Americans are stunned every time a new incident of gun violence takes place, but not enough to make changes. According to existing legislation, only law-abiding people of sound mind can obtain a firearm. The argument goes that criminals, by definition, do not abide by legislation, and *guns do not kill people, people kill people*. Despite the obvious, energy is directed at gun control, instead of directing energy towards finding solutions to the mental health crisis.

---

[78] What is the difference between a jail and a prison? People who are accused of committing a crime are placed in a secure facility, i.e. a jail, until trial and sentencing, or until they engage in a plea agreement. People who have been tried, convicted and sentenced of a felony, are placed in a security facility called a prison. Prisons are referred to as correctional facilities, penitentiaries, internment facilities, and jails.

[79] E. Fuller Torrey, M.D., Sheriff Aaron D. Kennard, MPAA, Sheriff Don Eslinger, Richard Lamb, M. D. and James Pavle, *More Mentally Ill Persons in Jails and Prisons Than Hospitals: A Survey of States*. National Sheriffs' Association and Treatment Advocacy Center, May 2010.

Recent Massacres in the U.S.

The gunmen who opened fire on a movie theater in Denver, CO in July 2012, the Sikh Temple in Oak Creek, WI in August 2012, and the Sandy Hook Elementary School in Newtown, CN in December 2012, all used a combination of military-style assault rifles and handguns.[80] The deranged gunman who ambushed and killed two volunteer firemen and wounded two others in Webster, New York when they responded to a house fire on 24 December 2012 used a similar .223-caliber Bushmaster AR-15 style assault rifle as the one used in the Newtown massacre ten days earlier. Police found that he had other types of guns, which had been acquired from a woman who bought them for him several days before. As a convicted felon it was illegal for him to purchase or own firearms.[1] Based on published reports, all three perpetrators were mentally-challenged.

The perpetrator of the Denver theater massacre was under the care of a mental professional. The perpetrator of the Newtown massacre was mentally challenged and apparently his mother was about to confine him to a mental institution for treatment. The shooter of the firemen in Webster had served 17 years for killing his 92-year-old grandmother in 1981. The perpetrators of the Newtown massacre and the shooting of firemen in Webster, NY killed their own mothers before they acted against other victims.

More recently, we had the shooting on 11 October 2017. in Las Vegas, and the school massacre in Florida on 14 February 2018. At least 59 people were killed and about 500 were injured in the shooting rampage in Las Vegas, from the 32nd floor of the Mandalay Bay Resort and Casino

---

[80] Wade Michael Page, the perpetrator of the attack on the Sikh Temple committed suicide after being shot by a responding police officer. Page had been tied to white supremacist groups and had a history of alcoholism, according to press reports.

by a deranged perpetrator who had taken 23 guns to his hotel room unnoticed, in a carefully planned attack who committed suicide.[81] The young perpetrator of the shooting at the Marjory Stoneman Douglas High School in Parkland, Florida, had given multiple signs of his plans, and had been reported to FBI headquarters, but they did not even inform the local FBI office of the reported threats by the deranged perpetrator. Despite being a minor, he was able to obtain a high-powered rifle, despite known behavioral issues. Psychiatrists had recommended admission to a residential treatment facility at least four years before he carried out the massacre.

Where is the problem? The proliferation of gun-ownership, the apparently large number of people with mental problems that are not receiving treatment, or a society that fails to seriously address these issues? The source of the problem may go back to the 1960s when left-wing psychiatrists had an epiphany: *confinement of the mentally ill constituted a violation of their constitutional rights.* They could be released and given a pill daily to control their mental problems. Not only are thousands of schizophrenics roaming the streets, but the entire society is suffering from schizophrenia derived from the interminable debate over taxes and the size of entitlement programs.

Although mass shootings grab national attention, there is an even more serious side to the availability of firearms. The domestic front is not peaceful. There are many nefarious actors, from criminal elements to home-grown extremists, in addition to a large number of mentally ill people that periodically make the U.S. resemble a war zone. For example,

---

[81] According to a published report, the perpetrator of the Las Vegas massacre told an UBER driver of his plans during a ride. Jim Hoft. Huge Breaking News; Vegas Killer Warned UBER DRIVER OF LOOMING "TERRORIST Attack at Mandalay Bay," – with Woman in Car with Him! The Gatewaypundit.com 31 May 2018.

in June 2014 two Las Vegas police officers were having lunch when they were shot and killed by a White supremacist anti-government extremist couple who wanted to start a revolution.[82] Despite the mounting need to address the challenge of mental illness, the growth of extremist ideology, and the availability of guns to people who should not have access to them, nothing is seriously done. Too many interest groups get into the debate and nothing is done. The country continues to move ahead without a bearing, led by politicians who have no idea of where "true north" or the "magnetic north" are, or the difference between the two.

Uber links to the massacres?

How do all of these mass shootings relate to Uber? In February 2016, UBER driver Jason Dalton, 45, who had no prior criminal record, randomly murdered six victims, and wounded several others at three different locations in Kalamazoo County in Michigan, shooting from his car. He held a regular job with the Raymond James company as an insurance adjuster, and had a wife and two children. What set him off? A rider told police and Uber investigators that James had started driving dangerously after receiving a phone call, leading the rider to abandon the car as soon as he could.[83]

On 14 February 2018, Nikolas Cruz, a 19-year-old expelled student opened fire and killed 17 students at the Marjory

---

[82] Cynthia Johnston, Killers of Las Vegas cops harbored anti-government ideology, *Reuters*, 9 June 2014; Nicole Hensley, Las Vegas police officers gunned down at pizza restaurant, one civilian killed, *New York Daily News*, 9 June 2014.

[83] Chris Killian, Jason Silverstein, and Stephen Rex Brown. Kalamazoo shooting suspect Jason Dalton was Uber driver, took fares in between massacres. *New York Daily News*. 22 February 2016.

Stoneman Douglas High School in Parkland, Florida.[84] An Uber driver delivered him to the scene of the shooting. She did not see anything strange or any indication that he was about to carry out the dastardly deed with an AR-15.[85]

On the other hand, an Uber driver prevented a mass shooting in Chicago in April 2015, using a lawfully licensed concealed weapon, which according to Uber rules, he was not supposed to carry while driving for the company. The Uber driver shot and wounded the gunman in Logan Square as he opened fire on people. The Uber driver was not charged by police, as he had a legal license for his weapon, and he acted to protect people under attack.[86] [87] This company rule is unenforceable for both, drivers and riders. It is well-known that many Uber drivers carry concealed weapons for self-protection. Drivers talk to each other, including at Uber offices. They discuss this issue regularly.[88]

Considering the thousands of Uber trips in the course of a single day, plenty of bizarre things occur, some involving acts of extreme violence. For example, in July 2017, a husband and wife started an argument while riding in an Uber, then the husband pulled out a gun and fatally shot his wife.[89] She

---

[84] Carlin Becker. Uber driver who dropped off the Florida school shoote3r before his massacre breaks her silence. US/rare.us/rare-news/across-the-us-a/Uber. 28 February 2018.

[85] Asher Klein. An Uber Ride, a Massacre, a Confession: How Investigators Say the Florida School Shooting Unfolded. *NBC5/Chicago*. 15 February 2018.

[86] Geoff Ziezulewics. Uber driver, licensed to carry gun, shoots gunman in Logan Square. *Chicago Tribune*. 20 April 2015.

[87] Adam Bates, Cato Institute. An Uber driver with a concealed handgun prevented a mass shooting in Chicago. 21 April 2015.

[88] Personally, I do not believe that it is a good idea to violate the law, as well as company policies. Weapons can make an already dangerous situation much worse.

[89] Peter Holley. Husband accused of fatally shooting wife while riding in Uber. *The Washington Post*. 4 July 2017.

was sitting in the front passenger seat, and her husband had taken a seat behind the driver. The incident took place in Seattle, Washington. The perpetrator told the driver to continue driving, and eventually told him to let him off. The driver called police, and the perpetrator was picked up near the drop-off point. Based on news reports, the perpetrator was drunk at the time.

Attacks on Uber drivers

One of the most famous cases of an attack on an Uber driver took place in Miami, Florida. A drunk young female physician, tried to hijacked an Uber car that arrived at her location for another person. She attacked the driver verbally and physically, but the entire incident was recorded. The doctor was not arrested, and arrived at a settlement with the driver. However, her Uber account was suspended, and was harassed by numerous callers, and her employer put her on administrative leave. The case went viral, and classified as *"an arrogant, drunk, little brat."* This case is only one of many videos on YouTube about attacks on Uber drivers.[90]

Another famous case was a physical attack on an Uber driver by a drunk senior marketing manager at Taco Bell. The perpetrator was arrested, and was fired by his employer. The incident started when the passenger was so drunk that he could not enter the address where he was going, and could not verbally tell the driver his destination either. When the driver asked the passenger to leave the car, the physical attack on the driver started. The passenger reportedly filed a law suit against the driver for illegally recording the incident without permission! The Uber driver sued the passenger claiming

---

[90] ABC. Doctor Accused of Attacking Uber driver.: "I'm ashamed." *ABC News*. 28 January 2016.

assault, battery and infliction of emotional distress.[91] [92] Only in the USA!

Another Uber driver was no so lucky. A 16-year-old girl attacked and killed an Uber driver with a stolen knife and machete in Chicago in May 2017.[93] Based on news reports, there was no provocation in any manner. He picked up the passenger at a Walmart in Skokie, Illinois, and a few minutes into the ride, she started stabbing him. The driver got out of the car and asked for help in the lobby of a condominium building, but help arrived too late to save him. He was able to describe what happened; the Uber app had the name of the client. The perpetrator ran away, shedding part of her blood-stained clothing, but was picked up by police. Apparently, she had stolen the knife and machete at the Walmart. Technically, the 16-year-old perpetrator should not have been able to ride an Uber by herself because she was under 18 years old. This rule is violated all the time. Hundreds if not thousands of school kids are picked up at schools by Uber drivers, and the rides are charged to a parent's credit card. Often, multiple students are picked up at schools and driven home or elsewhere. Uber may claim that drivers are encouraged to report violations of this rules, but it just about never happens. Drivers need the money...

There are multiple cases of Uber drivers attacked by riders all over the country. They have been attacked with bricks, knives, and other objects. For example, an Uber driver picked up a rider at a Manatee County, Florida, location. Within

---

[91] Uber Driver Attacked by Drunk Passenger. YouTube.com TYT. The Young Turks. 3 November 2015. Over 885,719 views as of 21 January 2019. https://www.youtube.com/watch?v=Q0xjkkBOijk

[92] Hailey Branson-Potts. Man, who attacked Uber driver while drunk files $5-million lawsuit. *Los Angeles Times*. 18 January 2016.

[93] Grace Wong, Susan Berger, and Brian L. Cox. *Chicago Tribune*. Girl, 16, accused of killing Uber driver with stolen knife, machete. 1 June 2017.

minutes the driver was punched as the rider attempted to hijack the car. The driver jumped out of the moving vehicle, but fortunately, a sheriff's deputy witnessed what happened, and gave chase. The passenger crashed the car several times, and eventually tried to escape on foot while being chased by law enforcement officers.[94] According to Uber management, drivers are abused more often than passengers. Although generally rider's complaint about their ridesharing experiences, and driver behavior, drivers are more likely to be the targets of abuse and assault by passengers. Riders know that Uber has their credit card numbers and other personal information, which is made available to police if anything happens... *there is no place to hide!*

Internationally, there have been multiple physical attacks on Uber drivers by taxi drivers. For example, in Spain there have been multiple taxi strikes in a number of large cities, including Madrid and Barcelona, to demand that the regional governments ban Uber and other rideshare companies for unfair competition.[95] In South Africa, an Uber driver was killed, and dumped in a field, after an attempted hijacking, and another Uber driver was attacked with acid in 2017.[96] In Mexico City, protesting taxi drivers physically attacked Uber drivers in July 2015, outside the airport. Video posted on YouTube showed people throwing eggs and flour inside the Uber cars, ripping outside mirrors, and inflicting other damage. Violent anti-Uber protests took place in Paris, France, in 2015. French taxi drivers overturned cars, burned tires, and blocked access to airports and train stations. In

---

[94] Samantha Putterman. Uber driver attacked and carjacked by rider in Bradenton, deputies say. *Bradenton Herald*. 28 August 2018.

[95] Natasha Lomas. 'Anti-Uber' taxi strikes kick off again in Spain. https://techcrunch.com/2019/01/21/anti-Uber-taxi-strikes-kick-off-again-in-spain/

[96] Uber driver killed, dumped in field near Daveyton. *Times*. 23 August 2017.

some cases, protesters contacted Uber passing as passengers, and once picked up, lured the drivers into preset locations where they were physically attacked by waiting taxi drivers.[97] Similar attacks took place in the United Kingdom and Germany against Uber in June 2014.[98]

According to Uber, despite all the protests, the number of Uber customers in Europe was doubling in size every six months in the 20 cities where the system is operational.[99] However, drivers have been faced with violence from Taxi drivers just about everywhere. In addition to the exposure to crime driving for Uber, they have to deal with systemic reaction from the taxi establishment that refuses to accept that conditions are changing, and the world does not remain the same for ever and ever.

Uber drivers killed in 2019 (sample)

In the first three months of 2019, three was a string of Uber drivers killed. These incidents illustrate that despite a system where clients pay Uber directly using credit cards - which means that the company has the name, address, phone number, and other key pieces of information that can be used to identify anybody who assaults a driver – assaults do happen. In addition, drivers do not carry cash, or collect cash payments, which takes away a reason to attack a driver for robbery. Yet, at least four drivers were killed, perhaps by demented people, or people on drugs or drunk. These are the details:

---

[97] Kim Willsher. Anti-Uber protests turn violent in France. *Los Angeles Times*. 25 June 2015.

[98] Nico Hines. Anti-Uber Protests Shut Down Euro Cities. *Daily Beast*.11 June 2014.

[99] Ari Shapiro. Across Europe, Anti-Uber Protests Clog City Streets. *National Public Radio*. 11 June 2014.

- **David Rosenthal**, 58 years old, found dead in Denver. Apparently, he was a victim of a carjacking by two individuals. His car was used in an armed robbery of a convenience store in Cheyenne, Wyoming, and a Wells Fargo Bank in Park City, Utah. The two perpetrators were arrested by police a few days later in Oregon. One was a suspected illegal alien from El Salvador.[100] [101]

- **Ganiou Gandonou**, a 27-year-old Uber driver was stabbed to death in the Bronx on Saturday 2 March 2019. He was found dead in his black Toyota Camry. He had been driving for Uber since January 2017.[102] [103]

- **Musba Shifa**, a 43-year-old who drove for both, Uber and Lyft, in the D.C. Metro area was found dead in his car in Delaware. He had been reported missing for six weeks.[104] Born in Ethiopia, this driver had gone missing since 19 January 2019. He was last reported on the 1300 block of W Street NW, D.C. on 18 January.[105]

---

[100] Chuck Hickey. Denver man killed in carjacking was working as Uber driver. *Fox31*. 26 February 2019.

[101] CNN. Uber driver shot and killed in a carjacking. *CNN News*. 27 February 2019.

[102] Emma G. Fitzsimmons and Ashley Southall. Uber Driver Is Stabbed to Death in the Bronx. *The New York Times*. 3 March 2019.

[103] AP and Michael Nam. Uber driver found stabbed to death in his car in NYC leads Taxi Driver Federation to offer $3000 reward for the arrest of his killer. *AP and Daily Mail*. 3 March 2019.

[104] Matthew Stabley. Missing DC Ride-Share Driver Found Dead in Delaware. *NBC4Washingtron*. 3 March 2019.

[105] KYTV News. Missing DC Ride-Share Driver Found Dead in Delaware. *NBC KYTV News*. 4 March 2019.

- **Beaudouin Tchakounte**, a 46-year-old Uber driver assassinated in the D.C. Metro on 27 August 2019. A passenger high on PCP in a pool ride shot and killed Uber driver Beaudouin Tchakounte, and passenger Casey Xavier Robinson, on Indian Head Highway, Oxon Hill, Prince George's County, Maryland. The incident took place on 27 August 2019, around 9:45 pm. Cameroon-born Uber driver Tchakounte, was 46 years-old and the father of four children ages three to 15. He had been driving for Uber for three years.[106] [107] [108] [109] [110]

PCP – What is it? Also known *as "Angel Dust,"* Phencyclidine, is a mind-altering drug that can cause hallucinations, or distortions in a user's perception of reality, and violent behavior. It is typically smoked, but may be taken by mouth, snorted, or injected. It is addictive. It appeared in the market in the 1950's as an anesthetic and tranquilizer. It was discontinued in 1967, and manufacturing and distributing it is illegal. The Drug Enforcement Administration (DEA) has made numerous arrests of PCP traffickers. For example, in February 2014, the DEA seized almost 100 gallons of PCP in Los Angeles, with an estimated street value of about $1 billion. According to the DEA, Southern California is considered as a key manufacturing center, from where it is distributed all over the country. In March 2018, nine people were indicted in the DC Metro Area for distributing PCP, fentanyl, cocaine, and firearms. The FBI, AFT, DEA, and the D.C. Police Department participated in the investigation and arrests.

---

[106] Lyn Bui and Justin Jouvenal. Ride-share driver and passenger killed in Md., police said. The Washington Post. 28 August 2019.

[107] Gina Cook, Derrick Ward, Jackie Benson, and Justin Finch. Uber Passenger shoots, kills Driver and man sharing ride in Maryland: Police. NBC News. 28 August 2019.

[108] Scott Broom. He drove Uber 7 days a week for a better life, now he's dead. WUSA9. 29 August 2019.

[109] Lynh Bui. Man accused of killing an Uber driver and passenger told police he 'messed up,' court documents say. The Washington Post. 29 August 2019.

[110] Mike Murillo. Prince George's Co. man accused of killing 2 during Uber ride says he 'messed up." WTOP. 29 August 2019.

Beaudouin Tchakounte was a practicing Catholic, who worked very hard, seven days a week, to take care of his family, including paying to send his children to Catholic schools. His wife, a registered nurse, described for the press how Beaudouin sacrificed to provide his children the best possible life that he could afford.

There are several issues associated with this tragic event that are worth mentioning. The arrested assassin, Aaron Wilson, Jr. 42 years old, was booked on first and second-degree murder. In violation of Uber rules, apparently the credit card used to book the ride was listed to a woman, who based on a police statement, is the killer's mother. According to Uber rules, the

Beaudouin Tchakounte
Epistemic Injustice – Uber Driver Assassinated
27 August 2019

person who books a ride, is supposed to be present during the ride. This rule is violated all the time, in some cases with the driver's acquiescence, and other times without his knowledge. When it happens, the driver may or may not know that the passenger is not the person listed in the Uber app. Assuming that Uber conducts a background check on new clients – which it does not – there would be some way of protecting drivers from possible criminal activity. When a rider other than the person who actually books the ride is picked up by a driver anything can happen.

In this particular case, the arrested perpetrator of the crime had previously been sentenced to five years in jail after pleading guilty to a robbery count in 1998, and had other violations on his criminal record. Uber provided police the phone number and other details of the person who actually booked the ride. Police contacted the individual, who turned out to be the mother of the arrested perpetrator, and police found him in a backroom of his mother's house.

I personally experienced a similar situation. I accepted a ping and went to pick up the passenger. It turned out that the person waiting for the ride was not the person who booked the trip. I did not find out until I engaged in conversation with the passenger. I learned that he was a convicted felon who had served time in prison. Nothing happened, but I alerted Uber about the experience, and the potential dangers when the passenger turns out not to be the person who booked the trip. In

Aaron Lanier Wilson, Jr.
Assassin
Euphemism: "Suspect"
Picture by Prince George's County Md.
Police Department

my case, the passenger could have attacked me or cause some kind of criminal violation. He did not. However, the potential was there for some kind of incident. (see vignette #5, in the Appendix). Without a doubt, rules have a reason for existence, but they are not worth anything if they are violated all the time, with or without the knowledge of the driver and/or Uber, or both. Then again, when a traditional taxi cab is flagged by a would-be passenger, they do not have any idea of who is requesting a ride. This kind of incident can happen, and is one of the significant exposures that drivers have. *Is it worth it? Does compensation received by drivers justify this level of exposure?* Life is what it is...

Uber drivers sexual attacks on passengers

According to a CNN report dated April 2018, they uncovered at least 103 cases of sexual assault against passengers in the United States alone, although there are multiple similar reports from countries all over the world where UBER operates.[111] Some cases found by the CNN investigators involved cases of drivers with multiple sexual attacks on riders going back as long as five years. Based on the report, Uber is facing several potential class action lawsuits for failure to properly vet drivers before they are accepted as "partners."

Uber's internal investigators

According to a CNN report dated 21 January 2019, Uber has a team of about 60 investigators who are poorly paid for the work they do, and are stressed out due to the volume of work they are expected to handle. According to the report, these investigators are supervised by about 15 team leaders or supervisors, who are just as stressed out as the people they supervised. Based on this report, it is safe to conclude that there are more cases of sexual assault, rape, verbal and physical threats, thefts, and serious traffic accidents than what is reported by the news media. The problems are not only in the U.S. and Canada, but across all the Uber operations overseas.[112]

There is very little information available in the open domain regarding how the challenges associated with ridesharing are shared with taxi services worldwide.

Uber discloses the facts about 2018

On 5 December 2019, Uber published a comprehensive 84-page report on sexual assaults and related incidents in

---

[111] Sara Ashley O'Brien, Nelli Black, Curt Devine, and Drew Griffin. CNN investigation: 103 Uber drivers accused of sexual assault or abuse. CNN. 30 April 2018.
[112] Sara Ashley O'Brien, Neil Black and Drew Griffin. Stressed out and at risk: Inside Uber's special investigations unit. *CNN*. 21 January 2019.

2018. The number of rides with incidents represented a very small fraction of all the rides: 0.0002 percent. There were 3,045 sexual assaults out of 1.3 billion rides in 2018. Although in most of the incidents the drivers were the perpetrators, riders assaulted drivers in 45 percent of the reported incidents. The number of incidents dropped from the previous years, despite an increase in the number of rides. Uber has taken steps to address the problem by incorporating an emergency button on the app, and by implementing more thorough background checks, including frequent picture verification of who is driving cars. The key to understanding the problem is society at large. Uber and other driveshare providers function with all the societal challenges that affect the United States and other countries where they operate. Proliferation of gun ownership, drug use, alcoholism, people with untreated mental illness, and the release from prison custody of criminals that are unable and/or unwilling to rejoin polite society, cannot be blamed on Uber or any of the other driveshare companies.[113] [114]

In the 5 December 2019 report Uber disclosed that law enforcement was not notified in every instance of rape and/or sexual abuse. The stated reason was that victims are often reluctant to notify law enforcement because they fear that they may be victimized again by the very efforts to bring to justice a perpetrator. Public opinion, the news media, and regulators have a difficult time accepting this excuse.

---

[113] Yoel Minkoff. Uber releases sexual assault statistics. *SeekingAlpha*. 5 December 2019.
[114] Morgan Winsor. Uber reveals nearly 6,000 incidents of sexual assaults in new safety report. *ABC News*. 6 December 2019.

So what?

Insurance coverage is the Achilles heel, and principal vulnerability, for the ride-share sector. Couple the need for normal vehicle insurance (collision, uninsured motorist, liability), the need to have life insurance coverage is evident by the tragic assassination of drivers with small children. Medical and dental insurance, workman's compensation in case of injury at work, short-term and long-term disability income insurance, are beyond a basic necessity. Bad things occur for no particular reason. Life is unfair. *Poop happens!* There is no way to cover all of these needs with the income derived by ride-share drivers under current conditions. A normal employer would provide access to these types of insurance, and would either provide at company expense coverage, or would share costs with the employee, or at least would provide some form of group insurance at cheaper rates to employees. However, in the case of driveshare companies like Uber, since the drivers are self-employed, there is no coverage. The driver's families are left to deal with the consequences of crime and happenstance all by themselves.

These are the facts:

- There are over 320 million firearms in private hands in the U.S. but there is limited information on who owns them, and if they are legally qualified to own them.
- Mentally-challenged individuals can easily get hold of weapons and use them with criminal intent on a daily basis.
- The challenges associated with mental illness are not unique to the U.S. Every country is affected by behavioral and emotional disorders, and how to address the challenge.

- Between 12 and 16 million out of about 326 million people in the U.S. suffer some form of mental illness.
- Too many interest groups get into the debate over gun control and emotionally challenged individuals, yet little or nothing is done about the multiple challenges associated with these issues.
- Rideshare and Taxi drivers are often victimized by the conditions under which they work – and there are no easy solutions – as long as society fails to address the overall mix of problems, coupled with a cowboy mentality and glorification of violence.
- Uber and competing drive-share companies need thousands of drivers, and the high rate of turnover makes the shortage even more critical. Failure to carry out due diligence before they approve new driver-partners will come back to byte them if they do not come up with a viable solution. (This situation may well cost Uber it's operating license in London.)
- The peculiar business arrangement between Uber and drivers is an obvious way of avoiding responsibility, particularly on safety issues. Amazingly, the court system in the U.S. has failed to create a case system that addresses the legality of the arrangement once and for all.
- The number of incidents like the ones covered in the CNN report, and Uber's report released on 5 December 2019, represent much less than one percent of all Uber trips. Considering that over one billion trips take place annually, it is incredible that nasty incidents do not happen more often.

INFAMOUS UBER DRIVERS

 Uzbekistan native Sayfullo Saipov, worked as a driver for Uber – He is famous for ramming a Home Depot rental truck into a crowd of mostly civilian tourists in a New York City bicycle path on 31 October 2017.[147] [148]

 Jason Brian Dalton was charged by police for randomly killing at least six people from his Uber car on 20 February 2016 in Kalamazoo County, Michigan. Forty-five-year-old was charged with murder, assault, and criminal use of a firearm. Several Uber passengers called police and notified Uber that he was driving erratically.[149] [150]

(U) FBI Photo of Harbir Parmar.

Uber driver of Indian origin Harbir Parmar, of Howard Beach, Queens, New York, was sentenced to three years in jail for kidnapping and groping a female passenger on 21 February 2018. He dropped her off on the side of I-95, near New Haven, Conn. The victim was a young Japanese woman with limited knowledge of English who was drunk at the time. Parmar had a history of wrongdoing working as a driver for Uber, including overcharging passengers by entering wrong information on the Uber app. The court sentenced Parmar to pay back over $3,600 in fraudulent fees. Uber customers had filed complaints about being overcharged for their rides, and for false cleaning charges, as the alleged that victims had vomited in his car.[115] [116] [117]

---

[115] Indian-Origin Uber Driver Kidnapped Woman Passenger To Boost His Fare. *Press Trust of India*. 15 March 2019.

[116] Stephen Rex Brown. Uber driver who kidnapped, groped passenger sentenced to 3 years in prison. *New York Daily News*. 24 June 2019.

[117] NBC. Uber Driver Sentenced After Kidnapping Sleeping NYC passenger. *NBC*. 25 June 2019.

• V •

Uber and Law Enforcement

There are multiple examples of wrongdoing by Uber drivers listed on the Internet, not only in the U.S., but in neighboring Canada, the UK, and numerous other countries. There are a few examples of how Uber drivers rose to the occasion and alerted law enforcement when they witnessed vile criminal acts. With their assistance, passengers engaged in criminal activity have been arrested. These Uber drivers should be commended for their assistance to police so that victims of crime could be rescued, and criminals could be taken off the streets.

Uber drivers to the rescue

Uber driver Keith Avila rescued a 16-year-old girl from a sex trafficking organization after listening to a conversation between three passengers in Elk Grove, California, as he drove them to a Holiday Inn Hotel. The two adult women accompanying the minor turned out to be her pimps, based on the topic of their conversation. The driver called police after dropping off the passengers, and related the details of the conversation he had listened to. Police arrived and quickly and arrested the women, who turned out to be engaged in child sex trafficking, for pimping and pandering. A "John" was arrested for having sex with a minor.[118]

---

[118] Dan Gunderman. California Uber Driver discovers sex trafficking ring led by two females after hearing unlawful conversation in car. *New York Daily News*. 29 December 2016

In August 2017, another Uber driver alerted police about a potential pimp abusing young girls at a J.W. Marriott hotel in Phoenix, AZ. The driver assisted police in a sting operation that nabbed the perpetrator of the heinous crime, who was involved in drug trafficking. The arrested criminal had been trying to recruit the Uber driver to participate in his criminal enterprise prostituting young girls and distributing of methamphetamine. [119]

In May 2019, an alert Uber driver in Allegheny County told police about the location of a vehicle that had been involved in a deadly hit-and-run incident in Penn Hills, PA. Police had been searching for the car for several days and had requested assistance from the public. The Uber driver spotted the car, took a picture, and called the police department with the location.[120] In June 2019, another Uber driver in Huntsville suspected that criminal activity was taking place and alerted police. As a result, a sodomy suspect was arrested.[121]

Another Uber driver in Midvale, Utah, rendered assistance to a police officer who had been knocked to the ground out by a criminal during an attempted arrest. The Uber driver stopped, got out of his car, and went over to help the police officer. He then followed the suspect to a nearby housing building until police reinforcements arrived and made the arrest. The suspect was found to be in possession of narcotics and associated paraphernalia.[122]

---

[119] Monique Griego. Phoenix Uber driver helps police take down suspected pimp in undercover sting. *12 News NBC*. 30 August 2017.

[120] Uber driver helps police locate car involved in deadly hit-and-run. Channel 11. Allegheny County, PA. *WPXI.Com News*. 10 May 2019.

[121] WAFF 48 Digital Staff. Huntsville Uber driver helps lead police to sodomy suspect. *WAFF*. 20 June 2019.

[122] RaeAnn Christensen. Exclusive: Uber driver helps unconscious officer; tracks suspect in Midvale. *2 KUTV*. 28 February 2019.

Uber assistance to law enforcement

In addition to drivers who decide on their own to do "the right thing," the company is assisting law enforcement with criminal investigations. Although some people may consider these actions as "corporate snitching," the organization is doing the "right thing." Uber has hired regional Law Enforcement Liaison officers to handle relations with local, state, and Federal law enforcement authorities.

So what?

Uber receives a lot of bad press from multiple incidents of wrong doing by drivers, as well as for accidentally driving perpetrators of incidents of mass casualties. Considering the huge volume of business on a daily basis, much less than one percent of all the rides results in an incident of significant consequence for good or evil. Uber should establish an effective campaign to enhance the corporate image of the company as a responsible corporate citizen, not only in the United States, but in all the countries where it is active. As Tx Zhuo mentioned in one of his articles, *the name Uber is synonymous with bad PR, and for good reason.* As he points out, despite all the blunders, Uber is still considered *safer than most taxi services.*[123]

---

[123] Tx Zhuo. What Uber Needs To Do To Fix Its Reputation. Fast Company. https://www.fastcompany.com/3042107/why-ubers-success-means-nothing-if-it-cant-fix-its-reputation (Last accessed on 20 July 2019.)

U.S. Library of Congress Collection
1914 Ford Model T

My paternal grandmother, Mercedes Bacardi de Fermoselle, owned several Ford Model Ts, which she used to operate a fleet of taxis in Santiago de Cuba. After WWI broke out, it became very difficult and expensive to obtain parts. She decided to dismantled the vehicles to sell them as spare parts, and earned a substantial profit. Picture of my grandmother and one of her cars was taken in 1914 or 1915.

• VI •

Diversification or Speculation

Background

The American automotive industry grew during the 1920s through innovative techniques, such as the assembly line introduced by Henry Ford, which dropped the per unit cost of production. There were multiple auto manufacturers, but General Motors (GM), Ford and Chrysler each held between 20 and 25 percent market share. Smaller and less competitive companies slowly began to disappear. With the enactment of the National Labor Relations Act in 1935, and the Creation of the United Auto Workers Union (UAW), the collective bargaining process brought about better wages and better working conditions, but the only way industry could afford to cover the additional costs was to continue growing and kicking the liabilities of the pension plans forward.

During WWII the assembly lines were redirected to support the war effort. As soon as the war ended in 1945, manufacturers went back to producing cars. Over 21 million cars were built and sold in 1945. The U.S. auto industry was not only building for the domestic market, but was exporting all over the world. GM, Ford, and Chrysler, set up factories in Europe and Latin America to meet local demand, thus reducing the export of cars made in the U.S. Foreign competitors in Europe and Japan rebuilt their factories and began to produce for their markets and for export. They built smaller and more fuel-efficient cars, and introduced innovations as they build new factories. American factories were old, whereas the rest of the world had new factories, which gave them a competitive edge.

By 1970, several factors merged to torpedo the American auto industry. Consumers demanded safer cars, after successful litigation by Ralph Nader forced the industry to rethink car designs with safety in mind.[124] New government regulations forced the industry to invest in environmental technology, while the UAW aggressively approached collective bargaining with higher demands for wages and benefits. An embargo of oil exports to the U.S. imposed by the Organization of Arab Petroleum Exporting Countries (OAPEC) in response to U.S. backing of Israel during the Yom Kippur War in October 1973 precipitated a new crisis. The devaluation of the dollar, plus the new-found power of OPEC, led to much higher fuel prices, which triggered a demand for fuel efficient vehicles. American companies were behind other producers in fuel efficiency, pushing buyers to purchase imported cars.

A stock market crash in 1973-1974, plus the political and economic uncertainty emanating from the Watergate Scandal, further destabilized the automotive sector. Reengineering vehicles to comply with new government efficiency regulations added costs. Shortages of fuel, fuel rationing programs, and the state of the economy reduced the demand for vehicles. The automotive industry in the middle of the economic mess, denominated "*stagflation*" had to phase out front engine/rear wheel drive to more efficient front engine/front wheel drive designs. Japanese fuel-efficient cars took advantage of the consumer rejection of gas guzzlers contributing to a drop in

---

[124] Ralph Nader, a left-wing activist, and Harvard Law School graduate published in 1965 *Unsafe at Any Speed*, an analysis of how American auto manufacturers, particularly GM, were making cars that were unsafe. Nader should be given credit for making the U.S. automotive industry improve car design, which ultimately rendered them more competitive.

American car sales that lasted until the 1980s when fuel prices dropped. By 1985, the average car made in the U.S. improved its mileage performance from an average of 13.5 miles a decade earlier to an average of 17.4 miles per gallon of fuel.

When fuel prices went down in the 1980s, the American automotive industry went back to producing larger vehicles and successfully introduced minivans, SUVs, and more pick-up trucks, with Chrysler leading the way after recovering from near death. Foreign manufacturers followed their lead, as the American public forgot the experience of the 1970s and bought the larger vehicles. Minivans, SUVs, and pick-up trucks became popular through the 1980s and 1990s. When fuel prices went back up around 2008, the gas-guzzling SUV and pick-up truck culture went into crisis. Once again, factories making the large fuel guzzlers were shut down, bringing about another crisis. By 2008, Japan was producing over 5.5 million cars, China 9.3 million, and U.S. production had decreased to 8.75 million, while Germany produced 6.0 million.

President George W. Bush's Administration provided Chrysler and GM $17.4 billion in loans in December 2008 to keep them from going into bankruptcy. In exchange, they had to implement a plan to regain competitiveness. Over one million direct and indirect jobs were at stake. President Obama's Administration provided $43 billion in additional funds in exchange for more concessions. With this assistance, both car companies started a recovery, leading to profitability and recovery of the funds provided by the government, as the companies emerged from bankruptcy.

There is another side to the story of the American automotive sector. Since the energy crisis of 1973, the leading German, Japanese, and Korean manufacturers have invested in vehicle factories in the U.S. The most interesting aspect of these factories is that several of them produce the top ten cars with the highest percentage of American content. For example, Toyota turned out to be the leader in the 2010 lineup of vehicles with the highest percentage of American components, not one of the three American companies (GM, Ford, and Chrysler). The American companies – however that is defined - have a high percentage of parts made in Canada, Mexico, Japan, and other countries.

Just because the three American vehicle manufacturers lost market share since 1973 to foreign companies, it does not necessarily mean that autoworkers have lost their jobs to foreign workers. While the rustbelt lost jobs, Alabama, Georgia, Indiana, Kansas, Kentucky, Illinois, Mississippi, South Carolina, Ohio, Texas and West Virginia benefitted from foreign investment to produce cars in the U.S. BMW, Honda, Hyundai, Kia, Mercedes-Benz; Nissan, Toyota and Volkswagen have manufacturing plants in the U.S. In the meantime, Detroit lost about 25 percent of its population, and so have other key population centers in the old rust belt.

The health of the automotive manufacturing sector in the U.S. is not necessarily as bad as it is portrayed to be. Just because the three American giants are not anywhere close to what they once were, does not mean that all is lost. Foreign companies manufacturing in the U.S. repatriate their profits, but so do GM and Ford from their own business operations overseas.

Hybrid and electric cars

Toyota introduced in 1997 the first viable hybrid vehicle to the Japanese market. Audi introduced a hybrid into the European market about the same time. Ford, GM, Honda, and Toyota, were pushing to introduce hybrids into the American market by 1999, and the Toyota Prius entered the market in

2000, followed by the Honda Civic Hybrid in 2002.[125] Electric vehicles first appeared in the market in the late 19th century, but were displaced by the internal combustion engine. Once again in the 21st century interest returned to the production of efficient electric vehicles. Tesla delivered its first electric cars into the American market in 2008. Mitsubishi launched its first all-electric car into the Japanese market in 2009.

Self-driving technology

The rapid growth of rideshare introduced into the market in 2010 by Uber, created conditions that led to R&D investment into self-driving technology. The future of Uber and other ridesharing companies are inextricably linked to the automotive sector. In February 2015, Uber opened a robotics research facility in Pittsburgh to explore building self-driving vehicles. Within three months, new controversies started, as the company poached about 50 employees from the Carnegie Mellon's National Robotics Engineering Center. Within two years, modified versions of a Volvo sports utility vehicle equipped with Uber technology come out of the Pittsburgh facility, together with new speculation about safety... *haste kills!* Uber was accused of lifting self-driving technology from Waymo, a company associated with Google's parent company Alphabet.

By then, Uber was about to cross its 5 billion trip milestones, as the company problems continue to build up: fraud allegations, resignation from the Uber Board members associated with sexual misconduct, and CEO Travis Kalanick was forced to resign by key investors. And then.... an Uber self-driving Volvo XC90 SUV killed a pedestrian in March 2018 in Tempe, Arizona. The vehicle was going about five

---

[125] Brad Berman. History of Hybrid Vehicles. Hybridcars.com. 14 June 2011.

miles per hour faster than the 35-mph limit authorized in the zone, and it did not even slow down to avoid hitting the pedestrian. There was a driver behind the wheel, but the SUV was in autonomous mode. Prior to this accident, at least 37 crashes had taken place in the previous 18 months.

After the accident, all testing was stopped, as the company examined what went wrong, and the NTSB and other jurisdictions launched separate investigations. Other companies conducting parallel research on self-driving vehicles stopped their own testing to reevaluate the concept, including Waymo, GM, and Intel. The international news media provided ample coverage to the Tempe, Arizona, accident. Preliminary reports indicated that as part of the testing, an automatic braking feature had been disabled, and the system had not handed control to the driver that was monitoring the test. Everything happened so fast that there was no way to avoid the accident.

Estimates that by 2020 around 10 million self-driving vehicles from different manufacturers would be on the road is unachievable.[126] Private and government entities involved in research include BMW, Bosch, Caterpillar, Defense Advanced Research Projects Agency, Delphi, Ford Motor Company, Google, John Deere, Mercedes-Benz, NASA, Nissan, Tesla, Volvo, and Uber. The advent of reliable and safe self-driving vehicles may be inevitable, but not necessarily in the near-term.[127] [128] [129] Uber and competitors will continue to require drivers for a long time to come.

---

[126] Jeff Plungis. Self-Driving Cars: Driving into the Future. *Consumer Reports*. 28 February 2017.

[127] Luke Collins. Self-driving cars and the future of the auto sector. *McKinsey Podcasts*. 2016.

[128] Marc Saltzman. Car Trends and Lifestyle: Self-Driving Cars- Ar we there Yet? *AARP*. 7 February 2018.

[129] Scott Corwin and Derek M. Pankratz. Forces of change: The future of mobility. *Deloitte Insights*. 16 November 2017.

According to press reports, when people see an Uber driverless vehicle out for tests, they frequently signal employees in the vehicles with rude gestures and even road rage. Based on published reports, the same is happening to Google's autonomous vehicles, including slashing of tires and even threatening with guns on "safety" drivers inside the vehicles. One of the articles quotes Eric Meyhofer, the head of Uber's self-driving car unit about these incidents. According to published reports, these incidents have been captured by cameras on the vehicles.[130]

Car sharing

What is car sharing? It involves short-term car rental. Instead of purchasing vehicles and paying for maintenance, parking, and insurance, people would have access to networks that make them available by the hour, by the day, or by the week. The difference between car sharing and regular car rental companies is that vehicles are available at strategic locations, and can be borrowed for more limited amounts of time. They are available at Metro stations parking lots, special bays, or parking lots in the D.C. Metro. Car sharing is not a new invention.

As far back as right after WWII, the concept surfaced in Western Europe, initially in Zurich, Switzerland. However, the concept slowly died out, possibly because there was very limited profit, or no profit at all, and demand simply was not there. A similar bicycle ride sharing concept surfaced in the 1960's, but the same people who promoted the idea, essentially killed it by stealing them, and dumping them anywhere. As computer technology developed starting in the mid-1980s, it became increasingly possible to track their location, and

---

[130] Isabel Asher Hamilton. Uber says people are bullying its self-driving cars with rude gestures and road rage. *Business Insider*. 13 June 2019.

the users. Smart cards, GPS, and related technologies made it possible to track the bikes more effectively, and the same applied to other motor vehicles. New car sharing companies, such as, City Car Club, Flexcar, GoGet Carshare, StatAuto, Yandex, and Zipcar, came about, but traditional rental car companies bought them out. Avis and Enterprise, for example, invested in car sharing companies and expanded their operations.[131] [132]

Car sharing has spread all over the world, with the top cities where the concept is available are Tokyo, Moscow, Beijing, Shanghai, and Guangzhou.[133] Automakers, in part due to their concerns about the future of car ownership and the potential impact on their business, have created their own car sharing business. They include BMW, Daimler Benz, and Volkswagen, while other companies, including GM, have invested into ridesharing, namely Lyft. Avis-Zipcar worked out a business agreement to test the concept of Uber drivers using Zipcars.

This trial could be important to address the requirement that Uber drivers use vehicles that are no older than five years old, which limits the potential number of drivers to those who have credit worthiness to purchase and finance a vehicle. Cars used for Uber add up mileage quickly, depreciate faster than normal, and require more frequent maintenance. Based on published information, Uber drivers pay $7 monthly membership fee, plus $12 hourly to use a Zipcar. Based on my experience, that proposition is unfeasible. Drivers do not make enough money to cover the costs of these concepts.

---

[131] A brief history of car sharing. The City of Portland, Oregon. 20 October 2011.

[132] Susan A. Shaheen, Daniel Sperling, and Conrad Wagner. A short History of Carsharing in the 90's. researchgate.net. January 1999.

[133] Ilya Khrennikopv. Here Is the Future of Car Sharing, and Carmakers Should be Terrified. *Bloomberg*. 8 February 2019.

At best, a drive-share driver makes about $20 per hour gross, and having to pay $12 hourly, would drop driver income to less than minimum wages. In addition, Uber drivers do not have a steady workflow and have periods in which they are idle or trolling hopping for the App to beep.[134] Uber signed an agreement with car-share startup Getaround, allowing Uber clients to rent cars through the Uber app for self-driving for a short time. Uber customers can unlock cars from the Getaround system through the Uber app. Considering that Uber has never made a profit, the company continues to explore creative new ideas in the hope to eventually find the right mix of services to become profitable.[135]

Uber Bike and e-scooters

Uber made a business decision in 2018 to purchase the bicycle and e-scooter-share company Jump for a reported $100-to-200 million.[136] Lyft had already entered the market ahead of Uber.[137] The scooters operate with a battery-powered boost.[138] Uber is now renting JUMP electric scooters through the Uber app. Customers simply use the Uber app in their cell phones to find an available scooter, enter the QR code

---

[134] Nathan Bomey, Uber, Zipcar sign car-sharing deal. *USA Today.* 8 February 2017.

[135] Sasha Lekach. Uber launches its own car-sharing service, Uber Rent. *Marshable.com* 11 April 2018.

[136] Micah Toll. Uber launches first electric scooter share, offers free rides in first week. electrek.com. 3 October 2018. (Last accessed on 6 March 2019). According to Bloomberg, the price was closer to $200 million. See: Nick Summers. Uber wants to make its own electric scooters. https://www.engadget.com. 31 August 2018. (Last accessed on 6 March 2019).

[137] Trevor Mogg. Uber's first electric-scooter service takes on Lyft in Santa Monica. https://www.digitaltrends.com. 3 October 2018. (Last accessed on 6 March 2019).

[138] Sasha Lekach. Uber acquires electric-assist bike-share company Jump. Marshable.com. 9 April 2018.

icon in the Uber app on the handlebar, and they are on their way... at up to 15 miles per hour.

According to one study, when the Uber riders were given the alternative to rent a scooter, about 10 to 15 percent shifted to renting a scooter instead of riding in an Uber car to their destination. However, Uber increased the number of scooter trips by 15 percent, which more than made up for the loss of revenue from Uber cars. Tourists are increasingly using electric scooters instead of ride sharing options with Uber or Lyft.[139] The average fare for a ride is between $2 and $4. Uber management speculate that in about ten years, no one is going to own a car, but in the case of e-scooters, Uber entered the market late, as multiple companies have been in the market for some time, renting both, electric bikes, as well as the scooters. However, Uber's *Advanced Technologies Group (ATG)* and *MicroMobility Robotics* division are investing heavily to develop more efficient ways to operate autonomous electric bikes and scooters and achieve efficiencies in the process of recharging batteries.[140] According to a Bloomberg report, Uber wants to design and manufacture its own e-scooters.[141] [142]

As in other business ventures, Uber has been under regulatory attack related to e-scooters. For example, 4 November 2019, Los Angeles suspended the company's license to rent e-scooters and bikes. This situation opens the door for another costly legal battle. The city wants the company to

---

[139] David Alpert. Scooters are taking cars off the road, a survey says. Greater Washington. 25 October 2018.

[140] Micah Toll. Uber is working on autonomous electric bicycles and scooters, opens robotics division. electric.com. 21 January 2019. (Last accessed on 6 March 2019).

[141] Nick Summers. Uber wants to make its own electric scooters. https://www.engadget.com. 31 August 2018. (Last accessed on 6 March 2019).

[142] Joshua Brustein. Uber is building its own scooter to compete in frenzy. *Bloomberg Businessweek*. 30 August 2018.

provide information on all rentals as a way to ensure that the rules are being followed. Uber claims that the city unfairly is seeking internal company information, and is tinkering with personal information by demanding how consumers are using the services in real time, and resembles a government surveillance program. California's leftists seem to be hell-bent on destroying Uber and competitors like Lyft in one way or another.

Although e-scooter renters are responsible to wear a helmet and respect traffic laws, seldom to riders use a helmet, and there are no standards at the Federal level, and each state, and each jurisdiction either require scooter riders to ride in sidewalks or in streets. The liabilities are huge, and the number of accidents is piling up.[143] [144] The scooters are showing up everywhere, triggering numerous problems. Some people look at them as a new public nuisance. Apparently, the security mechanisms can be tinkered with and the scooters can be hijacked by criminal elements.

There are numerous legal questions, and the number of accidents is piling up.[145] The first recorded accidental death in the D.C. Metro area linked to a scooter took place near Dupont Circle on 21 September 2018. The 20-year-old rider on a Lime scooter was hit by an SUV. Between January 2013 and August 2018, according to NBC, more than 95,000 people went to emergency rooms due to hoverboard and electric scooter injuries.[146] [147] One of the tragic outcomes of

---

[143] Uber. Introducing JUMP scooters. Uber.com.

[144] David Murrell. Brace Yourself: The Dockless Bike and Scooter Scourge is Coming. *Philadelphia Magazine.* 4 March 2019.

[145] Zukerberg & Halperin. DC Scooter Accidents Keep Rising. zukerberghhalpering.com (Accessed on 6 March 2019).

[146] Aimee Cho, Carissa DiMargo, and Andrea Swalec. Man Killed Near Dupont Circle in DC's First Fatal Scooter Crash. NBC4 Washington. 21 September 2018.

[147] Paul Gessler. Scooter safety on minds of riders after man on scooter struck, killed in DC. *CBSWUSA0.* 21 September 2018.

the scooter frenzy in the D.C. metro was the death of 66-year-old Saul Edmonds in October 2018, when he tumbled down a Metro station escalator in his electric scooter.[148] The number of public complaints are increasing, as pedestrians complaint about scooters are being ridden on sidewalks, and they are left all over the place, creating a hazard, as pedestrians could trip as they try to bypass them.

According to a study on e-scooters conducted between 5 September and 30 November 2018, in Austin, Texas, in 936,110 rides, at least 192 people were injured requiring a visit to a hospital emergency room. The e-scooters were used for a total of 182,333 hours. At least 15 percent of the injured were found to have suffered traumatic brain injuries, since only a small percentage of riders use helmets. The study was conducted by Austin authorities and the Center for Disease Control and Prevention (CDC).[149] About 8 percent of the injured rides had to spend at least 48 hours interned in a hospital.[150]

In another study conducted in California in 2018, using records of emergency room use by people injured riding e-scooters in Los Angeles and Santa Monica. According to the findings, at least 249 riders were injured and had to go to an emergency room for treatment. At least 8.4 percent of the people injured were pedestrians who were struck by e-scooter riders. For comparison, about 5,000 people are killed riding motorcycles and 840 people riding bicycles in 2016.[151] There

[148] Fox5. Family of 66-year-old Saul Edmonds grieve the tragic death. Fox5. 13 October 2018.
[149] Sharon Jayson, Kaiser Health News for CNN. Injuries prompt CDC investigation into e-scooters. https://www.ksl.com/article/46503589/injuries-prompt-cdc-investigation-into-e-scooters. 4 March 2019.
[150] *Alexander Stoklosa*. The First Ever E-Scooter Safety Study Results Are In, and They're Terrible. *Car and Driver.6 May 2019.*
[151] Sarah Holder. Electric Scooters Sent Nearly 250 Riders to L.A. Emergency Rooms Last Year. Is That a Lot? *Citylab.com.* 29 January 2019.

are legitimate reasons to be concerned about e-scooters, tightening of regulations cannot be blamed exclusively on leftist California politicians.

Although the percent of riders injured in both studies was less than one percent, when millions of people ride e-scooters annually, the number of injured is significant. According to the Consumer Product Safety Commission's National Electronic Injury Surveillance System (NEISS), over 550,000 people were injured in 2017 riding skateboards and bicycles. According to an article in the Insurance Journal, litigation related to e-scooter injuries in on the increase. In general, injuries to e-scooter riders were the result of lack of adherence to traffic laws and warnings by companies that rent them. Scooter rental companies are facing litigation for gross negligence, but companies claim that riders waive liabilities when they rent one.

In addition to riders getting hurt, pedestrians are being hit, and they are tripping over scooters left on sidewalks.[152] Another article published in the Insurance Journal points out that injury lawyers are chasing scooter accidents, which is bound to increase litigation.[153]

In D.C. scooter and bicycle riders are not required to wear helmets. Scooter riders have to be at least 16-years-old, but the scooters are not considered vehicles. They are defined as motor-driven cycles. They are allowed to use bike lanes. They are permitted on sidewalks, with the exception of the area known as the Central Business District (Defined as the area south of Massachusetts Ave N.W. between 23rd Street on the west, and 2nd Street on the East, to the Mall and D Street S.W.) Dockless scooters are all over the place in the D.C.

---

[152] Janet Lorin. Who Pays for Injuries Blamed on E-Scooters? *Insurancejournal.com*. 29 January 2019.
[153] Anousha Sakoui and Edvard Petterson. Injury Lawyers Chasing Scooter Accidents, in Search of Insurers. *Insurancejournal.com*. 12 June 2018.

Metro area, and the numbers are increasing.[154][155] Just about all jurisdictions in the D.C. Metro area have been forced to review regulations. For example, the Arlington Va. County Board opened a pilot program, and decided to ban scooters from sidewalks, which is contrary to the regulations in D.C. As DC Metro jurisdictions consider enacting new regulations, in other jurisdictions, as for example, New York, e-scooters are considered "unregistered motorized vehicles," which are technically illegal on sidewalks and streets, although apparently police are choosing to ignore people using them to avoid confrontations, waiting for new guidelines.[156]

The principal scooter companies are Bird Rides, Bolt, JUMP (Uber), LimeBike (Uber), Lyft (Motivate), Scoot, Skip and Spin, and Waybot's scooters, but their numbers are increasing. In Arlington, VA, as of March 2019, there are at least seven Dockless electric scooter companies operating in the county.[157] The e-scooters have already been deployed to over 100 cities. Sooner or later the chickens will come home, as people complain to elected officials about scooters left all over the place on sidewalks, potentially becoming road hazards for pedestrians, particularly people with disabilities.[158] Based on CNN article published on 22 November 2019, e-scooters are riding into serious trouble and are being increasingly

---

[154] David MacMillan. Arlington VA fails to protect pedestrians, riders in new scooter program. https://www.medium.com. (Last accessed on 6 March 2019).

[155] Fox5. Alexandria considers Dockless bikes, scooters. *Fox5*. 9 October 2018.

[156] Gordon Chaffin. Scooter owner offers observations after 160 miles. dccommutertimes.com. 23 October 2019. (Last accessed on 7 March 2019.)

[157] Bolt joins Arlington scooters; Top scooter complaints so far? Washington Informer. 6 March 2019.

[158] Scott Kirsner. Are we letting our sidewalks be turned into giant scooter rental lots? *Boston Globe*. 16 June 2019.

regulated and banned by local jurisdictions all over the world.[159]

So what?

There have been plenty of ups and downs in the automotive sector for over a century, but technological advances have always come out, and been implemented. If the markets want driverless vehicles, eventually viable technology will come about. However, the rideshare sector of the economy cannot be dependent on the advent of technology for survival. Solutions to all the challenges affecting rideshare have to be implemented on the basis of what is available right now, without depending on what may come about at some point in the future. Uber should stop investing in R&D in this area, and wait till the auto manufacturers come up with their own solution. Each sector should stay in their own lane.

---

[159] Julia Buckley. E-scooters suddenly appeared everywhere, but now they're riding into serious trouble. *CNN* • 22nd November 2019

• VII •

View from Behind The Windshield

Ubering around the Nation's Capital presents a unique perspective of reality, and the contrast between areas of extreme wealth, and areas of extreme poverty. It is all visible to anybody who wants to see what has been building up for years. *"Reality,"* is defined as: *the state of things as they actually exist, as opposed to an idealistic or notional idea of them.*[160] The current *"reality"* did not appear overnight. The problems have been building up since the 1960's, and repairs cannot be made overnight.

Homelessness

There are homeless encampments all over the District of Columbia, and the situation seems to be growing worse, but is still far from conditions in San Francisco, Los Angeles, and Santa Monica, California. A similar situation is building in New York City, and other parts of the country. Frankly, if I had not been driving around for over three years, I never would have become aware of the homeless tragedy.

The average person normally does not go to some of the areas I have visited. I have witnessed the situation spreading practically all over the Capital since 2015. One of the sad things is that the news media apparently does not care about the situation. As a result, Americans are uninformed about what is going on around the Nation's Capital. The D.C. Metro Area is a microcosm about what is going on, despite it being

---

[160] The Cambridge Dictionary defines reality as the actual state of things, or the facts involved in such a state.

one of the most economically strong areas of the United States.

Economic mismanagement

For many years, America was impoverished, in part, due to substantial political and economic mismanagement. Americans tried to fix the world while neglecting the home front, and it showed. While the country's economy reigned supreme in the world, domestically the future was uncertain. An estimated 46.5 million people lived in poverty, and median family income continued to decline, reaching a low point in 2008.[161]

Just as it was in 1965, about 15 percent of the population continued to live in poverty, despite the so-called *War on Poverty,* and all the social legislation enacted since the 1960's. Wages were flat, or retreating. In 1999-2000, the median income was $54,473. By 2011 the median income had dropped to $49,434, increasing slightly towards the end of the year to around $51,413.[162] The financial crisis of 2008, had a definite negative impact on the income of American families. Uber was created in the middle of the financial crisis that started in 2008.

As of December 2013, Americans had endured 59 months of above 7.3 percent unemployment.[163] One of the consequences

---

[161] *Who is considered poor in the U.S.?* In 2011, a single person under 65 years of age living with an income of less than $11,702, or a couple with two children with an income under $22,811. About 25 % of all jobs paid less than $23,000, and about 50% of all jobs paid less than $34,000 annually. See: U.S. Bureau of the Census, *Income, Poverty and Health Insurance Coverage in the United States: 2012*, released 17 Sept. 2013.

[162] United States Census Burau, Median Income of Households Using Three-Year Moving Averages 1999-2011.

[163] Terence P. Jeffrey, "54 months: Record Stretch of 7.5%+ Unemployment Continues," *CNSNews.com*, 6 July 2013. The situation improved slightly

of high unemployment is that the unemployed and their families lose access to employer-provided benefits, including medical, dental, vision and other types of insurance, as well as access to 401-K retirement savings plans. Uber had a large pool of potential drivers in 2010 when it commenced operations due to the economic situation.

Without a doubt, conditions have improved since the elections of 2016. The economic figures reported at the end of 2018, confirmed that recovery continued, with employers creating 312,000 new jobs in the last month of 2018, plus an upward revision of 58,000 for October and November. The unemployment rate rose to 3.9% from 3.7%, but that was good news as 419,000 workers joined the labor force. Many had not yet found work, but the flood of job seekers suggests the U.S. still isn't at full employment. Why? People who had stopped looking for employment have returned to actively "looking for employment," drawn by more openings and rising pay. However, despite all of these figures, homelessness is visible all over the D.C. Metro Area within a short distance of the White House and the Capitol Building. *Why?*

Drug addiction

D.C. has the worse drug addiction crisis in the country, and the situation has been going from bad to worse between 2015 and 2019.[164] According to the Center for Disease Control (CDC), there were an estimated 64,000 drug overdose deaths in the U.S. in 2016.[165] According to current estimates, about

---

by mid-2014, but for lower-wage labor earning less than $15 per hour the situation was about the same.

[164] Christopher Ingraham. CDC releases grim new opioid overdose figures: 'we're talking about more than an exponential increase.' *The Washington Post*. 21 December 2017.

[165] For example, Keith Humphrey, of Stanford University, is quoted by Christopher Ingraham in his article published by the Washington Post

175 people die in the U.S. every day due to illegal drugs. According to the Office of the Chief Medical Examiner (OCME) in D.C., there was a 100 percent increase in fatal narcotics overdoses from 2015 to 2016 (114 to 231 deaths). And the crisis continues to grow. In 2017, the number of drug overdose deaths climbed to 70,237 nationwide. D.C. experienced one of the highest number of deaths in the country due to drug abuse, estimated at about 44 victims per 100,000 inhabitants. Deaths among Afro-Americans increased 127 percent from 2015 to 2016.[166]

The news media and academia blame the Trump Administration for the trend, when he was not even in power in 2015 and 2016![167] According to at least one published article, Uber drivers can be witnesses, as well as unwitting direct participants in the crisis.[168] A dealer/pusher can call an Uber, and use it to distribute drugs with multiple stops during a point to point ride. How many times does this happen nationwide? Nobody knows! There have been a small number of documented cases, but nobody knows to what extent there has been an *"Uberization of drug trafficking."* What are the potential legal implications for Uber drivers when a passenger is using the system to deliver narcotics to their clients?[169]

---

on 21 December 2017, blaming President Trump, when in fact, it was President Obama who was at the White House from 2009 till January 2017.

[166] Government of the District of Columbia. Office of the Chief Medical Examiner. Opioid-related Fatal Overdoses: January 1, 2014, to December 31, 2017. Report date: 22 January 2018.

[167] President Trump has done more on the subject of fighting the opioid crisis than former presidents, see: Allan Coukell. President Trump Signs Bipartisan Bill to Fight Opioid Crisis. PEW. 24 October 2018.

[168] Brian Anderson. How Uber is changing drug dealing. *Motherboard.* 26 May 2016.

[169] Several articles have been published of cases were police actually arrested an Uber passenger for felony possession of narcotics. See: Uber

As a driver I had an interesting experience. I picked up a passenger in Silver Spring, Maryland, and drove him to a location in D.C. The passenger told me that he is a store manager at the mall where I picked him up, but he was on his way to a more profitable part time job selling "legal" marijuana at a nightspot in D.C., and normally that makes him about $1,000 per night. It is an all cash business, but although the "business" is "legal" according to local laws, it is illegal, under Federal law. Because the banking system is regulated by the Federal Government, they cannot accept deposits derived from an illegal activity at the Federal level. Thus, it is a cash business, and the cashflow and profits remain hidden from both, *"the government,"* and criminal elements who target the drug dealers to get their cash. Thus, the "system" has created an underworld where criminal elements target each other to get their hands on the cash. In the meantime, the Internal Revenue Service (IRS) has no way of taxing the cashflow. Local law enforcement and federal law enforcement officers are caught *betwixt and between* in this mess.

I let my rider talk, but was careful not to stick my nose into the security issues related to the flow of illegally acquired funds. My passenger went on to describe his clients, which included off-duty policemen out of uniform from several area jurisdictions. They enjoy their grass while off duty. Apparently, local jurisdictions in the DC Metro Area fail to require frequent unannounced drug testing of cops. If they were required to *"piss in the cup"* once in a while in an unpredictable way, would they be smoking grass? The ride

---

driver gets an assist in drug bust. *Miachaeltravels.* 8 December 2017; and Howard Cohen. This Uber passenger picked the wrong driver to take him to buy drugs. *The Miami Herald.* 2 December 2017; and Ariel Zilber. Six-person 'drug ring used fake Uber stickers on their cars to avoid suspicion while dealing heroin and cocaine to over 100 customers.' *The Daily Mail.* 3 May 2017.

was otherwise unremarkable. *It is incredible what rideshare passengers are willing to discuss with drivers!* Obviously, my rider had no idea of my background, and my links to Uncle Sam in one capacity or another going back 51 years.

This situation is a contributor to an increase in the number of homicides in D.C., which went up by 38 percent in 2018 over 2017. In the first month of 2019, the homicide rate in D.C. increased by 64 percent over 2018 (from 11 to 18). Property crime totals went up by 13 percent, all crime total by nine percent, according to the Metropolitan Police Department.[170] As of the end of February, the overall DC homicide rate was up by nearly 88 percent. This situation is not unique in the country. San Francisco, California, as well as other metropolitan areas in the states have a similar or worse situation than the D.C. Metro Area. Homicides in NYC went up by 14 percent in 2019, drive-bys a 50 percent spike in February 2019. As of the end of February 2019, the NYPD reported 52 murders, compared to 38 in 2018.[171]

So what?

Ubering around the D.C. Metro Area provides an unusual, but very sad view of the economic situation in the country, despite important improvements since 2017. Other than people who work directly in programs to assist the poor, drivers for Uber and Lyft get to troll around the region and witness conditions that most people do not even know exist. Economic improvements are visible since 2015, but the numbers of homeless and the number of people panhandling at intersections, do not seem to decrease. Some faces linked to

---

[170] D.C. Government. Metropolitan Police Department District Crime Data at a Glance, as of 31 January 2019.
[171] Homicides in NYC cup 14% this year, driven by frightening 50% spike in February. New York Daily News. 5 March 2019.

particular street corners disappear, but others remain there week after week, month after month, and some including the "combat veteran" panhandling at the corner of Lee Highway and Washington Boulevard, in Arlington, Virginia has been there for at least six years.

The improvements since 2016, are real, but opposition politicians are into denial. Instead of focusing on fixing problems, they are into "resistance." In the meantime, there are homeless people all over the place begging for help. There are panhandlers at key intersections in D.C., Arlington, Fairfax, Alexandria, Montgomery, and Prince Georges counties in Maryland and Virginia. Between narcotics addicts and mentally challenged people, the local scene is not pretty. *It is visible everywhere for people who want to see!*

According to the Metropolitan Washington Council of Governments, homelessness decreased in the region to about 10,480 people, a six percent decrease from 2017 (or 648 people). In May 2016, the number of homeless was 12,215, an increase of 592 people from 2015. In D.C., the number of homeless is estimated at about 7,473. The number of homeless in Arlington, Virginia stands at about 232, despite efforts to reduce the numbers by the Arlington Homeless Services Center. In Alexandria, Virginia, it is estimated that there are about 226 homeless individuals as of 2018, of which about 53 are children. In Montgomery County, Maryland, one of the wealthiest counties in the United States, there were about 69,755 people (6.7%) who live under the Federal Poverty line. An estimated 70,780 people are food insecure. (Not sure where their next meal is coming from). According to a 2018 census, there was a drop of six percent from a similar census taken in 2017.

The nation's child poverty rate has fallen to 18%, but that still means that there are about 13 million children living in poverty, including 33 percent of Native Americans. They are not visible in the DC Metro Area because there are no "Indian" reservations in the vicinity... so they are out of the mind for elected officials. However, there are another 33 percent of African-American children and 25 percent of Hispanic/Latino children living in poverty. They are definitely visible. Despite economic improvements since 2016, the percentage of children growing up in poverty is very high. The states with the largest improvements in the recent past are Iowa, North Dakota, Arkansas, Montana, and the top improvements have been achieved in Colorado, with a 25 percent child poverty reduction.

As of 17 December 2018, there were at least 552,830 homeless people in the U.S. representing a small increase over the previous year, after several years of steady decreases. The increase in drug addiction and the limited assistance to the mentally challenged contribute to the problem. Ask any UBER driver about what they see as they troll around waiting for the next ride.

Panhandler on the corner of Lee Hwy and Washington Blvd in Arlington, Va. On 29 June 2013. Six years later, he is still there as of May 2019.

(The picture was taken by the author, No known restrictions on publication.)

Homelessness in the DC Metro Area

A scene from Pennsylvania Avenue N.W. Wash. D.C.

This homeless person was on the grounds of the US Capitol, across from the US Supreme Court on 10/12/2013. As policymakers engaged in gridlock and the government remained "closed," multiple poor people roamed the streets of the Capital. Like other homeless, this woman pushes a grocery store cart with her meager belongings through the streets of the Capital. (The picture taken by the author, No known restrictions on publication.)

This is a picture of a homeless person at the corner of 19th and M Streets NW, Washington, D.C. on 10/12/2013. This is another example of the hundreds of homeless and mentally-challenged individuals roaming the streets of the Capital pushing a "liberated" grocery store cart with his belongings. (The picture taken by the author, No known restrictions on publication.)

Homeless encampment under the Whitehurst Freeway in N.W. D.C. near Georgetown. Picture taken by the author on 7-7-2019.

Homeless living in a tent on 23rd St. NW. in a bridge over Virginia Avenue.

Homeless encampment at a park located between 20th and 21th Streets N.W.

Homeless sleeping on Pennsylvania Avenue. View towards the White House. The tower on the left is the Old Post Office building, now the Trump Hotel.

Homeless encampment under the Whitehurst Freeway near the intersection of K and 27th Street, NW, Washington, about two blocks from the Watergate building complex and about ten blocks from the White House. Speaker of the House Nancy Pelosi lives in an apartment about two blocks from this location. Without a doubt she passes this area practically every day. The D.C. Government shut down the encampment and put a wire fence around it, but within days the homeless were back.

**Homeless looking for food in a
trash container, within a couple of
blocks from the U.S. Capitol**

Homeless on 1st Street, NE, in Washington, D.C. The CNN
address in D.C. is located at 820 1st Street, across from the
homeless encampment. However, CNN, to my knowledge
has never sent a camera crew and a reporter to talk to this
people and record their stories. How can they be helped if
the news media does not seem to care about their predicament?

Homeless person at the corner of 15th St. and Constitution Avenue, NW. across from the Washington Monument. He sleeps on top of a grill from where hot air comes out from the government building's heating system. In a clever way, he tied all four corners of a canvass to the grill, creating a "roof effect" and trapping some heat under it. On this day in January 2019, there was snow on the ground and the temperature dropped to 4° Fahrenheit.

Homeless sleeping on a bench on Pennsylvania Ave. N.W. Washington, D.C. right between the Capitol Building and the White House. The picture was taken in January 2019, when the temperature fluctuated between 11° and 28° degrees Farenheight.

HOMELESSNESS IN THE D.C. METRO REGION

• VIII •

Cultural Decadence

> "Every kingdom divided against itself is headed for destruction."
>
> Matthew 12:25

Rideshare and the *Social System*

The American *"social system"* is comprised of the norms, values, and ethics that govern interrelationships between all individuals, races, ethnic groupings, formal and informal organizations, family groups, economic classes, religious affiliations, and institutions that form the structure of the nation. The *"system"* comprises multiple *"subsystems"* of people and groups that have affinities that bring them together. The *"social system"* embodies multiple complex components that interact with each other based on traditions, shared thinking, passions, and collective wisdom, which transmitted from one generation to another constitute the *culture* of the nation.

What is *civil society*? It is a concept with multiple components and variables. It involves shared values and interests, as well as *un-coerced* collectively negotiated actions of a community of people. It includes the private and the public sectors, non-governmental organizations, religious and professional organizations, labor unions, advocacy groups and numerous other institutions and organizations that voluntarily bring together people with similar affinities, interests, purposes or values, whatever they may be. There are many definitions, but what they all have in common is *respect for the rights of other members of society*, as well as classical liberal values, and respect for democracy.[172]

Then and now

One of the most interesting political science studies of the U.S. was written by British jurist, historian, and statesman, Viscount James Bryce (1838-1922) in the mid-1880's, with the title *The American Commonwealth*. Bryce was concerned about British ignorance and misunderstanding of the former colonies.[173] At the time, there were about 60 million people in the U.S. and the Union consisted of 38 states and territories that were later to become states. Bryce's transcendental study described the American political system and American society. Americans were optimistic about their future, and

---

[172] *Liberal* values defined as supporting free markets, civil liberties, and the ideals of the American Revolution and the Constitution– *not far-left politics*!

[173] James Bryce's book is considered one of the three basic studies of the United States system of government, the others being *The Federalist Papers*, consisting of a series of 85 essays published between 1787 and 1788 by James Madison, Alexander Hamilton, and John Jay, outlining how they perceive that the new government would function under the U.S. Constitution; and Alexis de Tocqueville's *Democracy in America*. Born in France in 1805, de Tocqueville was a historian and political thinker who traveled to the United States and wrote about his experiences and observations of life in the young nation. The book was published in two volumes in 1835 and 1840. He wrote highly of the U.S. Constitution, and applied many of his observations later on in France, when he participated in writing a new Constitution for the Second Republic in 1848. One of de Tocqueville's most important observations was: *"there is no country in the whole world in which the Christian religion retains a greater influence over the souls of men than in America, and there can be no greater proof of its' utility, and of its conformity to human nature, than that its' influence is most powerfully felt over the most enlightened and free nations of the earth."* If he were writing about the U.S. in 2014, would de Tocqueville be able to make the same observation?

the economy was expanding, even if there were periods of recession. America was *respected* and was progressively increasing its' influence in world affairs. A new preeminent world leader was being forged, opined Bryce. He was correct in his assessment. Without a doubt, the 20th Century was the American century, with the American economy becoming the most advanced economy in the world, and with the United States becoming the preeminent world power after WWI.

If Bryce conducted a similar analysis in 2019, he would be more concerned about the American ignorance of their own country's history and the widespread misunderstanding of the Constitution in which the country's political and economic systems rest. Back in the 1880s, British elites assumed that the U.S. was a vulgar, uncultured, and rustic country barely starting to industrialize. In 2019 Americans seem to be deconstructing the country, with an increasingly vulgar culture, with schools that are barely educating young people. The economy was suffering from a process of de-industrialization. In world affairs, the U.S. has been losing influence as the economy deteriorated and military conflicts overseas ending inconclusively, or never coming to an end. American civil society was challenged internally and externally in ways that could not have been predicted back in the 1880s. The move to destroy statues of historical figures, from Cristopher Columbus in New York City, to Confederate Generals in New Orleans, to murals depicting George Washington in the San Francisco area, is indicative of the level of rampant stupidity around the country.

Uber was founded in 2009, at a time when the economy was in desperate need to introduce creativity, particularly making use of advances in computer science and IT, to invent new concepts that make use of the new power now available. *Gentrification* or the recovery of rundown neighborhoods in Washington, D.C. and other cities near downtown areas may not have made much progress without the ridesharing technology. In these neighborhoods there is little or no parking, and whatever exists is unaffordable. Public transportation is not fully developed. Uber and copycats made it possible for millennials to move to *"gentrified neighborhoods"* and be able to afford transportation without having to own a vehicle. Uber provided a new freedom to move around at an affordable price for work and leisure. The introduction of electronic scooters and bikes has helped people to move around in these areas, while introducing multiple new challenges.

American society has been increasingly willing to allow people the freedom to live their lives however they want, even if it involves self-destructive behavior. *Live and let live!* The spirit and letter of the American Constitution supports the notion of personal liberty, with the rational assumption of reciprocity and respect for other people's rights. Uber is not in the business of dealing in the social issues that affect the nation, but it can play a positive or negative influence. When Uber drivers decide to deny service to people because they have a MEGA hat on, they become part of the problem, not a solution. The same applies if drivers deny service to a rider because they have a Hillary Clinton hat on. The Civil Rights Act of 1964 listed a number of protected classes, but that group has to be expanded to include the current make up of society. Muslims, Koreans, Iraqis, Iranians do not have a historical presence and were not included in the 1964 legislation... But they are a fact of life now. Political groups were not included either, not were homosexuals. Does that mean that it is perfectly legal to discriminate against them? Obviously not!

Cultural values

Predators, cheaters and sociopaths are not necessarily willing to provide *reciprocal tolerance* under an umbrella of pluralism and respect so that everyone benefits. Loudmouths and bullies have been allowed to have their way. Particularly serious is the growing intolerance of those who preach tolerance. They only remember the First Amendment to the Constitution when it suits them. At times it is not clear if American society is suffering from cultural decadence, or advancing towards a progressive "Utopian" multicultural, tolerant, pluralistic society, where there is no difference between right and wrong. Some writers have obsessed with comparing the American experience since the 1960's as a predictor of a fate similar to that of the Roman Empire.[174] Some aspects of the recent American experience are dreadful, but it is far from reaching the level of disruption suffered by the Roman Empire.

American cultural values have been deliberately torpedoed by snake-oil salesmen promoting morals, lifestyles, and behavior contrary to those of established in mainstream society. These include the *hippie* movement that emerged in the mid-1960, the associated drug culture, and the general nihilistic mayhem that followed. In other words, the masses were indoctrinated with the idea that *morality does not inherently exist*, and all moral values are abstractly contrived. Sadly, the *turn on, tune in, and drop out* culture started in the 1960's has taken hold and is a big contributor to economic problems affecting the country, particularly high drug use, which produced in 2017 an estimated 70,000 deaths from drug overdoses. Compare that with the approximately 58,000 American casualties during the ten-year Vietnam War. Where are the mass movements and demonstrations comparable to

---

[174] During the 3rd century AD, the Roman Empire suffered military defeats, plagues, civil wars, Barbarian invasions, corruption, abuse of power, insecurity, economic decline, religious discord, unrestrained immigration, government confiscation of private assets, famine, and the inability to recruit and maintain an effective military, and finally Rome fell and was sacked in 410 AD.

the anti-war movement of the 1960's? Traditional moral order has turned into *obscene moral disorder and destructiveness* that has nothing to do with creating a more tolerant and pluralistic society.

War on Drugs

Since the late 1960's, narcotics addiction has increased exponentially, despite a very inefficient "war on drugs," which has never been carried out forcefully, and as a result, it has failed miserably. Instead, the opposite has taken place, including the legalization of marijuana as a "solution" to the problem. What the country desperately needs are leaders with gonads, willing to instruct law enforcement to plow under drug trafficking organizations (DTOs). When over 70,000 Americans die in one year as a result of drug addiction, it is irresponsible and inhumane not to do something about it. After allowing the current situation to build for about fifty years, something more effective has to be done.

The principal drug linked to deaths from overdose is Fentanyl, a synthetic opioid, estimated to have caused about 39% of the deaths, but Meth is the principal killer. Most of the Meth is manufactured in Mexico and smuggled over the border into the US. The number of victims were adding up year after year... Finally, in 2018 the number of deaths from drug use declined somewhat from the previous year. The slight decline is linked to stricter border control under President Trump. *How many more people have to die before the "war on drugs" is played out for real?*

Drug Overdose Deaths in the US
Source: Centers for Disease Control and Prevention (CDC)

2018 – 68,557 drug overdose deaths – First decline in many years!

2017 - 70,237 drug overdose deaths, of which 47,600 were linked to opioids (67.8 percent)

2016 - 60,000 + drug overdose deaths, with a fivefold increase in deaths involving synthetic opioids, such as fentanyl

2015 – 47,000 + drug overdose deaths, with a 137 percent increase in deaths involving synthetic opioids

Mental illness

The challenges associated with mental illness are not unique to the U.S. Every country is affected by behavioral and emotional disorders and how to address them. To start with, diagnosing a mental illness and the degree of impairment is complicated. Based on published statistics, somewhere between four and five percent of Americans are affected by some form of mental illness, with the highest concentration in the 18-to-25-year-old bracket. As of November 2015, there were about 320 million people living in the U.S. of which between 12 and 16 million suffer some form of mental illness.

According to the *Diagnostic and Statistical Manual of Mental Disorders*, there could be around 11.4 million adults with serious mental illness.[175] Most of these people are not institutionalized, and many have not even been diagnosed as

---

[175] Twenty percent of Americans are mentally disturbed, 19 January 2012. http://rt.com/usa/disturbed-mental-illness-study-225/; U.S. Census Bureau, POPClock Projection, 29 December 2012; See National Institute of Mental Health's National Comorbidity Survey, and Substance Abuse

suffering from a mental illness. The "system" to take care of the mentally ill is broken, which compounds the problem of establishing and enforcing gun control legislation, because there is no complete database of people who should not have access to guns. Rideshare functions with that background, but it should not be allowed to add to the mix of challenges by tolerating any type of discrimination.

The issue of criminal insanity is highly controversial, as the legal profession uses *"cognitive"* insanity as a means to defend lawbreakers. Many people who commit crimes are not able to discern right and wrong, are mentally impaired, and are incompetent to stand trial. The issue is further complicated by mentally challenged criminals, who clearly are not mentally competent. Instead of ending in institutions that can provide needed care, they end up in jail instead.

Based on a study carried out in 2010, using 2004-2005 data, it was determined that there were three times more seriously mentally ill persons in jail and prisons than in hospitals. It was further determined that at least 16 percent of inmates in jails and prisons (about 319,918 individuals) have a serious mental illness. In 1955 there was one psychiatric bed for every 300 Americans. In 2005 there was one psychiatric bed for every 3,000 Americans, of which the majority was filled with court-ordered "forensic cases," and not readily available.[176]

What happens when the large population of criminally insane individuals complete their sentences? They are released without any kind of follow up or treatment, which

---

and Mental Health Services Administration's National Survey of Drug Abuse and Health (NSDUH).

[176] E. Fuller Torrey, M.D., Sheriff Aaron D. Kennard, MPAA, Sheriff Don Eslinger, Richard Lamb, M. D. and James Pavle, *More Mentally Ill Persons in Jails and Prisons Than Hospitals: A Survey of States.* National Sheriffs' Association and Treatment Advocacy Center, May 2010.

leads to a high rate of recidivism. And they are out there... and do call for ride-sharing services, and some are, without a doubt, driving Uber, Lyft, and similar services, because it is practically impossible to avoid making them driver-partners.

Gun violence

Americans are stunned every time a new incident of gun violence takes place, but not enough to make changes. According to existing legislation, only law-abiding people of sound mind can obtain a firearm. The argument goes that criminals, by definition, do not abide by legislation, and *guns do not kill people, people kill people.* Despite the obvious, energy is directed at gun control, instead of directing energy towards finding solutions to the mental health crisis.

So what?

Extremists at both ends of the political spectrum share similar traits. Pathologically insecure and marginalized crackpots cluster in paramilitary and right-wing militias at one end, and left-wing unruly mobs at the other end of the spectrum demonize each other. Irrationally, they see the world in absolute and uncompromising terms with no grays or middle ground. Fanaticism is leading to the creation of a complex phenomenon that is resulting in *virtual ungoverned spaces* throughout the country where antisocial extremists rule. Uber functions within the overall framework prevalent in American society, so it should not be a surprise when a driver or a passenger gets attacked, or when a mass murderer gets driven to where they plan to carry out a massacre by an Uber driver. Obviously, Uber and other rideshare companies are not responsible for the conditions under which they have to operate.

• IX •

Rideshare's Top Vulnerability

Limited to non-existent insurance coverage for drivers is the most serious vulnerability for the rideshare sector of the economy. The problem is shared by Uber, Lyft, and their competitors. Drivers lack the most basic insurance policies, particularly legally mandated payroll coverage: workman's compensation, unemployment insurance, disability, survivor benefits, and health insurance. Accident insurance is generally inadequate when compared with the exposure for drivers who are on the road four or five times the normal mileage of non-professional drivers. This situation is the principal trigger for regulators in multiple jurisdictions who want to force this sector to adhere to legal requirements that apply to most employers. Insurance coverage is the *Achilles Heel* of the drive-share sector.

Ride-share drivers have operated for about nine years without basic insurance coverage. In September, 2019, Uber started to provide some insurance protection for drivers while they have their app turned on. Limited as they may be, these types of insurance coverages make Uber a pioneer in granting some limited insurance coverage to workers in the gig economy. This indicates that Uber management is aware of the challenge and is trying to do something about it, in part due to government regulator pressure in some jurisdictions, such as California and New Jersey, but it may be too little and too late.

With a population of 326 million people in the United States, it is a numbers game... An infinitesimal percentage of people are touched by tragedies, but tragedies occur daily, and any of them can become a catalyst for conflict. Insurance coverage against multiple perils is a *sine qua non* – absolutely necessary! This flaw in the basic business model can lead to the downfall of Uber and the principal competitors in rideshare.

Drivers by the very nature of their job are more exposed to all kinds of perils than most people. Perpetual recidivists, including criminals with some form of mental illness, are allowed to roam freely to continue victimizing innocent people. It only takes a relatively small number of mentally unfit people to produce episodic tragedies. Anybody can make the wrong judgement, misinterpret or misunderstand facts, act based on inadequate knowledge, or simply make a mistake. There is a chain of cause-and-effect tragedies that unfortunately are part of the compass of daily life not only in the United States, but in all sixty-six countries where Uber is operating. There are demoniacal people who take delight in upsetting the peaceful course of life. Apocalyptic predictions are not justified, but without a doubt, something has to be done to stop the tragic never-ending chain of events that are leading to catastrophe. The situation is not just the product of *happenstance* or *happenchance,* or part of a complex plot. The possibility of something going wrong somewhere is high.

As long as there are no accidents, the issue of lack of insurance coverage is a "non-problem." But when an unfortunate accident happens unexpectedly, and a vehicle is damaged in a collision, possibly causing personal injury or death, it is too late. The issue stops being hypothetical and changes to a *"here and now"* as a significant challenge for drivers, their riders, and rideshare companies.

Disability insurance. In the event that a driver becomes disabled due to something that happens while they are working, i.e. trolling or driving a passenger, they can be covered, if they agree to purchase insurance out of pocket. Disability payments to replace income can go up to

$500 per week. Considering that drivers have been attacked by criminal elements and others have been the casualties of accidents, it makes sense for drivers to carry disability insurance. Yet, few if any drivers have disability insurance. Normally, employers are required by law to provide this type of insurance. Regulators will press gig economy companies to adhere to legal requirements, or will force them out of business. Public opinion will side with the regulators.

Medical coverage. Drivers now are able to purchase medical coverage through Uber, which was not previously available. There is a copay, and coverage can go up to $1 million. It is not clear if coverage has been made available at some kind of discount to drivers and their families, and if Uber Technologies provides any kind of subsidy. Coverage is limited and costly. Most drivers do not have medical insurance for themselves or their families. Taxpayers should not have to pay for coverage through MEDICAID for Uber drivers and their family members.[177] Public opinion will side with regulators on this issue.

Survivor benefits. After several incidents in which Uber drivers have been killed and their families left destitute, the company has made it possible for them to purchase life insurance coverage in the event they are killed while on the job. Survivor benefits are set for a maximum of $150,000. The cost is not cheap, and is based on mileage. The average driver goes about 3,000 miles per month, and would pay about $120, which is not cheap for drivers who make a gross income of about $2,500 monthly. Net income, as previously explained, is a lot less than that. After paying for fuel, maintenance, road and property taxes, and normal wear and tear and

---

[177] MEDICAID is a jointly funded Federal and state government program to provide medical insurance to families with limited income. The program provides free health insurance to about 74 million low income and disabled people.

depreciation, drivers barely earn minimum wages. Public opinion will definitely side with regulators.

Insurance providers. Uber technologies is not an insurance company, although perhaps it should be, considering the large number of people involved in what is without a doubt, a business with considerable exposure to criminal activity and accidents. As the company states in its communications with drivers on the subject, all coverage is provided by outside parties, namely Atlantic Specialty Insurance Company, a member of OneBeacon Insurance Group, and Affinity Insurance Services. Coverage is limited and policy terms are outlined in each individual policy. Recently James River, the insurance provider that has provided coverage to Uber for several years announced that they are cancelling the policy. They simply could not make any money due to the large number of incidents associated with rideshare.

Traffic accidents. Road traffic accidents do happen, although as a percentage of the number of the vehicles on the road, the incidence is relatively low. Nevertheless, catastrophic accidents happen annually. The causes are directly related to driver experience and behavior, including decision-making-ability, and human factors, such as reaction speed, and physical handicaps, including visual and auditory acuity.

Risky practices, including distractions from cell phones, tinkering with a GPS, and texting while driving are contributors to traffic accidents. By the very nature of taxi and rideshare activities, drivers are challenged by taking a passenger from pick-up point to their ultimate destination, at times to places that are unfamiliar to the driver. Chatting with passengers is another potential distraction, particularly when passengers insist on giving instructions to the drivers that contradict what the GPS is instructing the driver to do. Additionally, weather conditions, visibility, speed and multiple other factors contribute to driver exposure to collisions. Every now and then, some information filters to drivers about the experiences suffered by other drivers involved in an accident, but unless a very significant accident happens and is covered by the news media, little is learned about the experience.

YEAR	NUMBER OF VEHICLE ACCIDENTS	NUMBER OF FATALITIES	PERCENTAGE INCREASE / DECREASE
2010	5,419,000	32,999	-3.5 % ▼
2011	N/A	32,479	-2.3 % ▼
2012	N/A	33,561	2.6 % ▲
2013	N/A	32,719	-3.3 % ▼
2014	N/A	32,675	-0.09 % ▼
2015	N/A	35,092	10.5 % ▲

According to the National Highway Traffic Safety Administration (NHTSA), more than five million vehicle accidents take place annually in the United States, and about 2.2 million people are injured. Between 33,000 and 35,000 die from their injuries. The estimated cost of accident injuries tops $1 trillion dollars annually. About 30 percent of the accidents are caused by speeding. On average, claims for property damage average $3,000, while on average claims for bodily injury is about $14,650. About 10 million vehicle accidents take place annually, counting parking lot scrapes and other minor accidents all the way up to multiple car pileups, and serious incidents resulting in fatalities. (The version of the Uber app released in 2018, provides drivers on the lower left side of the GPS screen the top speed for the road, and if they are speeding, the speed is flashed in red above the legal speed to alert them to slow down.) The longer drivers are on the road, the incidence of accidents increases.

Based on published articles, insurance companies do not want to have anything to do with rideshare operations, not even when drivers are trolling for rides. They do not want to handle coverage during rides, thus leaving drivers exposed to potentially huge liabilities and damage to their vehicles. The fact is that drivers are facing $1000 deductibles provided by Uber, in addition to no access to rental vehicles paid by insurance while their cars are being repaired, and the potential for huge liabilities associated with accidents. Without a doubt, most accidents produce limited damage below the $1,000 deductible. Most Uber drivers make around $100 to $150 per day on average. That means that drivers would have to pay for repairs a sum equivalent to their gross income from driving for about two weeks. Accidents are catastrophic for the average Uber driver.[178]

A driver can ignore the risk and pretend that they are the best driver on the road, but at the end of the day, the more anyone drives, the more likely it is that they will get into an accident. Calculating accident compensation for injured passengers includes not only the cost of medical treatment, and additionally loss of work days, compensation for injuries, pain, and suffering. In cases of wrongful death, the figures skyrocket. The Internet is full of advertisement by lawyers whose practice is totally dedicated to accident law, which produces for them considerable income profiting from accidents. This situation drives up costs.

An average driver not involved in rideshare or any form of professional driving has on average an accident every 17 years. The number of drivers actively driving for Uber has been estimated at about 163,000 to 175,000, as of 2017, but these figures are low. In the D.C. Metro Area, there are an estimated 10,000 drivers working part and full time. The rate of turnover is huge, which causes the company to be permanently recruiting more drivers. There are no reliable figures as to the causes for the high turnover. With such a large number of drivers on the road for extended periods of time results in numerous accidents. That is the nature of the

---

[178] (The deductible for UBER is $1,000 and the deductible for Lyft is $2,500.)

beast. There are no published statistics, but the insurance companies are not stupid. They know the numbers, and that is why they avoid selling insurance to Uber and Lyft drivers.

Uber provides drivers insurance coverage at company cost, through James River Insurance, based in Arizona. The insurance coverage has a $1000 deductible, which means that for most accidents there is no coverage at all. Most accidents cause damage reparable under the deductible, and that money comes out of the drivers' pockets. Based on a review of complaints posted on the Internet, Uber insurance through their service provider stinks. However, James River has already announced that they will no longer do business with Uber.

These comments are a sample of what Uber drivers and riders have posted on their experiences with James River, the company contracted to provide insurance coverage:

> *Stay away from James Rivers If you are driving for UBER don't rely on James Rivers to help you.*

> *UBER should use a better insurance.*

> *JAMES RIVER IS WORTHLESS COMPANY*
> *Horrible support/insurance system*
> *This company sucks*
> *Fake and bad*

> *There is a $1,000.00 deductible that YOU have to pay before they can send you x amount over that. My damage was estimated at $900 so MY UBER SCAM INS. wouldn't send $ THIS INSURANCE IS FRAUD*

Horrible app just like the insurance company itself Once again UBER and their ways left me speechless.

My wife and I were in a crash while riding with UBER. I immediately reported the incident and a few days later a rep. from James River Ins. called to get details and whatnot. It seemed easy enough. She assured me they would be paying for any medical bills we incurred (my wife needs PT). Everything was going well until our case was transferred over to their PIP department. I completed the paperwork the requested of me and called with questions. Our rep. has not returned one phone call or email (dating back to May 22nd). The supervisor hasn't returned a call or email. I called the supervisor's supervisor, but I'm not getting my hopes up.

This is literally the worst insurance company in this country. They refuse to answer phone calls in a timely manner, and that includes the managers. They literally gave us no explanation on why we were at fault, (which our primary insurance and every other opinion we have gotten says it wasn't our fault) and they literally made the decision out of thin air.

Worst insurance company ever. Was riding in UBER and was in an accident. They do not communicate and refuse any help.

The man handling my account is incredibly rude, slow, and only returns a small percentage of my calls.

Worst insurance company ever. Only insurance company willing to cover UBER.

Worst insurance situation of my life. I was stalled out; my claim was not being followed through on by anybody at James River consistently during the whole process.

This company is terrible the worst customer service in their claims department, they never answer the phones & it typically took 1-2 days to respond to emails/voice mails. It's taking them almost 2 months to settle my claim.... which I'm still dealing with.

WHAT UBER TELLS DRIVERS ABOUT INSURANCE
(As of 12 August 2019)

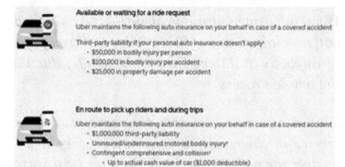

FROM THE UBER WEBSITE
(As of 12 August 2019)

"Uber maintains commercial automobile insurance that covers U.S. partner drivers that operate under the "Ridesharing" or "Transportation Network Company" ("TNC") model through **Uber's TNC subsidiaries, Rasier LLC and its affiliates.** *(1) This coverage does not apply to partner drivers who are licensed livery or black car operators or taxis, which may be requested through the Uber mobile application. Those livery partners maintain separate commercial automobile insurance pursuant to local law. Due to differences in local laws, we maintain separate policies for Ridesharing by state.* **These policies are only applicable to partner drivers of Rasier LLC (1) and its affiliates in the United States.** *The first page is for the policy covering the period of time from accepting a trip until the trip has ended and the rider(s) has exited the vehicle. The second page is for the policy covering the period of time from logging on to the Uber Partner app until accepting a trip."*

On 8 October 2019, James River Insurance informed the market that it had notified Uber's subsidiary Rasier LLC and related companies that it was cancelling effective 31

December 2019, all insurance policies issued to them.[179] The business relationship with Uber accounted for an estimated 45 percent of the insurance company's business. The coverage was due to expire at the end of February 2020, but James River was forced to take action due to huge losses associated with the Uber accounts.

J. Adam Abrams, CEO of James River, explained that the company was forced to terminate the underwriting because the relationship was not profitable.[180] In just about the same way that ride-share has not been profitable for Uber, the insurance claims made it impossible to continue the relationship. The relationship between Uber and its subsidiaries and Allstate, Farmers, and Progressive, continues in several states. Based on comments published in the insurance media, Progressive plans to continue insuring Uber for now.

So what?

- Uber does not provide transportation services of any kind – Uber is a *"technology company"* – or so the company claims in *Quixotic outbursts!* In polite society this is called *heifer dust.*
- Uber does not own, lease or charter any vehicles for the transportation of passengers; drivers are freelance independent contractors, they own or lease their vehicles, and are responsible to have their own

---

[179] Bernard Goyder and Christopher Mundo. James river to end Uber coverage early after losses. *The Insurance Insider.* 8 October 2019. NOTE: Uber set up Rasier LLC, as it has set up other subsidiaries, like UberAcht and Uber 8, to deal with specific market situations. Uber then acts as a "holding company."

[180] Brenda Bouw. James River Shares Sink After Insurer Cancels Policies Issued to Uber Subsidiary. 9 October 2019. https://www.thestreet.com/investing/stocks/james-river-shares-sink-after-insurer-cancels-policies-issued-to-uber-subsidiary-15120873 (Last accessed on 11 October 2019).

insurance. Insurance coverage through Uber starts when the driver turns on the app and ends when it is turned off.

- Insurance companies sell their coverage to "normal" drivers who are not involved in any kind of business with their vehicles, and if they do, they are expected to disclose the use of the car to their insurance provider, or their coverage may be invalidated. There are special insurance packages for professional drivers... at a much higher cost than what the average person pays for a car not used for business.

- Even if the Uber app is on as the driver trolls for riders, their own personal insurance "possibly" covers them – not any insurance through Uber – However, are the insurance companies willing to accept this arrangement? It does not look like it! Finding alternative coverage after an insurance company cancels a policy is difficult and very costly. Driveshare drivers cannot afford expensive insurance coverage. Driving without insurance is illegal.

- When the driver has accepted a passenger, the Uber insurance provides "limited" coverage with a $1,000 deductible – But why does Uber insist that drivers provide information about their own personal insurance coverage if in fact, that insurance would not cover Uber or the drivers?

- The risks of Uber drivers are very significant in case of an accident, and insurance companies want to stay away from the risks associated with ride-share operations such as Uber and Lyft.

- Uber announced in late 2018 that they are testing insurance coverage through such companies as Progressive, but only in a few states. In September 2019, Uber introduced new insurance packages available for purchase by drivers, but the fees are high, in line with the vulnerabilities that affect ride-share. The fees are high and beyond the driver's ability to pay without making extreme sacrifices, but Uber management deserves some kudos for trying.

X

War on Uber

Regulatory attention to the ride-share sector and Uber in particular was predictable.[181] [182] [183] [184] [185] States will enact labor laws to address the practices of the so-called "gig economy." California leads the way and others will follow. There are real consequences when rideshare companies, such as Uber, deny drivers basic protection earned by American workers through many years of struggle by classifying them as independent contractors. Legislation enacted to counter the "gig economy" will bring about collateral damage to other sectors of the economy that have relied on contracting out work, from barbershops and beauty parlors, to small newspapers, freelance journalists, and the home cleaning sector.

These efforts to exercise more controls over companies like Uber were foreseeable and unavoidable. What was avoidable were problems with regulators for concealing and shrouding facts when Uber was hacked by skillful criminals who gained access to information on company computers. Hackers are

---

[181] Caroline Spiezio. As the Gig Economy Goes Public, Labor Regulations Still Pose Risk. Law.Com. 20 March 2019.

[182] Joe Kennedy. Three Paths to Update Labor Law for the Gig Economy. Information Technology & Innovation Foundation. 18 April 2016.

[183] Orly Lobel. The Gig Economy & The Future of Employment and Labor Law. University of San Diego School of Law. San Diego Legal Studies Paper No.16-223. 10 October 2016.

[184] Wesley Dockery. The End Of The Gig Economy? California Labor Bill Could Drastically Affect Uber, Lyft. International Business Times. 11 September 2019.

[185] Jill Cowan. Why Newspapers Are Fighting California's Landmark Labor Bill. *The New York Times*. 12 September 2019.

always trying to breach defenses and exploit weaknesses in computer systems seeking illicit profit. Uber, like other organizations, was successfully targeted by hackers, who stole the personal data of an estimated 57 million customers and drivers in a massive breach in October 2016. Uber cannot be blamed for that. However, Uber was at fault by not disclosing expeditiously to the public what had happened.

Uber eventually had to fire the chief security officer and one of his deputies for not disclosing expeditiously what had happened. From this incident we learned that Uber had at the time at least seven million drivers and former drivers. The driver's license numbers of at least 600,000 drivers were stolen, but the company stated that Social Security numbers and credit card information was not taken. Uber denied that information on trips was stolen.

As a result of the incident, Uber had to negotiate with the Federal Trade Commission (FTC) and settle a lawsuit with the Attorney General of New York over data security disclosures. *Uber management thought they could cover the sun with a finger!* Mismanagement converted Uber from a victim of crime, to a violator of regulations, and was fined for violating legal requirements. This incident was *par for the course* and caused by annoyance and frustration operating within the regulatory environment. If you play with fire chances are that you will get burned. Uber got burned twice, by the hacker and the FTC for not following guidelines.

Compliance with labor laws

Multiple laws regulate the relationship between employers and workers, and they are not as malleable as rideshare managers think. The 40-hour work week officially became law with the signing of the Fair Labor Standards Act of 1938, which limited the workweek and established a minimum wage. The long struggle to achieve the 40-hour week can be traced back to 1791, when carpenters in Philadelphia went on strike demanding a 10-hour work day. As of January 2019, there were 29 states with a minimum wage higher than the Federal minimum wage of $7.25, which was set on 24 July 2009.

The original Social Security Act was signed into law in 1935, which has been amended multiple times since then, expanding coverage with additional social welfare and social insurance programs (Old-Age, Survivors, and Disability Insurance). This legislation cannot be ignored by rideshare companies. Both, employers and workers contribute to the program through payroll taxes. Independent contractors – *as already stated before* – have to pay the employer and employee FICA taxes.

Workers' Compensation is a form of insurance that provides wage replacement and medical benefits to employees injured in the course of employment and is required by law. It mandates survivor benefits to the dependents of workers whose deaths result from a work-related incident. People who are self-employed are excluded from workers' compensation in many states. Employer premiums are linked to the rate of injuries and illnesses in a workplace, to provide an incentive to employers to improve working conditions.

A large number of rideshare drivers have been killed and/or seriously hurt while on the job. Not having access to Workers' Compensation is not acceptable to the average American, regardless of political affiliation. Coverage is compulsory and employer violations can even result in criminal charges. Misclassifying workers as independent contractors is a potentially serious issue for employers. The Internal Revenue Service (IRS) has a test to determine if an individual is an employee or an independent contractor, based on the type of relationship between the employer and an individual, and so do each individual state.

Business enterprises have incentives to designate as 'independent contractors' individuals performing work for them. They can argue that labor laws are outmoded, but there are *serious consequences* resulting from tinkering with the law of the land. They can avoid paying the employer's share of Social Security Taxes and Medicare taxes, overtime pay, benefits such as holiday, sick pay, and vacations, and payment of unemployment compensation taxes, and workers' compensation insurance. But the chickens can and will come home sooner or later to roost.

The U.S. Department of Labor estimates that there may be 3.4 million employees that are improperly classified as independent contractors, when they should be reported as regular employees. Employers can be fined for failure to withhold income taxes and Social Security and Medicare taxes (FICA) and deposit the money with the appropriate Federal agency, namely the IRS. There are criminal penalties of up to $1,000 per misclassified worker and one year in prison can be imposed on the individuals responsible.

Connecticut's new regulations for ride-share

Under a new law in Connecticut that took effect on 1 July 2019, transportation companies (TNCs) are required to pay drivers at least 75% of the money collected from passengers, and companies are not allowed to keep more than 25% of the fees collected for a driver's work on any given day.[186] If the law is violated, drivers are entitled to file a civil suit to recover up to twice the amount of money due from their employers, plus reasonable attorney's fees and associated costs.

---

[186] TNCs, e.g. Uber and Lyft.

California's Assembly Bill 5

Traditionally, a "job" has been defined as a *"paid position of regular employment,"* or *"a specific task done as part of the routine of one's occupation, for an agreed payment by an employer."* It is defined by the *Cambridge English Dictionary* as *"the regular work that a person does to earn money."* The *Oxford Dictionary* defines it as a *"paid position of regular employment."*

Enter the so-called "gig economy," and the concept of a "job" starts to morph into some type of freelance work, as opposed to traditional permanent jobs, as part of a free market system, in which temporary positions are common and organization's contract independent workers are hired for short-term *"engagements."*

Uber Technologies, headquartered in California, is one of the entities that introduced the concept of using (not hiring) independent contractors instead of taking on workers and placing them on a regular payroll.[187]These concepts represent a very significant departure from tradition, and are regarded by labor unions and worker rights activists as a form of exploitation and denying workers their rights. Gig work in the United States is estimated to employ about 57 million freelancers whose work-life balance has been extremely and negatively affected.

Under a bill known as AB 5, all ride-sharing drivers would be considered as "employees" instead of "independent contractors." Based on several articles published on the proposed legislation, both Uber and Lyft, as well as any other ride-sharing company using the same schema could be bankrupted.[188] In a rare article published by Uber's

---

[187] Official title: *"Worker status: employees and independent contractors."*
[188] Graham Rapier. Uber and Lyft are fighting tooth and nail against a California bill that could make some drivers employees and bankrupt both companies. *Business Insider.* 21 June 2019.

Chief Executive, and Lyft's Chief Executive and President, the proposed legislation in California would cause serious damage to a growing sector of the economy.[189]

Under AB 5, for a person to be considered an independent contractor, their job description would have to pass a three-part test, based on the Supreme Court decision in May 2018 in *Dynamex v. Superior Court of Los Angeles County*. AB5 was endorsed by labor unions and multiple leftist groups.[190] Democratic presidential candidates Bernie Sanders, Kamala Harris, Elizabeth Warren, Julian Castro, and Pete Buttigieg endorsed passage of AB5.

And then, it happened... On 10 September 2019, the California State Senate passed the AB5 or *"Gig Worker Bill"* on a vote of 29 to 11. The Assembly passed the bill on a vote of 56 to 15. California Governor Gavin Newsom spoke in support of the legislation, which he signed into law, with the expectation that it would go into effect on 1 January 2020.[191] [192]

Governor Newsom described gig work as a creation of employers to erode people's basic labor protections by classifying them as independent contractors, such as worker's compensation, unemployment insurance, and other benefits. Proponents of AB 5 estimated that the State of California was losing about eight billion dollars annually from subsidizing the safety-net assistance for contract workers, according

---

[189] Dara Khosrowshahi (Chief Executive, Uber Technologies), Logan Green and John Zimmer (Co-founders, and Chief Executive and President, respectively, of Lyft. Open Forum: Uber, Lyft ready to do our part for drivers. *San Francisco Chronicle*. 12 June 2019.

[190] About 1,200 labor unions who belong to the California Labor Federation provided support for AB 5.

[191] Dustin Gardiner. California's AB% gig-work bill gets key backing from Gov. Gavin Newsom. San Francisco Chronicle. 3 September 2019.

[192] Alexandria Sage. California Senate passes bill to tighten 'gig' worker rule. Reuters. 11 September 2019.

to Assembly Member Lorena Gonzalez (D-San Diego) and principal author of AB5.

There are serious consequences to the enactment of AB5. Coverage of drivers under the Fair Labor Standards Act of 1938 and the Americans with Disabilities Act (ADA), will render ride-sharing as we have known it since 2010, unworkable.[193] Rideshare labor costs are estimated to increase by about 25 to 30 percent, which for companies that are not generating a profit, would mean bankruptcy.

The AB 5 bill was amended multiple times to exempt physicians, *repo* men, interpreters and translators, newspaper delivery workers, and about forty other professions, and designed to target specifically ride-sharing. DoorDash, Lyft, and Uber joined forces and each contributed $30 million to create a special fund to fight AB5, as it would torpedo ride-sharing. Their principal goal was to sponsor a ballot initiative to allow voters to have the final decision to overturn AB5 by a direct popular vote, which would take place in the general elections scheduled for November 2020. Uber shares tumbled by 5.74 percent, and Lyft shares dropped by 7.25 percent as a result of AB5.

Uber's Chief Legal Officer (CLO) Tony West reacted to the developments claiming that AB5 did not apply to rideshare companies, including Uber.[194][195] West had been fighting for

---

[193] The FLSA established minimum wage, overtime pay, mandatory record keeping, youth employment standards, and the 40-hour work week. The ADA prohibits discrimination against people with disabilities in transportation, employment, and protects the rights of employees and job seekers.

[194] Carolyn Said. Facing AB5, Uber's Tony West discusses improving drivers' lot. San Francisco Chronicle. 13 July 2019.

[195] Tony West was hired by Uber in October 2017, a former Assistant Attorney General in the Civil Rights Division of the Department of Justice, and former General Council for PepsiCo. His sister-in-law is Senator Kamala D. Harris (D-California), Democratic Presidential Candidate, and endorser of AB5.

months against AB5, prior to the IPO. He had stated that the California Supreme Court decision on the Dynamex case had for all practical purposes made AB5 the law of the land, and Uber had been working to improve conditions for drivers, including making sure earnings do not fall below a certain level. Discussions have mentioned a $21 per hour base, but that does not take into account the costs of maintaining vehicles, wear and tear, depreciation and other factors.

However, West did mention that Uber is aware of this challenge and will take it into consideration to come up with viable alternatives. West expressed what he described as driver preferences, including being able to set up their own schedules, and the ability to work without constraints for Uber, Lyft, and any other company. In a ballsy way, West expressed the opinion that Uber will not treat contractors (drivers) as employees under AB5, because the company is a "technology platform" for several different types of digital technologies, and not providing "rides," and as such, drivers are not part of the company "core business" and therefore not covered by the new legislation.[196] [197]However, as has been pointed out, Uber and other violators could be fined $1,000 daily per driver for violations of the law.[198] Uber has a history of playing hardball in multiple legal battles all over the world since 2010, and AB 5 will be another fight in the chain, but this time it looks suicidal. Nobody is expecting leftist politicians to give mercy to rideshare companies.

And things could get much worse for rideshare companies. Other states and local governments, including New York, Oregon, and Washington State have similar legislation to AB

---

[196] Michael Cleveland. California contractor law doesn't apply, says Uber. https://uberpeople.net/threads/california-contractor-law-doesnt-apply-says-uber.351070/ (Last accessed on 12 September 2019.)

[197] Sara Ashley O'Brien. Uber claims new California law still won't force it to classify drivers as employees. *CNN.* 11 September 2019.

[198] Ibid.

5 pending. The prime targets of the legislation are rideshare companies, particularly DoorDash, Lyft and Uber, which would suffer significant increases in operating costs, and possibly implode.[199] [200] On 20 September 2019, Uber filed a law suit against New York City for new rules limiting how much time drive-share drivers can spend on the road without a passenger, because it is arbitrary and threatens to undermine the Uber business model. The stock market reacted with a 3.6% tumble in Uber shares.[201]

New York City Regulations for Ridesharing

The New York City Taxi and Limousine Commission in 2018 voted to halt new for-hire vehicle license issuance for 12 months, and in 2019, they added another regulation that cuts the amount of time drivers can spend without a passenger in a car from 41% to 31% of the time, and another NY City commission enacted new minimum wage rules for ride-sharing drivers. The pay rate was set at $17.22 per hour after expenses. The new rules were set to become effective in mid-January 2019. A study conducted by the NY City Taxi and Limousine Commission had estimated that most ride-sharing drivers were earning about $11.90 hourly.

Lyft decided to take legal action against the NYC regulation, but the New York State Supreme Court ruled to uphold the enactment of the NYC Taxi and Limousine Commission in May 2019. The Independent Drivers Guild

[199] Gabriel Canon. California's controversial labor bill has passed. Experts forecast more worker rights, higher prices for services. *USA Today*. 11 September 2019.

[200] Chris Jennewein. Assembly Bill 5 Making 'Gig Economy" Workers Shift Employees Passes State Senate. *Times of San Diego*. 10 September 2019.

[201] Brandy Betz. Uber suing NYC over cruising cap rule. *SeekingAlpha*. 20 September 2019.

(IDG) in NYC supported the decision. Lyft decided to join Uber in October 2019 and sued New York City seeking to nullify the rule limiting the time drivers can cruise in the city without passengers as arbitrary and favoring taxis.

Uber took legal action against the NYC regulation that capped the number of rideshare drivers that went into effect in August 2018, but the challenge was dismissed on 1 November 2019 by the New York State Supreme Court. In the meantime, the Taxi and Limousine Commission extended the cap for another year.

The situation in New York City is going from bad to worse for rideshare companies, but the circumstances are not unique. Together with such developments as the enactment of California's AB 5 law in September 2019, the regulatory challenges continue to expand both, in the U.S. and in other countries. Fighting legal battles is costly, and fighting city hall traditionally has been a losing proposition. The idiom "can't fight City Hall" is a classic... *it is a battle that you can't win*. And DeBlasio likes screwing things up! On the other hand, an endless stream of rideshare cars was starting to clog the streets... and drivers had their income retreating. A free and open market should be allowed to figure out the solution... not government... but not in New York City. The taxi "medallions" are a government enforced racket.

New Jersey takes legal action against Uber

The Labor Department of New Jersey in early November 2019, took legal action against Uber (Rasier) with a claim for an estimated $523M in past-due payroll taxes covering a four-year period. In addition, Uber/Rasier are assessed as owing an estimated $119M in penalties and interest on the unpaid taxes. This claim relates to unpaid payroll taxes linked with disability insurance and unemployment compensation. Additional assessments may come in the near future related to failure to pay minimum wages and overtime pay to drivers.[202] Press reports about this new legal action plus other significant developments triggered another decline in Uber shares down to $26.21 at mid-day on 14 November 2019.

Challenges overseas: London

The London transport authority threatened to shut down Uber operations in the city since 2017. Uber employed an estimated 45,000 drivers in London, but that did not count. The authority questioned Uber operations, including the process to conduct background checks on drivers. It questioned the use of software to block the regulatory authority's ability to catch lawbreaking drivers.[203] And then on 25 November 2019, the London regulators gave Uber what was characterized as a "seismic blow," that caught the company "flat footed." Uber was given twenty-one days to shut down operations, with the possibility of an appeal. London has about 3.5 million riders who use Uber, making it the largest Market in Europe and one of the top five markets in the world for the company.[204] [205] (The top markets in the world are Los Angeles, New York City, San Francisco, São Paulo, and London. They produce about 25 percent of Uber's total sales.)[206] While Uber is under attack, other rideshare

---

[202] Brandy Bets. SeekingAlpha. 14 November 2019.

[203] Yoel Minkoff. Will Uber be shut out of London? *Seeking Alpha*. 22 November 2019.

[204] Brandy Betz. Uber's London license could be 'seismic blow' – Wedbush. *SeekingAlpha*. 25 November 2019.

[205] Tom Burridge. Uber loses license to operate in London. *BBC*. 25 November 2019.

[206] Kelvin Chan. Uber loses license in London over safety, vows to appeal. Associated Press. 25 November 2019.

competitors are moving into the London market. The issue is not ride-share. The issue is Uber and its business practices.

U.S. House of Representatives starts hearings

The U.S. House of Representatives' Transportation and Infrastructure Committee held a hearing on Wednesday 16 October 2019, as the start of an evaluation of the rideshare sector, according to committee Chairman Peter DeFazio (D-Oregon). Both Uber and Lyft elected not to cooperate with the congressional investigation.[207] [208] Based on published reports, Congressman DeFazio wrote to Uber CEO Dara Khosrowshahi and Lyft CEO Logan Green requesting their participation in the hearings, but both refused to participate:

"I intend to pursue legislative solutions to address numerous issues plaguing the ride hailing industry, many of which will be raised at this hearing. These include conditions governing your partnerships with States and local governments and transit agencies, the labor impacts of your business model, and disturbing reports of public safety problems among those who use your platform. If you do not send a representative to testify at the hearing, you leave the Committee little choice but to make these policy decisions without your input."[209]

Among the issues mentioned by Congressman DeFazio were sexual predation by drivers, inadequate background

[207] PYMNTS. Congress Calls Uber and Lyft to Ride-Hailing Hearing. PYMNTS.COM. 14 October 2019.
[208] Chris Mills Rodrigo. Transportation chairman wans Uber, Lyft against missing upcoming hearing. The Hill.16 October 2019.
[209] U.S. House of Representatives. Press Release. Chair DeFazio Urges Uber, Lyft to Reconsider Participation at Upcoming Hearing on Serious Issues Facing the Ride Hailing Industry. 14 October 2019.

checks, and inadequate wages. Based on released information, during the previous four year over 100 women were sexually assaulted by rideshare drivers. As Congressman Peter DeFazio put it after Uber and Lyft refused to testify at a Congressional hearing:

"The hearing should serve as a wake-up call to the companies that have flooded our roadways with disruptive technologies and investor capital that their days of operating with little policy and regulatory oversight in the transportation space are coming to an end... Perhaps they don't want to talk about what their model is doing to drive down wages and turn our transportation workforce from a skilled, trained pool of workers earning living wages to another casualty of the gig economy..."[210]

Congressman DeFazio is aware of how rideshare has made transcendental changes in the way Americans and people in other countries move around, but he wants to regulate the future of mobility. So is Highways and Transit Subcommittee Chair Eleanor Holmes Norton. Both are left-of-center politicians who are not friendly to *laisses fair* economics. Anti-competitive regulations affected the urban transportation sector all over the country, particularly in large cities since at least the 1930s. The rules went generally unchallenged, until the advent of Uber and rideshare in 2010. With the potential advent of autonomous vehicles in a few years, the entire transportation system is getting new attention.[211] Should self-driving cars be regulated at the state or Federal level? Roadblocks to innovation under the disguise

---

[210] Susan Heaveyity and David Shepardson. Ride-hailing companies Uber, Lyft won't testify before Congress. *Reuters*. 16 October 2019.
[211] The National Transportation Safety Board (NTSB) is looking at Uber's self-driving car that killed a pedestrian in 2018 in Tempe, Arizona. See Colin Dwyer, NTSB: Uber Self-Driving Car had Disabled Emergency Brake System Before Fatal Crash. *National Public Radio* (NPR). 24 May 2018.

of protecting the public good are bound to surface. The current push to regulate ridesharing is part of a much larger look at transportation in general, but it is too early to determine if regulators will learn any lessons from regulatory experience dealing with evolving market forces.

Chicago approves new taxes on rideshare

On 26 November 2019, the Chicago City Council approved a new surcharge tax on rideshare trips, under the excuse that the purpose is to ease traffic congestion. In reality, Mayor Lori Lightfoot was trying to establish an additional revenue stream for the city. Uber and competitor Lyft protested and offered alternatives, but without an active constituency to support rideshare they failed. This new financial challenge is in line with a war by regulators on the rideshare concept. If the regulators manage to bankrupt ridesharing companies, they will also kill the geese that lay the golden eggs... Mayor Lightfoot will have to find some other source for her $40 million revenue stream to support the city budget.[212]

Uber CEO puts his foot in his mouth

As if the Uber shares were not under considerable pressure after the release of the 3rd Quarter 2019 Financial Statement, and the sale of about 20 million shares by company founder Travis Kalanick, which was linked to a drop in price to about $25, Uber CEO Dara Khosrowshahi made a tactical mistake on an Axios interview on 11 November 2019. He called the

---

[212] Brandy Betz. Chicago approves a congestion tax. *SeekingAlpha*. 26 November 2019.

assassination of *Washington Post* columnist Jamal Khashoggi at the Saudi Arabian Consulate in Turkey a "mistake."[213]

The Managing Director of Saudi Arabia's Public Investment Fund, Yasir Al-Rumayyan, is a member of the Uber Board of Directors, representing the Saudi Arabian Government. The Saudis are one of the principal investors in Uber, with an estimated investment of about $3.5 billion. Although CEO Khosrowshahi attempted to correct his statement as a 'mistake,' it was too late to stop another campaign to boycott Uber. *If one of the company's main investors kills someone it doesn't really matter...* Karen Attiah, the *Washington Post's* Global Opinion Editor said, hinting that the statement justified another #Boycott Ubber campaign. A representative of a murderous regime was allowed to keep a seat on the Uber Board of Directors... when you're richh, your crimes become "mistakes"...[214] The new boycott was trending on Twitter in the days right after the statement was made by Khosrowshahi.[215]

So What?

Regulatory attention to the ride-share sector was predictable. The concept from day one disrupted the *status quo ante,* namely, the previously uncontested existing state of affairs. The taxi sector right off the bat went on the warpath.

---

[213] The US Central Intelligence Agency concluded that Crown Prince Mohammed bin Salman ordered the assassination of Khashoggi at the Saudi Consulate in Istanbul, Turkey. See: Shane Harris, Greg Miller and Josh Dawsey. CIA concludes Saudi crown prince ordered Jamal Khashoggi's assassination. The Washington Post. 16 November 2018.

[214] Melissa Quinn. Uber chief backtracks on calling slaying of Jamal Khashoggi a 'mistake. The Washington Examiner. 11 November 2019.

[215] Ross A. Lincoln. Uber CEO Defends Saudis After Jamal Khashoggi Murder: 'Doesn't Mean They Can Never Be Forgiven'. https.//the wrap. com. 10 November 2019. (Last accessed on 14 November 2019)

There are real consequences when taxi companies, often in bed with local politicians, have their business torpedoed by new technology. There are real consequences when rideshare companies, such as Uber, deny drivers basic protection gained by American workers through many years of struggle by classifying them as independent contractors. Labor unions would pro forma fight such practices.

The war with regulators and business interests affected by the advent of "rideshare" was easy to anticipate. In the climate resulting from a natural conflict, Uber management needs to be careful with how they handle public relations. Maintaining a favorable public image is vital for Uber when the company is in the middle of a legal battle with regulators. Uber has failed to cultivate a positive reputation with the news media and the public.

Uber has gone through melodramatic management incidents of mismanagement, sexual harassment of employees, and who knows what else. The scandals that led to the resignation of company founder Trevor Cordell Kalanick in 2017, shaped and framed the public perception of the company. The Uber image has been messy since 2010. In 2020 the future of rideshare will be decided, and Uber will have to deal with relentless attacks as it struggles to become profitable. Uber needs brand ambassadors to improve its reputation.

Consequences...
Definition: *The result, outcome, or effect of an action or condition...*

A self-evident potential consequence of AB5 is that the rideshare concept may be plowed under... The new California legislation makes fundamental changes to the rideshare model. The precedent will influence what happens in the rest of the country.

Thousands of ride-share drivers stand to lose their jobs. In San Francisco alone, there are an estimated 45,000 part time and full time Uber and Lyft drivers. Across the U.S. there may be as many as three million drivers. In London there are about 45,000 additional drivers. *What will they do then if Uber fails and closes shop?*

Before rideshare came about in 2010, the same people had other alternatives, including unemployment. Rideshare drivers have complained about the downside, including earning less than minimum wage, the high cost of repairs and maintenance, lack of insurance and normal benefits provided by regular employers, while enjoying flexibility of hours and being their own boss.

Some drivers have stated that they are working in the rideshare sector *out of desperation and lack of viable alternatives.* What will they do if Uber goes away?

XI

Uber After The IPO

An Initial public offering (IPO) is a stock market launch of shares of a corporation that is privately owned– normally by company founders, institutional and private investors. The process is referred to as "going public." Normally, IPOs are underwritten by investment banks. Through this process capital is raised for expansion. Companies normally raise capital for growth by either borrowing, or by selling equity (ownership). While companies are privately held, they do not have to disclose to the public internal information. However, that changes when companies go public through an IPO process. Very often there are "funky" share price movements, as investors speculate about the future profitability of the venture.[216]

People and institutions that invested in a company prior to an IPO see these events as an opportunity to recover and profit from their investments. Underwriters prepare a "prospectus" outlining internal financial data and estimates of future growth and profitability. The "prospectus" is filed with the Securities and Exchange Commission (SEC). Corporations new to the stock market may see their shares bounce up and down based on quarterly financial reports, and news that may have a significant impact on its future financial performance.[217] There are strict reporting guidelines established by the SEC to protect investors.

All business enterprises are faced with risks and uncertainties. Risks and hazards are a fact of life.

---

[216] Rhythmic, unconventional, rhythmic groove... up and down.

[217] For example, news about a stricter regulatory environment tend to drive down shares of rideshare companies.

Expectations, projections, predictions, and speculation about future profitability of the rideshare concept may not reflect reality. Uber management is well aware of that. So are the investors. Uber "bookings," have grown every year since the company was founded, and the growth continues. Rideshare is a growing sector of the economy, but that does not mean it is profitable, or at least not profitable under current conditions. And, the regulatory operating environment, is bound to become stricter in the future.

There is a growing demand for ride-share companies to abandon the practice of using independent contractors as freelance drivers. Companies like Uber will probably be forced to hire drivers as regular employees with a standard package of benefits sooner or later, depending on the locality or the state. At the national level, Congress may enact legislation forcing rideshare companies to change their practices. That would increase costs for rideshare companies, including Uber, by an estimated 25 to 30 percent when they are already operating unprofitably. While the affected companies are fighting this trend in court, the potential legal costs will further undermine profitability. On the other hand, some changes may reduce the costly *churn rate* of drivers.[218]

Is Uber a "Unicorn": "nickname" used for startups with private valuations of $1 billion or more that lose large amounts of money. The company's IPO was the 9th largest in U.S. history – selling 180 million shares, with a value of $8.1 billion. Since the IPO on 9 May 2019, after reaching a top value of $47.08 on 28 June, 2019, the value of shares dropped to $27.01 on 6 November 2019, or a drop of about 40 percent - the lowest price in the first six months after the IPO.

---

[218] The annual percentage rate in which employees, in this case freelance drivers, leave their employment.

Rideshare drivers can barely cover costs and are exposed to numerous perils as freelance self-employed contractors. They are not covered by workman's compensation which normally offers insurance for wage replacement and medical benefits in case of injuries in the course of employment, including wage replacement due to disability, and benefits to dependents. In most states workers' compensation statutes require that employers provide insurance to their workers. As far back as 1910, the first Uniform Workmen's Compensation legislation was enacted by an increasing number of states, and by 1920 all but eight states were mandating coverage. By 1963 all states had enacted legislation providing coverage to workers injured in the course of their employment. According to jurisprudence, workers are covered for assault while performing a job.[219]

As has been described in the previous pages, drivers have been assaulted, injured, maimed, and killed. Rideshare companies are not to blame for the social problems that exist in society, but precisely because of the dangers is that legislation forces employers to provide compensation for workers injured in the course of their employment. The Federal Employment Compensation Act provides mandatory protection for workers injured on the job. Businesses are required by legislation to pay for medical treatment, loss of wages, job-related injuries, and death benefits to dependents in all fifty states. There are severe penalties for employers who violate legal requirements. As freelance independent contractors, rideshare drivers have not been covered by these benefits.

Nevertheless, the future of rideshare is not necessarily bad. The number of consumers that use rideshare technology represents a fairly low percentage of the population, which means that there is ample opportunity to grow. On the second

---

[219] Implies a body of law and methods for interpreting law – case history.

quarter of fiscal year 2017, Uber handled ~889 million trips, as compared to ~1,677 million trips on the same period in 2019. Adjusted net revenue grew from $1,630 million in 2017, to $2,873 million in 2019, representing a year over year growth of 12 percent. Yet, most people have never used Uber or any other rideshare company.

Uber finally had its IPO on 10 May 2019. The market expectation was mixed. The company continues to bleed money, and that cannot be sustained forever. In the second quarter of 2019, Uber lost $6.56 billion.[220] Shares of the company dropped as much as 12 percent in extended trading in the NYSE right after the results were made public. Loss per share was $4.72.[221] The cumulative losses since 2010 will increasingly endanger the future of the company. Operating loses cannot be sustained forever.

2nd QUARTER 2019: BLEEDING CONTINUES

Uber shares listed in the NYSE dropped by 12.1% after the release of corporate performance on the 2nd quarter of 2019. The company had an operating loss of ~$656 million. By mid-October 2019, share price was down to around $30, as compared to the IPO price of $45 per share.

Uber revenue increased for the 2nd Quarter of 2019, as compared to the same period in 2018. Revenue increased by roughly 14 percent from year to year. Uber lost $739 million in 2018, and $5.5 billion in 2019. The company is reasonably justified in investing in R&D to develop new technology, and

---

[220] Uber Technologies. Form 8-K, Report to the United States Securities and Exchange Commission. 8 August 2019. (Note that net loss for the quarter, depending on how they are assessed, may be either $5.24 billion or $6.56 Billion.)

[221] Lora Kolodny. Uber shares slide after reporting disappointing quarterly results. CNBC. 8 August 2019.

grow the business, but the cost of business continues to grow and there is a finite number of investors willing to continue losing money with no end in sight.

Assets

In standard financial accounting, an "asset" is any resource – tangible or intangible - owned by the business enterprise. An "asset" is a *resource with economic value.* They represent "value," meaning that they can be converted into cash. Assets normally are used to generate income. Uber does not own the vehicles used for rideshare. The drivers and their lenders do. There may be as many as three million vehicles being used to deliver Uber services to clients. Nobody clearly knows the actual value of the fleet of vehicles used by Uber, but at an estimated low average value of $12,000 per vehicle, the value of the fleet may top $36 billion dollars. Considering that Uber requires that vehicles have to be less than five years old, this estimate is very conservative.

The drivers have been providing their own vehicles, which in most cases, they are financing. Vehicles depreciate rapidly, which means that there is a relatively short window to recover the investment and produce a profit. Uber and other rideshare companies have been using the assets owned by the drivers and their lenders, without the need to invest in these key assets to deliver services to the client base. What happens if newly enacted legislation requires that drivers be put on the payroll as regular employees? What about the vehicles? Drivers will have to be compensated for the use of their own assets, in addition to wages and benefits. How will this issue be addressed? The alternative would be that Uber purchase and provide the vehicles to the drivers, and the whole thing would then resemble a traditional taxi company... and that will not fly.

Not only is Uber bleeding money, most drivers are not even aware of what their costs are, and do not have a clear idea of how their vehicles depreciate until it is too late. Couple with a cumulative loss of $5,357 million from 1 March 2017 to 30 June 2019, where is the money going to come from to address this issue? Note that these losses represent only the past two years, but added to all the bleeding since 2010, the numbers are very significant, and hard to justify by pointing out that the losses represent an investment in growth. A cumulative loss of over $15 billion is a difficult pill to swallow.

The approximately 100 million consumers that use Uber services as of the end of June 2019, see as "the face" of the company the army of contractor-drivers. They are "the face" of Uber. They are the image of the company. They are the visual representation of a rideshare company, or the general idea that the consuming public has of the product, brand... and services provided by Uber. The appearance, reliability, and general characteristics of the drivers and their vehicles represent the image and "reputation" of the company.[222]

I frequently ask my passengers if they have any anecdotes, they wanted to share with me about their prior experiences using Uber. The vast majority had good experiences. They seldom had anything really significant to say, but the most frequent complaint was that drivers often had cars that had not been cleaned up in ages, frequently had bad smells, and AC units were not working properly. Considering that a large number of drivers spend well over 40 hours driving, an undetermined number of them actually sleep in their cars, and a large number are immigrants with different concepts of personal hygiene, this is important. If Uber were required to hire drivers as regular employees, and possibly required to

---

[222] "Reputation" is ubiquitous, spontaneous, and highly efficient mechanism of social control in natural societies. It is a subject of study in social, management and technological sciences. In this case, it refers to the opinion that people in general have about Uber.

provide them with vehicles, then the company would have to enforce standards of cleanliness and maintenance no protect the "assets" from an ever-faster process of devaluation. For a company to remain in business, "image" is a critical component, and a genuine asset. It is inseparable from business performance. Millions of times daily the Uber client base has contact with drivers and their vehicles, and that is how they acquired their "image," of the company.

Liquidity

The ease by which a company or an individual can convert assets to ready money or cash is referred to as "liquidity." It is a measure of how an entity can convert assets into cash to meet its obligations. Liquidity refers to the funds available to pay expenses. Uber shares continue to experience significant price swings in its short history after the IPO, leading to an apparent decline in investor assumptions and expectations. Uber generated sales on the second quarter of fiscal year 2019 of about $3.3 billion, but did not generate a profit, losing an estimated $2.70 per share. Investors speculated that the price per share would possibly drop to under $36. One day before the official release of the data, Uber was trading on 7 August 2019 at $39.75. Confidence on the future of the company seemed to be waning, to a great extent due to cash flow losses and a growing liquidity problem. Since then, the share price dropped to around $30.

Lyft, the prime competitor for Uber in the United States, was founded in 2012, and has, as of 2019, about 30 million riders, and about 2 million drivers. The company continues to experience revenue grown year-over-year, but like Uber, despite revenue growth, it cannot turn a profit. Like Uber, the number of active riders grew 41% from 2018 to 2019 to about 21.8 million. Lyft's co-founder, Logan Green, described the company's performance on the 2nd quarter of 2019 as a milestone *"on our path to profitability."*[223] Lyft reported revenue of $867.3, versus $504.9 in the same period of 2018. It had a net loss of $644.2 million in 2019, versus a net loss of $178.9 million in 2018. (The adjusted net loss was $197.3 million versus $176.5 million the previous year.) Lyft management projected a growth rate in sales of between 61% and 62% for 2019.[224] [225] Nevertheless, the same issues that affect Uber, apply to Lyft.

A liquidity crisis is normally hard to predict, but they are tied to lack of confidence. A deterioration in external financing conditions, due to a decline in investor certainty about future profitability can easily trigger a liquidity crisis. A steady operating loss could easily turn into insolvency (unable to pay its debts). Does Uber have assets that can be immediately liquidated to settle current debts if the company continues to lose money quarter after quarter? Is a credit pyramid building in the background, behind a façade that the company can "create" money and wealth?

Subscription Service

A subscription business model implies that a customer pays a recurring fee at regular intervals for access to a product or service. Businesses benefit from receiving monthly or yearly recurring subscription revenue from loyal clients.

---

[223] Seeking Alpha. Lyft, Inc. (LYFT) CEO Logan Green on Q2 2019 Results – Earnings Call Transcript. 7 August 2019. https://seekingalpha. com/article/4282970-lyft-inc-lyft-ceo-logan-green-q2-2019-results-earnings-call-transcript?li_source=LI&li_medium=liftigniter-widget (Last accessed on 8 August 2019).
[224] Lyft Announces Record second Quarter Results. *GlobeNewswire.* 7 August 2019.
[225] Lyft, Inc. Form 8-K, Report to the United States Securities and Exchange Commission. 7 August 2019.

The subscription model focuses on retention of customers and establishes a long-term relationship. Lenders, investors, and shareholders appreciate a business model which retains customers and receives the benefit of predictable and recurring subscription fees. As part of an effort to increase income and inject profitability to the company, Uber management started studying the possibility of creating a monthly subscription service for consumers of the multiple transportation means offered by the company, from rideshare to rental of e-scooters and food delivery. As far back as 2016, Uber started studying the concept.[226] [227] [228] The subscription under the name *Ride Pass*, was made available in several cities as far back as October 2018 for between $14.99 and $24.99 a month depending on location. In exchange, the members are given discounted rate fares. The concept did not seem to help the company to produce a profit by the 2nd quarter of 2019. Lyft has been testing the subscription concept, but very little has been discussed in the news media about the financial results. There are costs attached to all the speculative actions taken by both companies.

People have been slowly induced to accept the concept of subscriptions to receive the benefits of new technology. When this author graduated from college about 50 years ago, one normally subscribed to telephone service, electricity, gas and water. Then came subscriptions for cable television in the late 1970s, when previously television was free, but limited to about a dozen stations, including ABC, NBC, and CBS, with much limited transmissions of a small group of local stations. With the arrival of personal computers in the early 1980s,

---

[226] Taylor Leddin. Uber tests out monthly subscription plans. TheAmericanGenius.com. 30 September 2016.

[227] Andrew J. Hawkins. Uber introduces an Amazon Prime-style monthly subscription service. Theverge.com. 30 October 2018.

[228] Aditi Shrikant. Uber and Lyft unveil new subscription plans. But are they really worth the money? Vox.com. 31 October 2018.

consumers were forced to periodically invest in the purchase of updated applications, including operating systems, such as Windows, and then apps like Word. That was followed by call-in subscriptions to enter the Internet, which was later replaced in the 1990s by Internet subscriptions delivered to the home by coaxial cable. On and on, subscription services have proliferated, with an ever-increasing cost. Now Microsoft is selling subscriptions to popular operating systems and apps, instead of selling a product for a one-time price.

Add to the mix subscriptions to cellular telephony. Most households are paying a combined cost of at least $200 monthly to connect to the world via all the new technologies introduced in the past 50 years. Now rideshare wants to get consumers to subscribe to another service, regardless of how much they use the new services. At what point will consumers reach the point where they can no longer afford new subscriptions? Another new subscription to ridesharing services? What would be the churn rate in a ride-share subscription service? Would it entail a flat-fee or pay-as-you-go customized pricing structure?

The return on investment in a subscription to rideshare is questionable. Uber, for example, jacks up the price of a ride when demand increases due to weather conditions, or the end of a sports event or a concert, when a large mass of people is trying to return home. Subscriptions would imply that consumers would be exempted from price fluctuations, but that is precisely how Uber makes a "profit" by taking advantage of periods of high demand, even after sharing the uptick profit with drivers. Would the additional income potential from subscriptions more than make up for the loss of income by exempting subscribers from peak demand? Are consumers willing to accept another fixed cost and change their behavior? Would such a subscription service drive people from buying a personal car and use ride-sharing instead? Would such a plan force consumer to make a decision to marry

Uber or Lyft instead of using either company when they need a ride? Imagining a future world in which consumers can call for a driverless vehicle to pick them up and deliver them to their destinations... is it a trip too far... or a folly. (A total nonsensical absurdity!)

For companies like Uber and Lyft a subscription service looks like another costly and desperate attempt to find profitable activities and another departure from the core business. Investors continue to look at the sector positively waiting for the advent of driverless vehicles, which may be far away into the future, not around the corner. Working as a driver, depending on GPS through the Uber app to guide me to pick up passengers and deliver them to their destinations, I am aware of the multiple limitations. A day does not go by without having to deal with wrong instructions... *"Turn left at the corner"* ... but when you get to the corner it turns out that the GPS is suggesting an illegal action.

Regulatory environment

The regulatory environment at the federal, state, and local level in the U.S. has been growing to the point of becoming an unreasonable burden on the economy. The list of environmental regulatory agencies alone has been growing steadily since the 1960s. Regulations have derailed efficiency across the board, and limited the freedoms associated with *laisses faire* Capitalism. Transportation, financial services, banking, energy, consumer protection, and the complete legal environment all claim a piece of the action in rideshare. Fighting legal battles is costly, and fighting city hall traditionally has been a losing proposition.

The "system" is out to protect the *status quo* in in the transportation sector traditionally occupied by taxy services.[229] The "sharing" and gig economy, particularly rideshare is being targeted with or without reason across the board, and nobody can predict the outcome. Innovation is not always acceptable and not always an improvement over traditional ways of doing things. Passenger safety, liability insurance, labor laws, environmental concerns, consumer protection, pricing regulations, taxation, and other items are put in a blender to generate a complicated cocktail as the operating environment for rideshare. The concept that Uber is simply in the business of delivering a vehicle with a driver to consumers - as a facilitator (or connector) - in the sharing economy is under attack across the board. Uber is under attack as an unfair competitor, violator of local ordinances, perpetrator of deceptive business practices, a danger to public safety, non-compliant with statutory requirements, and a danger to public welfare.[230]

Diversification

Uber management has been making an effort to diversify the company (enlarging the company's range of products or fields of operation). For example, Uber Eats, has grown year-over-year by 140 percent. The number of restaurant partners reached ~320,000 at the end of June 2019. Uber Freight added new shipping customers since 2017. Uber Mobility, which includes JUMP, added new locations in the US and in Europe, including Paris and London. Uber's Advanced Technologies Group (ATG), claimed to have made progress

---

[229] Hannah Posen. Ridesharing in the Sharing Economy: Should Regulators Impose Über Regulations on Uber? https://ilr.law.uiowa.edu/print/volume-101-issue-1/ridesharing-in-the-sharing-economy-should-regulators-impose-ueber-regulations-on-uber/ (Last accessed on 16 October 2019.)
[230] Reeve T. Bull. Uber and the future of regulation. *The Regulatory Review*. 26 April 2018.

towards deploying self-driving vehicles in a joint business operation with Volvo using the XC90 SUV, which was designed to integrate ATG's self-driving system at the factory level, instead of as an add-on after-market concept.[231] Another addition to the list of services is "on-demand staffing," which Uber launching in Chicago with a new app. The idea is to match employers with temporary staff for shift work, or temporary workers at busy times, such as the Christmas rush.

Since 2016, Uber has been offering a helicopter taxi service or *"Ubercopter service"* in Sao Paulo, Brazil. [232] [233] This venture is shared with Airbus and a Saudi Arabia investment fund. More recently, Uber has been offering helicopter service to airports in the New York City area, like in Sao Paulo.[234] Uber has been linked to efforts to test a flaying taxi service in Los Angeles, Santa Monica, Sherman Oaks, within easy reach of LAX.[235] The jury is still out as to the profitability of these ventures. There are dangers in these ventures. An Uber-Copter crashed into a Midtown building in New York City within a couple of days of announcing the new venture, and immediately there were calls to shut down the idea before it even got started.[236]

---

[231] Uber. Form 8-K, Report to the USSEC. 8 August 2019, op. cit.

[232] Blake Schmidt. Uber lets you hail a helicopter in Brazil for $63. *Bloomberg*. 21 June 2016.

[233] Brad Haynes, Alberto Alerigi Jr. Uber offers helicopters to escape Sao Paulo gridlock. *Reuters*. 13 June 2016.

[234] Claire Ballentine. Uber Copter Will Now Fly You Over Manhattan Gridlock for $200. *Bloomberg*. 3 October 2019.

[235] Elijah Chiland. Uber plans to test a flying taxi service in LA: it could be up and running by 2010. 8 November 2017. https://la.curbed.com/2017/11/8/16624460/uber-air-flying-taxi-los-angeles (Last accessed on 17 November 2019)

[236] MissBees. Uber-Copter claims transportation is safe despite fatal midtown crash. 12 June 2019. https://thesource.com/2019/06/12/uber-copter-fatal-crash/ (Last accessed on 17 November 2019)

On 28 October 2019, Uber management announced the creation of a new financial division that will handle a new credit/debit card service, under the name "Uber Money." The new division will handle instant credit for drivers for services rendered (instant pay service), as well as a line of credit for fuel, maintenance, and other related expenses. In other words, now Uber wants to be a financial bank and enter the credit card business. It could turn out to be a profitable venture, but it is a very risky business.[237]

Apparently, Uber wants to build a financial empire starting with the approximately 100 million rideshare clients, and its approximately four million drivers world-wide. To accomplish this new task, the company is in the process of hiring more IT engineers with financial services background. In a way, it is an acceptance that a high percentage of drivers are living hand to mouth, and need instant access to their earnings, and the cards will help them to cope. Micro loans are already being provided to drivers in some countries as a way to keep them working for Uber. Cardholders will be a well below prime set of clients that may not be able to pay their credit card debt.

Just as in rideshare, competition is increasing rapidly, and Uber does not control the individuals working in these 'bets." As a result, it is very difficult to exercise discipline. Without internal discipline, no enterprise can really be successful. Any savings derived from avoiding overhead and administrative costs by using "contractors," have to be compared with the negative effects of not having full control over all the individuals that the enterprise needs to deliver its services to the clients. High turnover of these individuals has a high cost. Perhaps converting contractors to regular

---

[237] Hugh Son. Uber announces deeper push into financial services with Uber Money. *CNBC*. 28 October 2019.

employees could be a way of addressing the lack of discipline that is undermining the business. It would be a stretch... but in Spanish we have a saying: *No hay mal que por bien no venga.* (A negative can sometimes bring about a positive.)

Gentrification

In some parts of the country, the link between Uber and *Gentrification* has not been welcomed. The city of Oakland, California, for example, launched a war on Uber as part of an effort to slowdown and stop *Gentrification.* A campaign was mounted by local activists to stop Uber from moving into the city. An expansion of Uber was linked to accelerating *Gentrification*, with increases in rents and real estate prices, and driving the poor out. The company was accused of ignoring labor laws and undermining the power structure of the city by attracting suburbanites, and economic and race-based discrimination.[238] Leftists are out to find every angle to attack ridesharing.

Ride-sharing and public transportation

Uber has been blamed for a decline in the use of public transit systems.[239] For example, in Atlanta, rideshare was blamed for depressing ridership in MARTA and other transit agencies around the country. It has been alleged that the population that normally uses public transit has been pushed to the edges of urban areas where public transit systems are not available. It has been claimed that Uber is indirectly

---

[238] Oakland Launches War On Uber To Combat Gentrification. *Progrss.* 8 June 2017. https://www.progrss.com/communities/20170608/oakland-war-uber-gentrification/ (Last accessed on 19 August 2019.)
[239] Dan Whisenhunt. Transit expert says ride-sharing, gentrification may be behind decreasing MARTA ridership. AtlantaLoop. 6 June 2018.

responsible for transit systems ridership declines by 1.6% in Houston, 2% in Portland, 2.7% in San Diego, 2.8% in Dallas, 4.3% in Denver, 6.8 % in Baltimore, and 12.1% in Miami.[240] Again, leftist collectivists find every angle to attack rideshare.

Critical Key rideshare driver issues

Rideshare drivers are freelance or self-employed workers, and as such, they do not enjoy the most basic legally mandated benefits at the Federal and State levels. Without a doubt, this is the most critical issue affecting this business sector. (Please, do not call it an *industrial sector!*)[241] Employees in the U.S. benefit from legally mandated benefits, including Social Security, Medicare, Unemployment Insurance (to assist workers who lost their jobs through no fault of their own), and Workers' Compensation insurance, which provides financial support to people unable to work as a result of on-the-job accidents, and Minimum Wage requirements at the Federal and State levels.

Workers and employers are required to contribute to Social Security and Medicare. Rideshare drivers, are required to

---

[240] Bus ridership was down 3.9% and rail ridership was down 2.5 percent in 2017.

[241] The "economy" of a country includes all activities linked to the production, distribution, and consumption of goods and services and the supply of money. The Cambridge English Dictionary defines the economy as the system of trade and industry by which the wealth of a country is made and used. Investopedia defines economy as the large set of interrelated economic production and consumption activities which aid in determining how scarce resources are allocated. Economy is defined as *"a system of organizations and institutions that either facilitate or play a role in the production and distribution of goods and services in a society.* An "industry" is a sector of the economy that produces goods or services within an economy. It is referred to as the "secondary sector," or the manufacturing sector. Other "sectors" include the "financial sector," which provides financial services to other sectors of the economy.

contribute both, the employee and employer Social Security taxes. Companies that have 50 or more full-time employees are legally required to participate in the Family Medical Leave Act, which includes maternity leave, and time of for workers to recover from surgery or time off work to care for sick family members. Considering the exposure of rideshare drivers and their families to on-the-job accidents and criminal activity, lack of access to Workers' Compensation, is a very noteworthy challenge to ridesharing, easily correlated to a high rate of turnover, which is linked to the failure of businesses in the U.S.[242] [243] High turnover cuts into the bottom line of any company, including rideshare companies.

Rideshare Drivers do not benefit from typical employer provided programs. According to the Bureau of Labor Statistics (BLS), an estimated 70 percent of companies in the U.S. offer medical insurance, with some percentage of employer subsidization. Typically, employers cover an average of 82 percent of the premium of health and dental insurance policies. Group insurance premiums provide discounts to participants, which self-employed drivers do not have access to. Typically, companies promote higher levels of morale among their employees by providing other benefits. For example, short term and long-term disability insurance, and employer-funded retirements, such as 401 (k) and 403 (b)s accounts with some kind of matching program to incentivize workers to save part of their income for retirement. Paid vacations (paid time off- PTO), sick leave, and paid holidays are typically provided.[244] Life insurance is common, but not

[242] Jane Ann Reukauf. Walden University. The Correlation Between Job Satisfaction and Turnover Intention in Small Business. Walden University Scholar Works Doctoral Thesis. 2017.

[243] Bill Conerly. New Evidence That Low Employee Turnover Correlates With High Profits. Forbes. 19 April 2018.

[244] Most employers honor several national holydays, including New Year's Day, Martin Luther King, J. Day, President's Day, Memorial Day,

as common as health and dental insurance. Considering that in 2019 alone several Uber drivers have been killed on the job and their families were uncovered, this is a very significant reason for high driver turnover.

An increasing number of American companies offer tuition reimbursement assistance and other educational benefits. Uber introduced in 2019 some educational benefits for qualified drivers and their immediate family members. However, as self-employed workers they are not covered by paid time off, national holydays, and associated benefits. They do not get overtime pay, and many work long hours, which exposed them and their passengers when they work extended work hours. Based on published articles and driver interviews, many drivers regularly sleep in their cars.[245] [246]

These challenges associated with rideshare drivers and their income and lack of coverage under mandated and voluntary payroll programs are driving regulators to tighten the screws. It is estimated that the payment of these benefits normally adds at least 25 percent to payroll costs to employers. Contractors, including rideshare drivers, have not had access to these benefits since 2010. If Uber is losing money, and is unprofitable, how can the company afford these costs? Would consumers be willing to pay more so that drivers can have these benefits? Where would the drivers find employment if ride-sharing collapses and they lose their jobs?

4th of July, Labor Day, Columbus Day, Veterans Day, Thanks Giving's, and Christmas Day.

[245] Bruce Brown. Your Uber driver might be sleeping in his car at night, report reveals. Digital Trends. 27 January 2017,

[246] Juan Carlos Guerrero and Alexis Smith. 12-hour work days: A day in the life of an Uber rideshare driver. ABC7 News. 1 April 2019.

3rd Quarter 2019 Financial Highlights

On 4 November 2019, Uber reported its 3rd Quarter financial performance, and it showed that the company is not any closer to profitability.[247] Shares of the company fell about 5 percent. Nevertheless, some financial analysts saw some positive aspects, and believe that the company may reach profitability by 2021.[248] I do not see it that way. The company lost another net loss of $1.16 billion for the quarter. The company expects to lose about $2.9 billion in 2019. Gross bookings grew to $16.5 billion, representing a 29 percent growth over a year earlier. Earnings before interest, taxes, depreciation, and amortization (EBITDA) improved. Gross sales grew by 20 percent over the same 2018 period, and revenue growth accelerated. However, losses continued. And what the figures do not show is that the company is headed for more costly legal battles in the next 12 to 18 months, particularly in California and New York. In addition to problems with regulators, right after the 3rd quarter report it was announced that drivers in New York City are suing Uber for wrongfully deducting taxes and failing to pay a proper share of the income derived from rides. The suit was filed in a Manhattan District Court by the New York City Taxi Workers Alliance, which has about 22,000 members.[249]

---

[247] Lauren Feiner. Uber stock falls after quarterly results beat estimates, but losses topped $1 billion. *CNBC*. 5 November 2019.

[248] Bernard Keightley. Uber: Under-Appreciated Earnings Power. *Seeking Alpha*. 6 November 2019.

[249] Brandy Betz. Ride-share drivers in NYC are suing Uber. *Seeking Alpha*. 6 November 2019.

3ⁿᵈ QUARTER 2019: BLEEDING CONTINUES

Uber lost about another $1 billion in the third quarter of 2019. Shares continued to drop in value to about $27, from the IPO price of $45. Right after the financial results were announced, the lockup associated with the IPO expired, and co-founder Travis Kalanick and others dumped over $1.5 billion worth of shares, adding an additional downward trend on company shares.

So What?

Multiple analysts have published assessments of how they see the future for Uber and competitors. Analysts generally think that Uber is unlikely to ever produce a profit any time soon. Uber has lost more money than any venture in history. [250] [251] [252] [253] Analysts point out that the cost of doing business for Uber continues to climb. Uber CEO Dara Khosrowshahi has reacted to these negative assessments by stating that other companies, such as Amazon and Facebook, had rocky starts, but eventually became profitable. However, he has not provided explanations as to why the company has been so unprofitable. Like company founder, and Member of

---

[250] John Wilfredo Nono. Why You Should Not Invest In Uber (Or Lyft) Anytime Soon. *Seeking Alpha*. 27 August 2019.

[251] Richard Durant. Uber's Profitability Problem is Structural. *Seeking Alpha*. 21 August 2019.

[252] Len Sherman. Can Uber Ever Be Profitable? *Forbes*. 2 June 2019.

[253] Henry O'Brien. Uber: Payments & Profitability. https://medium.com/swlh/uber-payments-profitability-dc171ef10b80. June 2019. (Last accessed on 29 August 2019.)

the Board of Directors Travis Kalanick, as one would expect, do not comment about the growing picture that the company may have a flawed business model, and the alternatives are not very promising.

• XII •

Conclusions

To make no mistakes is not in the power of man; but from their errors and mistakes, the wise, and good learn wisdom for the future.

Plutarch

Knowing others is wisdom, knowing yourself is enlightenment.

Lao Tzu

Despite Uber becoming an *"eponym"* for rideshare, the company is unprofitable. Dragging a cumulative $15+ billion in loses, it was predictable that shares of the company would be trading well below the IPO price of $45.[254] The company's growth rate has been declining, and diversification efforts are a distraction from the core business. Uber eats is losing tons of money, for example. Many of the same freelance drivers work for other rideshare companies, with the result, that there is little that differentiates Uber from competitors. *It is the same drivers and the same vehicles!*

Uber management has difficulties defining what the company is all about, company rules are violated all the time, and the company continues searching for a way to define itself and produce a profit. Uber's *chief cook and bottle washer* admits that there is no way to predict if the

---

[254] As of 8 November 2019, shares were priced at $27.01.

company will ever produce a profit. The cash burn continues. Basic tenets or principles of the Uber concept, particularly the use of freelance self-employed drivers, are under attack by a coalition of leftist, labor union leaders, and seditious disgruntle drivers. Their actions to force rideshare companies to put drivers on a regular payroll may cause the demise of the concept. When riders who have come to depend on the concept are hit with higher prices, or the disappearance of the service, it may be too late. Drivers for whom rideshare, with all its faults, has provided them an income passes into oblivion, it may be too late for them to appreciate what they had.

Throughout this opus, I discuss my effort to understand what rideshare is all about. I talked with thousands of passengers and hundreds of drivers to find a point of shared humanity. I slowly gained knowledge, insight, and pattern-recognition. I drove over 9,000 passengers from September 2015, to December 2019. I earned top ratings from Uber. The entire process led to an intuitive grasp of reality, after dealing with the concept for over three years. *Uber notified me on 6 November 2019 that I had earned Platinum status!*

★	✓	⁒
Your rating	Your acceptance rate	Your cancellation rate
4.87	84%	0%

Does Uber now resemble the initial vision for the company back in 2009? Stating the obvious - Uber, like other rideshare companies- is in business to make money, but the company is unprofitable. Uber has lost more money than any start-up in history. Ride-share drivers are trying to earn a living, but hardly make any money, while being exposed to accidents and crime, without normal insurance protection. Are Uber managers and investors engaging in deceit, mystification of the rideshare concept, and bluffing? Are drivers deceiving themselves into thinking that they can really make money with the concept? Everybody and their grandmothers are pontificating with their own EBITDA scenarios, but most Wall Street analysts do not know what they are dealing with.[255] But their dreams are fading... The Uber financial fundamentals are very challenging. All the financial analysts looking at the numbers lack one fundamental piece of information. *What is it like to work inside the monster?*

The impact of rideshare in American culture, society and the economy since 2010 has been considerable, and well beyond what the people behind the advent of Uber could have expected. Rideshare has provided solutions to people in need. The physically handicap, people who are not within easy reach of public transportation, party goers after a night of drinking, elderly people trying to attend church services, people who cannot afford a car, suddenly had a viable alternative to traditional and costly taxi service. People with a wide variety of needs now have the means to solve their transportation challenges. Thousands of unemployed and underemployed people have an opportunity to work, even if only earning a limited income. How would all of these people deal with a sudden absence of rideshare services? What would regulators say if they kill the goose that lays the golden eggs? What would be the public reaction to a return to a world without this transportation alternative?

One could speculate about the advent of driverless vehicles, but that is a bridge too far now, bordering on a technical fantasy. Someday we may be able to put a man on Mars and return him back to earth, and someday we may be able to recover from the effects of aging. We are not there

---

[255] EBITDA: *Earnings Before Interest, Taxes, Depreciation and Amortization*. This is a key process used to valuate a company. It is part of a process to evaluate debt/equity, debt/capital, debt/assets, and debt/EBITDA.

now. The future of rideshare is not tied to driverless vehicles. But assuming driverless vehicles become a viable technology, the general public may be very hesitant to use the service. Insurance will be a life and death issue – literally. Insurance may already be the largest challenge faced by the driving-sharing sector, together with low compensation. All the issues that drivers face need to be addressed expeditiously, without waiting for a fast charging magical *Tooth Ferry* to appear bearing solutions to very critical challenges.

The *laissez-faire* or "market economy" provides the freedom to create a private business for profit in a competitive system without interference by government, that is, beyond a regulatory framework to protect the "public interest." Freedom is basic as a key enabler to a properly functioning economy. A basic tenet of the free enterprise system is that the market determines the price for all products and services, not the government. All of this happens under Capitalism, which allows in theory for competition, innovation, and private property. Market forces should determine the viability of ride-sharing in general, and Uber in particular, not government.

Uber is an example of how technological advancement and the entrepreneurial spirit can bring about progress. Sure, at times some concepts may sound like Utopian ideas, such as driverless vehicles, but that is precisely how ideas that at some point in history may have sounded impossible, and eventually became a reality. Wealth creation is a derivative of allowing the free flow of ideas and freedom for entrepreneurs to invest in new businesses. *This is not rocket science!*

There is a lot of hoodwinking and chicanery in most of the published analysis of the Uber phenomenon. Uber should be focused on the flagship product: *rideshare.* In a rapidly changing technological revolution, companies are forced to redefine what they are all about, but Uber cannot continue experimenting when it has not fully proven that the core business is valid. The core business continues to grow, and has delivered higher margins and profits, while other business, as for example Uber Easts losses money.[256] Rideshare companies – not only Uber – have not proven that they can operate at a profit. Again... *too many fingers in too many pies!*

What's Uber Technologies, Inc.? A *"technology company,"* or a transportation network company offering services that include ridesharing, food delivery, e-scooter and bicycle-sharing services, and now freight services. Any entity that fails to understand what they are all about will eventually face a debacle... Uber cannot be all things to all people.

The ancient Greeks had an aphorism: *Know thyself.* They inscribed it in the Temple of Apollo at Delphi. It was one of the 147 Delphic maxims. The Romans maintained the same aphorism... *Nosce Te Ipsum* – know yourself. At the other end of the world, Chinese philosophers came to the same conclusions. How can realistic goals be set without an understanding of what the company is all about?

Other Delphic maxims are: *"Know what you have learned," "Cling to discipline," "Consult the wise," "Pursue what is profitable,"* and *"Obey the law."* Enter the "Uber business rules...." Rules are defined as *"a set of explicit regulations governing conduct..."* According to the *Cambridge English Dictionary*, rules are defined as *"accepted principle of instruction that states the way things are or should be done, and tells you what you are allowed or are not allowed to do."*

In the case of Uber, drivers violate the rules thousands of times daily, and if they did not violate them, the company would lose considerably more money, drivers would not be able to earn a return for their investment in time and capital. The "system" produces most of the violations of basic rules.

---

[256] Although the core business is producing a profit, Uber will be forced by regulators to bring freelancer drivers into the company as regular employees sooner or later, and that could be a game changer.

The drivers simply answer a ping and go pick up a passenger. They have no idea of what comes next. It is Uber that places the drivers in a position where they are faced with deciding if they adhere to or violate company written rules. *Anarchy is endemic in rideshare!* Uber may lose its operating license in London as a result of all the anarchy in the way the company is operating in the city. (Although a large part of the problems stems from criminal elements taking advantage of flaws, or defects in the Uber app.)

All companies within the free enterprise system are exposed to changes in public policy, including being pushed out of business by legislation, regulations, or collateral damage. To influence public policy, corporations, labor unions, and so-called public interest groups invest hundreds of millions of dollars annually with lobbyists at the municipal, county, state, and Federal levels. The *Code of Federal Regulations* is over 175,000 pages long, and it continues to morph every day with new regulations added. The marketplace is transforming constantly, and every sector of the economy can be targeted by interest groups.

The rideshare sector could be plowed under by California's AB 5 legislation, despite a combined legal effort by affected parties to challenge it in court. The entire "gig economy" is facing a serious existential threat, and rideshare may not survive in its original form. Government intervention in the economy is a fact of life, and a necessary evil. The visionaries that created Uber may see their creation legislated out of existence.

There are limitations to the free enterprise system, as the public interest has to be protected and the national economy has to be kept in balance to maintain economic freedom. The Capitalist economy and the free competitive market are unconstrained up to a point, but government intervention and regulation is basic to protect "the system." Hopefully, regulatory constraints are based on sound judgement. But that may not be the case every time. Regardless, Uber and all the other rideshare companies have to comply with government regulations or they will be pushed out of business.

Are rideshare drivers for the most part a collection of losers who cannot find any other type of job? Why do people continue to drive for Uber when deep inside they know they are losing money? Is rideshare a key component of what is described as *freakonomics*?[257] One of the principles of "freakonomics" is that *"a lot of people are willing and able to perform a job that doesn't pay well."*[258] Visiting Uber offices in the Washington, D.C. Metro area one can come out with close to fully quantitative conclusions that Uber is scraping the bottom of the barrel to find drivers. Looking at the visitors one can come out with a speculative conclusion as to why mostly minorities and immigrants are signing up as ride-sharing drivers.

There is still plenty of room for the rideshare business to grow, based on an estimate that only about 43 percent of the population have used rideshare services in the previous 12 months.[259] As of August 2019, Uber had about 93 million monthly active users, up from 91 million in 2018. Beyond the rideshare core, both Uber and Lyft have diversified operations. Yet, they have not achieved profitability. Perhaps, it would make more sense to concentrate on the core business of ride-share and targeting key challenges, as for example, insurance.

As long as drivers can function without having accidents, fate is on their side. But statistically, about five million drivers have car accidents in a normal year, and about two million

[257] Steven Levitt and Stephen J. Dubner. Freakonomics: A rogue economist explores the hidden side of everything. *Harper Perennial.* New York: 2009.
[258] Tom Worstall. Freakonomics' Steven Levitt On How Inefficient Uber Really Is. *Forbes.* 20 September 2016.
[259]

result in permanent injuries. A lot of the accidents are caused by distractions, linked to irresponsibly fooling around with a cell phone. Phones are one of the biggest distractions, and that happens to be how rideshared drivers get their apps. In 2017, 37,133 people were killed in car accidents. Texting, talking to passengers, and adjusting radio, climate controls, and possibly GPS and Uber apps, may be a key contributor to accidents. About 16 percent of accidents are caused by distracted driving, according to the National Highway Traffic Safety Administration. Weather related car accidents accounted for about 22 percent of all the accidents. Rideshare drivers are out there during weather events, because that is when they tend to earn higher returns for their work. Drowsy driving is another major contributor to driving crashes. Rideshare drivers often push the limits of their ability to stay awake for the sake of earning more money.[260]

Confidence on Uber's potential profitability is waning, as it is evident that mounting losses will eventually lead to a liquidity problem. Investment money is not going to be around forever to cover operating losses, with the hope that at some point the company will become profitable, recover previous losses, and becomes a cash cow forever into eternity. The same analysis applies to Lyft and any other drive-sharing competitor.[261] [262]

To pay drivers more, ride-sharing companies have to charge more per trip. *How much price elasticity is there?*

---

[260] The source for accident information listed is the National Highway Traffic Safety Administration.

[261] Lyft, Inc. Form 8-K, Report to the United States Securities and Exchange Commission. 7 August 2019.

[262] Seeking Alpha. Lyft, Inc. (LYFT) CEO Logan Green on Q2 2019 Results – Earnings Call Transcript. 7 August 2019. https://seekingalpha.com/article/4282970-lyft-inc-lyft-ceo-logan-green-q2-2019-results-earnings-call-transcript?li_source=LI&li_medium=liftigniter-widget (Last accessed on 8 August 2019).

(Defined as the economic measure of the change in the quantity demanded of a product in relation to its price change= % of change in quantity demanded / % change in price.) [263] Without a doubt, except in cases where there is high demand, as for example when a large crowd leaves a football game, or a rock concert, or during a rainstorm, the public reacts swiftly to price for ride-sharing. Uber already has a dynamic pricing model to maximize profits at times of high demand. Customers accept, reluctantly, higher prices when it is obvious that demand for rides is high, but they can be alienated.[264]

On or about 13 November 2019, Uber founder Travis Kalanick sold about 21 percent of his Uber shares for about $500 million, triggering another slide in the value of company shares.[265] [266] [267] The sale was allowed after a legal investor lock-up after the IPO expired. Other Uber employee shareholders took advantage of the expiration of the lock-up to sell their shares of the company.[268] Uber estimated market capitalzation dropped from about $82B at the time of the IPO on 10 May 2019, to less than $47B on 11 November. This was a typical action for businessmen who create a company after it goes public and the legally required lock-up period expires. It is also a typical action for long-term employees to sell shares earned througth their contribution to the grown

[263] Op. Cit. Tom Worstall. Freakonomics' Steven Levitt On How Inefficient Uber Really Is.

[264] Zachary M. Seward. Uber economics: Sometimes the invisible hand slaps you in the face. *Quartz.* 13 December 20013.

[265] James Titcomb. Uber founder Travis Kalanick sells $500m state as shares slide again. *The Telegraph.* 11 November 2019.

[266] Tom Metcalf. Kalanick sells almost$1.5 billion of Uber in weeks after lockup. *Bloomberg.* 21 November 2019.

[267] Dara Kerr. Uber co-founder Travis Kalanick sells nearly $1B in company's shares. *Cnet.* 19 November 2019.

[268] For example, co-founder Garrett Camp sold 510,000 shares worth roughly $13.77 million.

of a company. However, financial markets and investors interpret these actions negatively, particularly when Uber is facing legal actions by regulators and politicians all over the country. The 25 November 2019 suspension of Uber's license to operate in London could be a sign of things to come in 2020.

Investment money is not going to be around forever to cover operating losses, with the hope that at some point Uber will become profitable, recover previous losses, and becomes a cash cow forever into eternity. Practically the same analysis applies to principal competitor Lyft.[269] [270] If Uber goes under, some of the same people who are critical of the company and the rideshare concept will be the first to raise hell when over a million people lose their way of earning a living, and millions more their way of getting around with more reasonable fees that traditional taxi service. About 23 percent of Uber drivers were unemployed before the started working for Uber as contractors. They may only make about $10 hourly after deducting their expenses, but they are earning something. If Uber goes under without a doubt there will be a line to the unemployment office, and then the finger pointing will start assigning fault for killing the goose that laid the golden eggs.

[269] Lyft, Inc. Form 8-K, Report to the United States Securities and Exchange Commission. 7 August 2019.

[270] Seeking Alpha. Lyft, Inc. (LYFT) CEO Logan Green on Q2 2019 Results – Earnings Call Transcript. 7 August 2019. https://seekingalpha.com/article/4282970-lyft-inc-lyft-ceo-logan-green-q2-2019-results-earnings-call-transcript?li_source=LI&li_medium=liftigniter-widget (Last accessed on 8 August 2019).

UBER SHARE PRICE AFTER IPO 10 MAY 2019

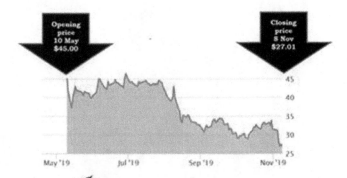

Unicorn: Nickname used for startups
with private valuations of $1 billion or more
that loose large amounts of money.

Two things are infinite: the universe and human stupidity; and I'm not sure about the universe.

Albert Einstein

Appendix

RIDE-SHARING IN THE NATION'S CAPITAL

A reference to national security and law enforcement in a book about rideshare may seem to be out of place, but it is not. Every day the unexpected happens, and national security is put at risk. People who should know better get into a rideshare vehicle, dial someone using their cell phone, and disclose secret information endangering national security. A description of the deterioration of conditions in the Nation's Capital, including increasing homelessness, and all that comes with it, is generally ignored. Uber is not at fault, but by examining certain driver experiences it is possible to illustrate how complicated life can be in *"the swamp."*

Pierre Charles L'Enfant
U.S. Library of Congress
LC-USZ62-32434

History. The Federal Capital, formally, the District of Columbia, is the brainchild of President George Washington. He selected the site for the new Federal Capital. A select group of commissioners was empowered to oversee the design and construction, and a deadline was set for completing the project by December 1800. French city planner Pierre Charles L'Enfant, was hired to design the city.

The selected area is located at the confluence of the Anacostia and Potomac rivers, as they discharge their waters into Chesapeake Bay. The area where the two rivers meet is affected by ocean tides, as the bay is at the same level as the Atlantic Ocean. When the rivers carry a large volume of water due to rains or melting of snow, at the same time that the tide is raising due to the rotation of Planet Earth and the position of the moon, low-lying areas flooded.

In an attempt to control the floods, the concept of building the "Tidal Basin" originated in the 1880s as a mean of flushing the Washington Channel, control tides, and avoid flooding. It was built by the Army Corps of Engineers. The Tidal Basin is better known for the National Cherry Blossom Festival that takes place every year in the Spring, but, as the name suggests, it was built to control tides and drain swamp area fed by the ties, rain, and melting snow.

Plan for the Federal District, c. March, 1791
Possibly drafted by Thomas Jefferson
Manuscript Division, Library of Congress

The Tidal Basin was built at the same time as the East and West Potomac Parks, and areas surrounding the Jefferson Memorial.

The Swamp. *Was the Capital located in a swamp area?* Not really, but close. Multiple politicians have made reference to Washington, D.C. as a swamp. For example, President Ronald Reagan in 1985, made the following remark: *"Sometimes it's difficult to remember, you didn't send us to Washington to feed the alligators, you sent us to drain the swamp. We didn't come to raise your taxes, but to lower them..."*[271] Presidential candidate Donald J. Trump first called for *"draining the swamp"* at a campaign rally on 17 October 2016, in Green Bay, Wisconsin. They were not the first to make such references going back about a century.

Thousands of tourists from all over the world travel to the U.S. Capital every year to visit the monuments, including the U.S. Capitol, the White House, the Lincoln Memorial, the

---

[271] "Reagan lauds Congress in fight with deficit." The Gainesville Sun (Florida), published this article quoting the President on 4 August 1985

Jefferson Memorial, the Vietnam and W.W. III Memorials, the Smithsonian museums, the Nacional Archives, the National Zoo, and numerous other sites. In 2015, the city welcomed over 21.3 million visitors.[272] Of these visitors, at least 2.14 million arrived from overseas. The top ranking of international visitors was China (300,000), followed by the UK (201,000), Germany (132,000), Australia (101,000), France (93,000), India (80,000), South Korea (77,000), Brazil (76,000), Italy (67,000), and Japan (66,000).[273]

Tourists destinations around the world make an effort to provide visitors their best services and their best image. They are well aware that tourists spend money, and tourism creates thousands of jobs. The Government of the District of Columbia, on the other hand, has been working very hard to turn the Capital into something that resembles a third-world developing country, rather than the Capital of the most advanced country in the world. It may not happen on purpose, but they fail miserably at providing visitors the best possible views and experiences.

In a previous section, pictures were provided of homeless people living on the sidewalks of some of the top thoroughfares in the city, like Pennsylvania Avenue, N.W., and even at the corner of 15th Street and Constitution Avenue, N.W., right across from the Washington Monument, and the White House.

Emily Post (1872-1960) and Amy Vanderbilt (1908-1974) have to be turning in their graves considering what is happening in the country. The two American icons on

---

[272] D.K. Shifflet & Associates. *Travel Market Insights*, National Travel and Tourism Office, U.S. Department of Commerce.

[273] The top tourist destinations in the world are Hong Kong (23.7 million visitors), Singapore, Bangkok, London, Macau, Kuala Lumpur, Shenzhen, New York City, Antalya, Paris, Istanbul, Rome, Dubai, Guangzhou, Phuket, Mecca, Pattaya, Taipei City, Prague, Shanghai, Las Vegas, Miami, Barcelona, Moscow, Beijing, and Los Angeles.

social behavior and etiquette could never have imagined public defecation and urination in San Francisco and Los Angeles, and definitely not in the Nation's Capital.[274] Post and Vanderbilt were concerned about such unacceptable behavior as spitting in public, which was only violated by baseball players, and shewing with the mouth wide open.

According to a study conducted by the U.S. Conference of Mayors in 2017, the District of Columbia had the highest homeless rate of 32 large cities, more than twice the national average -124 homeless for every 10,000 residents.[275] As of January 2018, it was estimated that about 6,904 homeless people were living in the streets of the Capital, of which about 1,781 were considered experiencing chronic homelessness.[276] [277] With the growing number of homeless camps, comes public defecation and urination, and not as some form of recreational outdoor activities. There are no facilities to address the issue. There are no permanent or portable toilets or public bathroom facilities in D.C. near homeless encampments.

Under the *Code of the District of Columbia*, § 22–1321. Disorderly conduct. (e) *It is unlawful for a person to urinate or defecate in public, other than in a urinal or toilet.* Nevertheless, in D.C. it is a non-citation, misdemeanor offense. The D.C. Council approved "two" pilot new public restrooms to address concerns about public health caused by public defecation and

[274] Kristin J. Bender. San Francisco paints walls to combat chronic public urination problem. *Associated Press (AP)*. 13 August 2015.

[275] Neal Augenstein. Homelessness in DC much higher than other cities, says survey. WTOP. 2 January 2017.

[276] United States Interagency Council on Homelessness. District of Columbia Homelessness Statistics. https://www.usich.gov/homelessness-statistics/dc/ (Last accessed on 19 August 2019.)

[277] Kfagley. District of Columbia's homeless population has significantly increased over the decades. Shelters to Shutters. 18 March 2018. https://www.usich.gov/homelessness-statistics/dc/ (Last accessed on 19 August 2019)

urination... When there are homeless encampments all over the city, and the residents relieve themselves right on the streets, obviously there is a real risk to public health.

It is irresponsible to allow the situation to continue. Ignoring the truth is no solution. The problem is real, and public restrooms are not available in areas of chronic homeless encampments. Public urination and defecation are not only a nuisance, but a health hazard, and the image of the city suffers. The situation is beyond embarrassing! It may be prohibited, but there is no enforcement. Willfully exposing a person's private parts for the purpose in the public view is illegal, but there is no law enforcement.[278]

When tourists visit the Mall area on weekends, the parks between the U.S. Capital on the East, and the Lincoln Memorial on the West, they run into an area packed with food trucks, with doubtful hygiene, and horrible looks. In addition to the food trucks, there are homeless, and people with mental challenges, drug addicts and alcoholics. The area resembles more and more a so-called *"Third World"* country's capital.[279] Perhaps the best terminology would be to depict the looks of the Mall area as something that one

---

[278] The return to barbarism is linked to Liberal and incompetent government, and a combination of other factors have created the current situation. The District of Columbia is one of the jurisdictions in the U.S. that has no government institutions that seclude people with intellectual or developmental disabilities. People with disabilities end up in jails because there is no other place to hold them. Mass incarceration of indigent people with disabilities is endemic, not only in the Capital, but in the entire country.

[279] The term originated during the Cold War to define countries that were not aligned with the United States, NATO members, or the Communist Bloc countries. The so-called "First World," included the United States, Western European countries, Canada, Japan, South Korea, and their allies, while the Soviet Union, the PRC, Cuba, North Korea, Vietnam, and their allies represented the so-called "Second World."

would expect in a developing or "Third World" country, not in the United States.

As a U.S. Foreign Service Officer, I served in Dominican Republic, Mexico, Argentina, Netherlands and Spain. I travelled throughout Latin America and Europe. I never saw anything like the situation in D.C. in Ottawa, Santo Domingo, Mexico City, Buenos Aires, Santiago, Chile, Lima, Panama, Bogota, San Jose, The Hague, Berlin, Madrid, Paris, Brussels, Rome, or Lisbon.

What would one expect to find in a Third World developing country? A high level of national debt? *The U.S. national debt just passed $23 billion in February 2019!* Crippling poverty, economic-inequality differences? Look at the pictures of homeless in downtown Washington, D.C. Rodent complaints are soaring in D.C. despite efforts to reduce the rat population. *Rats are overrunning the city!* Complaints reached an all-time high in 2017.[280] The city has earned the title as the fourth "Rattiest City," in the country, behind Los Angeles, New York City, and Chicago. The worse part of it is that it seems as if nobody cares.

What has happened in the Washington Mall since about 2009 is a disgrace. As of 2019, there are at least 450 food trucks that are licensed by the D.C. Government to operate in the city, and they compete to get a parking site smack in the center of the park area, right between the monuments. It is practically impossible to take a panoramic picture of the area without getting one of the food trucks in the picture! They offer all types of ethnic foods, including Asian, Barbeque, Caribbean, Cajun/Creole, comfort food, deserts, Ethiopian, Greek, Hawaiian, Indian, Indonesian, Italian, Japanese, Korean, Mediterranean, Mexican, Middle Eastern, Peruvian,

---

[280] Rachel Chason, John D. Harden, and Chris Alcantara. Rat complaints are soaring, and D.C. is doubling down on its efforts to kill them. *The Washington Post.* 23 August 2018.

Portuguese, Russian, Seafood, Spanish, Soul Food, Tex/Mex, Thai, Vietnamese, Venezuelan, and several other funky mix-styles.

Most of the owners and operators are recent immigrants, without a doubt, a good number of the people employed in the trucks are illegally in the country. (Note that there are plenty of illegal immigrants in the country from areas other than Mexico and Central America.) This is not an "immigrant issue." Even if they were operated by Native American veterans of the U.S. military, the food trucks would be out of place.

Do the food trucks belong in the National Mall? They function because the regulatory burden has been eased by the D.C. Government, and apparently the National Park Service, and the U.S. Department of the Interior have stayed out of the picture. The trucks may be considered by some as a "convenience," but they do not provide a good image. Personally, I think they desecrate the area.

The D.C. City Council approved legislation in December 2018 to crack down on food truck operators that monopolize parking spaces. The operators of the trucks have a fleet of junk cars that they pull into parking spaces to monopolize entire areas of the city. Some of the cars have accumulated hundreds of $30 and $50 parking tickets that go unpaid. At least one member of the D.C. Council has called the violations preplanned fraud. The sad thing is that with so many elected officials, including Members of Congress, nobody seems to care. A national treasure of American culture has been turned into a stinking mess.

FOOD TRUCKS IN THE MALL AREA

VIGNETTES
People don't know what they don't know

I am I, and my circumstances
(Yo soy yo y mi circunstancia)[281]

José Ortega y Gasset (1883-1955)
Spanish Philosopher

The following *"vignettes"* cover my experiences driving for Uber in the Washington D.C. Metro Area for over three years. Casual conversations with riders, and listening to their conversations *"in the open,"* illustrate society's exposure to potential nefarious and wicked actors. Discussions linked to criminal activity and potential national security threats happen in rideshare vehicles and traditional taxis. Although these incidents are infrequent, they do happen enough to illustrate how potentially dangerous is the environment in the D.C. Metro Area.

To put it in perspective, after driving over 9,000 passengers, in less than one percent (1%) of the rides something truly significant happened. Based on informal estimates, between 14 and 17 million rideshare trips take place daily. That works out to about 20 rides daily per driver. Based on these conservative estimates, in about 1,200 rides daily something unusual happens. That is less than one percent of all rides. If the average full-time driver handles about 600 trips monthly, something remarkable happens in their presence about six times in the course of a month.[282]

---

[281] From the book by José Ortega y Gasset, *Meditaciones del Quijote*. Madrid 1914. See: https://en.wikipedia.org/wiki/José_Ortega_y_Gasset

[282] Uber has an estimated 2.4 million drivers outside of the US. Estimates of Uber drivers in the US range between 700,000 and 800,000, but due to the high rate of turnover or churn, the actual number is difficult to ascertain. As many as 50 percent quit after a few months. Lyft may have about one million drivers in the US and Canada.

Intelligence is *"the collection of information of political or military value, which can be gathered through surveillance, reconnaissance, interception and monitoring of telecommunications, manipulation of the environment, espionage, informers, analysis, and evaluated conclusions drawn from the information collected.* Counterintelligence, involves *the collection of information to determine how foreign enemies collect intelligence, and their assets, i.e. spies.* Defensive Intelligence, or counterintelligence, encompasses defensive measures to protect our own information. Intelligence is a tool for national security, as well as for criminology. Law enforcement organizations need intelligence just as much as the sixteen national intelligence agencies tasked with protecting national security.

Deception, trickery, duplicity, double-dealing, and chicanery are part and parcel of the process of collecting intelligence and misleading enemies by manipulation and distortion of facts. Even in the Bible, there are warnings about the evil of deception, wickedness, lies and premeditated scams. (For example, Genesis 3:4-5, Psalms 101:7, Proverbs 10:9, 20:17, 15:4, 26:24-26, among other warnings.) Satan's malevolent brilliance and cunning are depicted throughout. The examples are provided to orient people to the standards of right and wrong.

Espionage is *"the act of procuring or gaining secret information without the consent, authorization, or acquiescence of the owner or proprietor of the information in a clandestine way."* Espionage has been around practically since the beginning of time. Egyptian hieroglyphs (pictographs and ideograms) and papyri denote the presence of espionage, intelligence and counter-intelligence in the Ancient World. The tradecraft of intelligence has expanded through the Hellenistic Age, the Roman Empire, and the Byzantine Empire... leading to the conclusion that espionage is the "second oldest profession." Superior force of arms, maneuverability, and discipline in warfare, are more-often-than-not, dependent on intelligence, collected through espionage. Over time, new additions to tradecraft have been introduced, from ever-improving secret communications, disguised writing, trick inks, to increasingly sophisticated telecommunications.

Unlike other countries, where intelligence services collect data on their own citizens, in the U.S. we have very clear definitions about what can and cannot be done against our own citizens. U.S. persons and permanent-resident aliens are protected under U.S. law from intrusion by government and infringement of their civil liberties. The information described in the vignettes that follow, were casually collected, without any intention to collect intelligence. *It just happened!* Nevertheless, they illustrate what happens in *"the swamp,"* encompassing the area inside the Washington Beltway (I-495).

The inhabitants of *"the swamp"* are not only corrupt members of the military industrial complex, elected officials on the take, and other nefarious actors involved in reprehensible activity. There are very stupid people who have no idea of what they are doing. There are plenty of despicable and immoral characters inside the Washington Beltway. The swamp cannot be emptied, bled, or drained easily. A package of ethics reforms would not sap the evil doers, because the challenges go well beyond what most people link to the abstract concept of *the swamp.* Multiple antecedents contributed to the current state of affairs, particularly our own attempts to correct problems by further tying out hands and blocking the very actions needed to flush out wicked, impious, and evil characters.

Excesses in intelligence collections during the Vietnam War in the 1960's and early 1970's brought about restraints on what law enforcement and intelligence agencies can legally do. The solution created even more problems. After the terrorist attacks of 11 September 2001, it became evident that there was a need to reevaluate restrictions to protect the nation from evil doers. While respecting the Constitution, the nation needs protection. Deficiencies in control and accountability of the intelligence and law enforcement community led to an environment in which the end justified the means, and excesses were the result. In hindsight, despite the excesses in the 1960s, numerous bad actors got away with murder. Nevertheless, the excesses resulted from the need to address domestic terrorism, inspired by foreign enemies who exploited our weaknesses. American leftist activists and would-be revolutionaries received training overseas to engage in terrorism within the United States. For example, in Cuba, under Soviet sponsorship back in the 1960's. The *Cold War* was the background for lots of efforts to undermine the United States in part by fomenting internal dissent.

Every human encounter is potentially intelligence "field work," including driving a rideshare vehicle. Every Uber rider is a *human research participant*, even if there is no formal arrangement. This plays out in both ways. Driver, as well as passengers, could be potentially conducting human research as they talk to each other.[283] Information voluntarily exchanged is operationally relevant socio-cultural data.

As a driver, I always tried to find a point of common humanity talking to people. However, just listening as riders talk to each other provides a window to an incredible amount of significant information that can have a serious impact on national security and law enforcement. In addition to national security issues, there is a very real danger of criminal activity that can affect both, drivers and passengers, particularly in "pools," when customers have no idea of who they are

---

[283] I am certified by the National Institute of Health (NIH), to carry out Human Research, by the NIH Office of extramural research. http//phrp. nihtraining.com/users/certificate.php

sharing the vehicle with. All the vignettes that follow took place unexpectedly. Everything just happened. There was no planning. Things just happened.

The Swamp

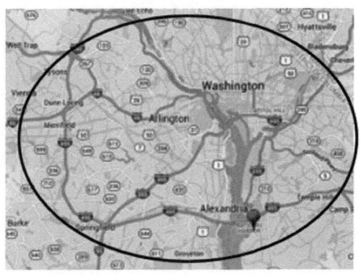

Vignette #1
Dangers of Ride-Sharing

On 18 June 2019, as directed by the Uber app, I went to pick up a passenger in Woodbridge, Virginia. I was looking for a lady with a Spanish name. I could not find anybody at the location pointed out by the GPS. I drove down about two blocks, passed the location that the app was pointing to, and turned around. I noticed a trailer park that possibly had the location number where the passenger was supposed to be. To my surprise, a man approximately 26 years old came over to my car and identified himself as the passenger.

This happens often, as parents call for a pick up for a child at school, a husband requests a ride for a spouse, or grown children request a ride for an elderly parent. My passenger identified himself with a Spanish name. I asked him if he spoke Spanish, and he answered back in some *gibberish* with a mixture of Spanish and English, and showed some astonishment that I spoke fluent Spanish, as well as English. I asked him where he was from, and told me that he was born in the U.S. of Salvadorian parents, who arrived in 1983, without a doubt, illegally.[284]

---

[284] At the time Central America was involved in a nasty civil war, as Communists with support from the Cuban Communist Government – as surrogates for the Soviet Union were attempting to take over the region. The war, compounded by economic circumstances triggered an exodus of illegal migrants to the U.S. as the US Government chose to ignore the situation and allowed it to happen. Thousands of Salvadorians entered the country they elected to settle in the Los Angeles area, for reasons of language and culture, and because local authorities – like Federal authorities – chose to ignore the situation. Salvadorian children and teenagers were bullied in schools by Mexican-American and Black American gangs. It did not take very long before the Salvadorians set up their own gangs as a defense mechanism. That was how Mara Salvatrucha (MS-13) was created in Westlake, Los Angeles, later spreading all over the country, and becoming a criminal gang. Another Salvadorian gang created about the same time was the 18th Street Gang,

The more my passenger tried to communicate, the more that he drifted in and out of *Spanglish*. It became rather obvious that he had a very poor educational background or some speech impediment, or both. He asked me where I was from, and some other related questions. He volunteered that he was born in Alexandria, Virginia, and had spent all of his life in the area, including three years in the penitentiary. I asked him about it, and he volunteered that he had been busted for a string of robberies when he was 15 years old, and had been tried as an adult. Traditionally, a juvenile under 18 years of age is tried in juvenile court, unless the offenses are so serious that it is determined that they should face the law as an adult. Under theft and burglary laws, a perpetrator that is under the age of 18 is dealt with through the juvenile justice system, not the criminal justice system. Juveniles convicted of a crime are normally released when they turn 21.

According to my passenger, he has been clean for nine years since he was released from jail. He earns a living as a tattoo artist, and works at a restaurant. He told me that he is the father of a five-year-old boy, who spent the Father's Day weekend with him from Friday to early Monday morning. He further explained, that he learned to tattoo while in jail, but did not explain if he attended any kind of formal educational program to learn the trade.

My passenger volunteered that he did not do any drinking over the weekend, while he had his child under his supervision, and claimed that he did not want his child to grow up and have a similar experience to his own. Although my passenger was somewhat incoherent, he managed to relate his story in the approximately 25-minute ride from Woodbridge to Fairfax City, along the Fairfax Park Highway. According to

divided into Revolutionaries and Southerners. Membership estimates go from 65,000 to 500,000.

Uber rules, driving a passenger without the presence in the car of the account holder is a violation of the rules. However, these Uber rules are not like the tablets inscribed with the *Ten Commandments* brought down by Moses from Mount Sinai. (Exodus 34.1)

What about the slogan: *"Once a Felon, Always a Felon?"* According to Virginia law (Virginia Code §16.1-305, and §16.1-306), any juvenile – regardless of age – at the level of a felony if committed by an adult, are not expunged and are retained for the rest of his or her life. The consequences are severe and long-lasting. *But who was I really transporting? Was I driving a criminal convicted of a violent felony?* Definitely, based on his story, he was not imprisoned for a misdemeanor criminal offense as a juvenile. He was convicted for a felony. There are consequences for bad behavior, one being that people like myself, who have an encounter with a felon, have to be on guard. Although situations like the one I am describing occur less than one percent of the time, they do happen to ride-share drivers. I had already driven over 8,200 passengers when I had this experience, and as far as I was concerned, it had never happened before to my knowledge.[285]

I decided to call the Uber 800 number and explain what happened, although once again, I was faced with a very nice lady on the phone, possibly in India, half-way around the world, who may not have understood what I was trying to

---

[285] Conviction for a felony carries a stigma. After someone pays their debt to society, they should not suffer discrimination. However, the high rate of recidivism overshadows those who are no longer engaged in crime, Felons are treated as second class citizens. They cannot own fire arms, are not allowed to vote, and suffer other indignities and heartaches. Finding sustainable employment is one of the principal challenges, which in turn can push them back to a life of crime because of their limited alternatives. Once released from prison they should not be punished for life, but due to conditions as they are, it is always potentially dangerous to deal with people who have been convicted of a felony.

explain. Namely, that a request for service was placed by an individual, who I only knew by a first name. However, that person placed the request for a ride for another individual, whose name was not recorded anywhere. Had I been victim of a crime or an attempted crime, Uber and police investigators could have traced the perpetrator possibly through the record of the person who requested the ride. Uber should have the full name, address, and credit card number to charge for the service. Nevertheless, nothing is known about the relationship between the requester and the passenger.

My passenger could have stolen the phone used to place the request, leaving behind no way to trace the identity. I requested to speak with a manager, but that did not go anywhere. I was told that the conversation was recorded, and a manager would be made aware of what happened. It is possible that Uber may cancel future use of the service by the owner of the account, but would that be fair? Although there was exposure, nothing illegal really happened. Would it be fair to further punish the passenger or his sponsor when in fact nothing happened, other than a possible violation of Uber rules? *But it happens all the time!*

These are samples of published details of Uber drivers attacked by passengers in the first six months of 2019:

- ~ 16 Jan 2019 – Two teenagers attacked and brutally beat a driver in Las Vegas when he refused their ride when the passengers looked underage.
- ~ 1 Feb 2019 – A driver was attacked and had his throat slit, and suffered cuts to his hands by a passenger with a knife in Tolleson, Arizona The driver was able to fight off the perpetrator, who got out of the car and fled on foot, but was later arrested and charged with attempted murder, and aggravated assault with a deadly weapon.

- ~ 19 Feb 2019 – A passenger attacked a driver in Wilmington, N.C. – The passenger requested the driver to pull to the side of the road alleging that he was sick and needed to throw up – a few minutes later the passenger grabbed the driver by an arm and demanded the keys to the car – The driver took off running on foot, and called police. The perpetrator was arrested for common law robbery.
- ~ 24 February 2019 – A driver was assaulted by a passenger in Englewood Cliffs, N.J. using the car's seat belt, without any prior discussion or altercation. Police arrested the perpetrator for aggravated assault and resisting arrest. The driver had to be treated by an ambulance crew.
- ~ 20 March 2019 – A driver was attacked by a passenger in Raleigh, N.C. after a verbal argument. The driver stopped the car and asked the passenger to get out, and a physical altercation ensued outside the vehicle. The passenger was arrested and charged with assault and damage to personal property.
- ~ 23 May 2019 – A driver was assaulted in Hanover, N.H. by a passenger who had been mistakenly picked up by the driver, confused about who of several people standing at the pickup point was the actual customer. The rider demanded a free ride, and forcibly tried to grab the car keys. After a short altercation the perpetrator ran away, and police could not find him.

Vignette #2
Where are the Natives?
What about our national security?

On Tuesday 4 September 2018, at about 3:30 PM I started a "pool," first, picking up a young lady from Baluchistan, Pakistan. She told me that she arrived in the U.S. as a political refugee, and described genocidal actions carried out by Pakistani security forces in her homeland. Baloch nationals have been fighting a guerrilla war seeking autonomy from Pakistan, all the way back to 1948, when the former British colony was reapportioned, creating India and Pakistan. Since 2016, some progress has been made in arriving at a reconciliation between the people of the region and the Pakistani central government, but fighting continues. The U.S. Government, Great Britain (UK), and Pakistan designated the *Baluchistan Liberation Army (BLA),* an *ethnonationalist militant organization,* as a terrorist organization.[286] My passenger made the point that her people were fighting back, and support their insurgency in order to survive. The U.S. Government has rejected the secessionist forces in Baluchistan, although it has expressed concerns over human rights abuses by Pakistan. Clearly, my passenger was a sympathizer of the Baluchi insurgency. A supporter of the Baluchistan Islamic insurgency should be on the U.S. Government watch list.[287]

---

[286] Federal Register (The Daily Journal of the United States Government). Designation of Baluchistan Liberation Army as a Specially Designated Global Terrorist. A Notice by the State Department 07/02/2019.

[287] There is very limited information in the public domain about the number of Baluchistan nationals living in the U.S. Nevertheless, Baluch activists have staged protests outside the White House against the visit of Pakistan's Prime Minister in 2014 and the United Nations headquarters in 2016. Indian intelligence services funded some of these demonstrations as part of their anti-Pakistan activities, based on published reports. Seehttps://www.geo.tv/

The young woman told me that she earned a Masters in Biochemistry, and wants to go back to school in America, but schools are costly, and she has to take some required courses by George Washington University before she can revalidate her degree. I suggested that she explore taking the pre-required courses at a Community College, which is much cheaper than large private schools. Then I thought about what I was hearing. The young lady was in fact talking about insurgents in her country, and she was engaged in an apology for their actions. Well, it just happens that the BLA has links to the Taliban, the prime enemy that American and NATO troops are fighting in Afghanistan, right across the border from her native Baluchistan (Pakistan). Was she properly investigated before she was issued a U.S. visa, assuming that she was legally in the country? I had no way of ascertaining her status in the country without her full name.

For whatever it is worth, Russian Information Warfare (IW), has promoted the concept that the U.S. is behind the BLA and the Baluch insurgency in Pakistan to destabilize that country through the use of terrorism. The Russians have used Russian TV to promote the idea as part of their psychological operations.[288] RT and Sputnik-News are two of the principal Russian media outlets used to disseminate Russian Information Warfare (IW).

As I drove her to her job in Crystal City, I received a message from the Uber app, telling me to pick up another rider for the pool. I picked up a Russian gal about 20 years old. I could not find out much about her because I was conversing with the lady from Pakistan, and she was on a

---

latest/191509-us-based-baloch-activist-says-he-heckled-pakistani-pm-on-behest-of-indian-spy-outfit-raw

[288] See: https://www.bing.com/videos/search?q=balochistan+republican+army&qpvt=balochistan+republican+army&view=detail&mid=2DB0F236D3303DA43A942DB0F236D3303DA43A94&&FORM=VRDGAR (Last accessed on 24 October 2019).

cell phone talking in Russian, which is how I found out where she was from. (I took Russian in High School and College.) Between dropping off the Pakistani rider, and delivering the Russian gal to her destination only about five minutes passed. I received another Uber ping to pick up another rider, which turned out to be a right, a Chinese national, at the same apartment building in Crystal City where I was delivering the Russian passenger.

At about 4:00 PM I picked up the Chinese national, after dropping off the Russian young lady. I learned from my Chinese passenger that he was in graduate school at George Washington University, working on a Master's degree in Computer Sciences. He had been in the U.S. for about a year and a half, and still needed another semester to complete his degree. Typical of a "pool" ride, within a few minutes, I received instructions to pick up another rider by the Metro station in front of Arlington Cemetery. This rider turned out to be another young lady born in St. Petersburg, Russia, where she works as a waitress at a water park tourist destination- or so she told me. She was on a short visit to the U.S. with several stops. The following day she was scheduled to depart for New York City.

Where else in the United States can an Uber driver be faced with experiences like this? For someone who has worked for Uncle Sam for about 51 years in one capacity or another, the whole experience had me generating more and more questions in my mind. Anyone linked to one of the sixteen intelligence agencies in the U.S. Government would be concerned about the geopolitical complexities of this experience.

Was my Baluchistan passenger legally in the country? Did she have ties to an organization that uses terrorism as an "equalizer" in irregular warfare? Was she properly vetted before she was allowed into the country? Could she be developed into a "source" for intelligence on what Baluchistan residents in the U.S. are up to? What about the Russians? What are the chances of meeting two young Russian women driving Uber within minutes of each other? It just happens that I may have enough knowledge of Russians to try to figure out what they were talking about on their cell phones. What about the Chinese student getting an advanced degree in IT? Was he sent to the U.S. by the PRC intelligence services to squeeze as much advanced IT knowledge as possible from Americans, to then turn it around and use it against us? Could an incidental encounter be used to develop a potential source of intelligence?

It would make sense to have informers and/or undercover agents working as ride-share drivers, in an effort to identify potentially threatening situations worth investigating. In just about any other country in the world, that would happen. But in the United States, that would be clearly defined as a violation of basic human rights… till something happens, and the intelligence community is instructed to *walk the cat back* to figure out where things went wrong. That is precisely what happened after 9/11/2001, when the intelligence community failed to analyze numerous hints that a terrorist attack was imminent. By then, close to 3,000 people were dead, and thousands more were wounded, and numerous *First Respondents* were contaminated by asbestos and other substances that led to cancer and other diseases surfacing years later.[289] *Only in America!*

---

[289] As of August 2019, about 3,000 first responders to the tragic events of 9/11/2001 have died as a result of inhaling carcinogens mixed with the dust. In other words, over 6,000 people have died as a result of 9/11/2001. Have we learned any lessons? Does anyone care that we are dealing with double the fatal casualty tally?

Vignette #3
January 2016
Ride from a BMW auto body shop, 8427 Lee Highway, Fairfax, Va. to the Executive Office of the President on 17th Street N.W. in Washington, D.C.

In January 2016, I accepted a ping from the Uber app, and received instructions to pick up a passenger from a BMW body shop on Lee Highway, in Fairfax, Virginia. The passenger was a white male that appeared to be

Executive Office the the President Building was originally the U.S. Department of State U.S. Library of Congress |

about 30 years old. The Uber app instructed me to take him to 600 17th Street NW, in Washington, D.C. The address rang a bell, but I could not place it, but I started driving in that direction. Before long, I noticed that he was placing a phone call with his cell phone. It did not take me very long to figure out that he was talking to someone about President Barrack Obama's schedule, and spilling highly classified information. The address where I was taking him turned out to be the Executive Office of the President of the United States. I had been there several times in the course of my work. The last time, back around 2010, to interview a DIA official on the subject of *Methodology for Analyzing Insurgency*, trying to identify lessons learned from about eight years of fighting in Afghanistan and Iraq, for an **unclassified** paper I was writing at the time.[290]

My passenger discussed with the person at the other end of the phone several venues to hold a meeting between U.S. Government officials and senior IT company officials. Both,

---

[290] Methodology: *"the systematic, theoretical analysis of the methods applied to a field of study."*

the companies and the government, had reasons to discuss certain security features of cell phones that made it very difficult for law enforcement to investigate acts of terrorism.

The genesis apparently was a historic showdown between industry and the FBI, triggered a month earlier by a terrorist attack on 2 December 2015. Two terrorists, Syed Rizwan Farook and his wife Tashfeen Malik, killed14 and wounded

FBI picture of terrorists
Syed Rizwan Farook and Tashfeen Malik.

22 other people, all state employees, at the Inland Regional Center in San Bernardino, California. The FBI and California law enforcement authorities had recovered computer equipment and cell phones to track the terrorists' activities prior to the attack, but were unable initially to crack security protections embedded by manufacturers.

The priority was to identify quickly if coordinated terrorist attacks were planned with Jihadist associates. Although the terrorists had tried to destroy their personal electronics, including cell phones, computers, and hard drives, they had not been completely successful.[291] [292] The FBI was initially unsuccessful hacking into an Apple iPhone 5C captured after a shootout with police in which both terrorists were killed.
The manufacturer demanded that the FBI obtain a search warrant or subpoena before they were willing to cooperate.

If the IT companies tried to set up a meeting on their own, the Anti-Trust Division of the Justice Department

---

[291] Story so far: Apple-FBI battle over San Bernadino terror attack investigation: all the details. *Los Angeles Times.* 19 February 2016.
[292] Joel Rubin, James Queally, and Paresh Dave. FBI unlocks San Bernadino shooter's iPhone and ends legal battle with Apple, for now. *Los Angeles Times.* 28 March 2016.

would object. The government had to organize the meeting to avoid legal challenges. Apparently, President Obama was interested in participating in some way in such a meeting. My passenger and his interlocutor were discussing details of such a meeting, including when and where, and what role President Obama could play.

My passenger was discussing where to host such a meeting, and if President Obama should go to open the meeting, give a keynote speech during a lunch, or attend at the end of the day to close the meeting. Specific times and locations were discussed, which provided critical information that could be used by nefarious actors to target the POTUS. *Just incredible!*

The moment the conversation ended I questioned my rider if he had any idea of what the U.S. Secret Service would do if they learned of what he had just done. Instead of being apologetic, he became *cocky,*[293] in other words, he became overly self-confident and arrogant. I told him that we were not going to get anywhere discussing his actions, but suggested that he take a look at one of my books which was right in front of him, in the back pocket of the passenger seat: *It's a Jungle out There! Memoirs of a Spook.* I told him to look at the pictures... and then we could go back to discuss his actions.

He flipped though my book, and centered on the pages with pictures... *"Oh! You are here with President Carter, President Bush, Vice President Mondale, Vice President Quail, and... hey, a picture with Bill Dailey, and he is giving you some kind of award...."* I told him - You are correct! – He answered back – *"He was Chief of Staff at the White House when Clinton was President!"* – I said – You are correct again! – But he was Secretary of Commerce when he gave me that award. By then, the young fellow was about to crap

---

[293] Conceited or arrogant in a bold and imprudent way.

in his pants. I told him – Look I am not going to turn you over to the Secret Service... that would be the least of your problems. If Michelle Obama heard what you did, she may look for a broom in one of the White House closets and use it to smack you over the head for placing her husband's life in danger! When I finally delivered him to his destination, he took off like a bat out of hell...

So what? How often do situations like this take place while riding in a taxi or rideshare Uber or Lyft vehicle in the course of a day, a week, or a month? Is there any way to stop the exposure of national security information by stupid people who somehow obtained a security clearance? As already shown in previous sections of this book, the number of foreign visitors, legal and illegal immigrants, and foreign diplomats is huge. The possibility of intelligence spillage is huge. I do not have a solution, other than strict enforcement. In Russia, China, Cuba, or North Korea a violation of this type without a doubt would end up with a death sentence.

Vignette #4
Mystery ride with a senior staffer
of Russian Television (RT)
Pool Ride from Roselynn, Northern VA to
Massachusetts Ave and 14th Street NW, Wash. D.C.

The Russian government-owned international television network (RT), is formerly known as *Russia Today*. It was launched in December, 2005, to focus on worldwide audiences as a prime propaganda machine, and integral part of *Information Warfare* (IW). In other words, RT spins the news cycle in support of the Kremlin, together with Novosti, Tass, and the entire government-control news media.

Mikhail Lesin
Died of blunt force trauma 5 Nov 2015 in Wash. D.C.

RT operated out of an office in downtown Washington, D.C. near Chinatown, at 1325 G St. NW, Washington, D.C.

The person credited with the creation of RT was Mikhail Yuriyevich Lesin, who was then a top adviser to Vladimir Putin. He was later dismissed in 2009 by President Dmitry Medvedev, but returned to RT when Putin was reelected in 2012, to leave the organization once again in December, 2014, apparently after a falling out with Putin. Lesin made a fortune as head of the state-controlled Gazprom-Media, and he and his family members lived the life of a Russian oligarch, including investing large sums of money purchasing American real estate. Based on unclassified news reports, Lesin was scheduled to disclose information about the link between RT, intelligence services, and the inner workings of Russian Information Warfare to the U.S. Department of Justice in Washington in early November, 2015.

The day he was to meet with U.S. Government officials for a tell-all expose of the unrelenting Russian effort to disrupt the information environment world-wide without regard for the potential consequences, he was found dead in his Dupont Circle hotel room in D.C. He may have died of injuries resulting from a drunken fall, or he may have been whacked by Russian intelligence operatives.

Most people only became aware of Russian Information Warfare (IW) after the 2016 presidential election, but Russians have been using Information Warfare tools as far back as the 1920's during Soviet times in a remorseless effort to disrupt through propaganda and disinformation. As a result of the Russian invasion of Crimea in 2014, sanctions had been put in place by the U.S. and allies against Russia, and Russian oligarchs and high-level officials.

With that background, I was intrigued by an unintentional encounter driving an Uber pool, in the presence of two other riders with a senior RT operative, who volunteered that he worked for the organization in the heart of our Capital. It was around 7 p.m. and raining when I picked him up in Rosslyn,

Virginia, a suburb located just across Georgetown. I drove across the Wilson Bridge over the Potomac back into DC.

I had one of Putin's despicable minions sitting next to me! The *Русское сообщество* в dc – (Russian collective in D.C.) may claim to be involved in art exhibitions, scientific forums, educational projects, and music festivals, but they are not necessarily educators, scientists, and journalists involved in any kind of cooperation with or society. Their Russian-American cultural activities are a cover for espionage and other nefarious activities.

I was surprised, and ready to exploit the opportunity, but had other people in the car, which limited my ability to play a cat-and-mouse game with someone who claimed to be primarily a *sportscaster*. He looked the part. He was tall, blond, spoke perfect English with a slight British accent, and had all the traits of a professional expert in exaggerations and reporting something close to the truth that turns out to be what in the vernacular would be classified as disingenuous *bullshittery.*

He was an expert in "small talk," or polite conversation about uncontroversial matters, and use the chitter-chatter to elicit information from unsuspecting interlocutors. I could deal with that, but was constrained by the presence of other people. Nevertheless, I was able to find out that he had been posted to an RT office in New York City, as well as to the one in Washington. He could be recalled back to Russia to assist with the coverage of the 2018 FIFA World Cup (*Fédération Internationale de Football Association*), which was to be held in Russia. It sounded like something plausible, but it resembled a case of typical disinformation.

I teased him with some Russian language small talk, but I simply did not have enough time to start a meaningful conversation to find out what he was really up to before I dropped him off at his destination near Massachusetts Avenue and 14th Street NW, in Washington.

I still had the other two passengers in the car. He may have been one of the *baddest* of villains working for the Antichrist, but I did not have a commission from Uncle Sam to engage in a more aggressive effort to figure out what he was up to. After disclosures of Russian tinkering with the U.S. elections in 2016, more sanctions against RT came about. RT and its employees operating in the US were required to register as foreign agents with the Justice Department under the Foreign Agents Registration Act.

So what? RT America had previously been singled out publicly in January, 2017, as participating in the conspiracy to tinker with the 2016 elections. In February, 2018, RT was dropped by two signal broadcasters in the DC Metro Area, and went off the air in the Capital region. Draining the swamp in Washington involves more than bringing under control corrupt corporate lobbyists, corporate media, "ruthless *onepercenters*," corrupt politicians, and other vile creatures. It includes foreign intelligence operatives and associated hideous creatures. It is really *A Jungle out there!*[294]

---

[294] Title of one of my previous books: *It's a Jungle Out There! Memoire of a Spook.* (2008).

Vignette #5
Woodbridge, to Springfield, Virginia
January 2016

I accepted an Uber pin to pick up a rider in Woodbridge, near the campus of Northern Virginia Community College (NVCC). Two Afro-American males in their twenties entered my car, and told me that they were going to Springfield Mall. I told them I had their destination in my GPS. I did not want to engage in conversation with them while driving in a heavily congested Interstate 95.

They continued their conversation, which had started before they entered my car. They were discussing a recent arrest of a friend, facing possibly as much as twenty years in jail. Apparently, their friend was charged with a drug trafficking offense. The thrust of their conversation centered around their friend's girlfriend, who had enough knowledge of the facts, that if she were to testify, could result in a long sentence. The question they were discussing was essentially how to keep the young lady from turning into a snitch. They repeatedly said that their friend's girlfriend could put him away for twenty years.

Without a doubt I was dealing with a couple of very dumb young men who would engage in such a discussion in front of a person who they did not know. By the way they were talking I could guess they had very limited education. I became naturally interested in the discussion, since they could be involved in criminal activity to silence a potential witness. On the other hand, my presence listening to their conversation was dangerous, since at some point they could get wise and understand that they had let the cat of the bag, and I could testify against them and their friend in a trial.

So what? How often do situations like this arise in a rideshare vehicle or a taxi? It can happen anywhere in the country, not just in the D.C. swamp. I am not aware of any specific instructions from Uber to drivers about what to do if faced with a similar situation. Should they call police and Uber to discuss what they heard? Obviously, time would be lost from work, which for most rideshare and taxi drivers is a valuable commodity. Would they really want to get involved in a legal case, in which they could be compelled to testify at trial... resulting in more loss of time? Perhaps they should be some form of compensation for drivers, as well as some program to offer them security, as they would become a target for criminal gangs, or drug trafficking organizations (DTOs).

Vignette #6
16 November, 4:07 P.M. to 10:00 PM
McLean, Va. to Duke University
Medical Center, Durham, N.C.

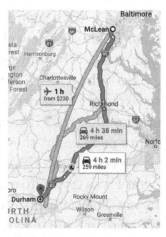

I accepted a trip on Friday, 16 November, 2018, from McLean, Va. to Durham, N.C. right in the middle of the Washington, D.C. rush hour, before the start of a long weekend. Why accept a 5-hour plus drive? First, I had no idea of what I was getting into when I accepted the drive. Second, it was a mother with three children ages 6 to about 14, and they were going to the Duke Medical Center because another son, age 18, was to undergo a bone marrow transplant. I could not complicate matters anymore, so I accepted the trip.

I took Dolly Madison Blvd to the Washington Beltway, known as I-495. This is a wide highway with four lines in each direction, and a toll road in the middle with an additional two lanes in each direction. The tools are "dynamic," meaning that they go up and down, depending on the volume of traffic. I drove from the Tysons Corner area on I-495 to I-95 South. The traffic on the main road was at a standstill. The toll on the E-ZPass lanes was up to $6.00. Once I turned South on I-95, once again I had to make a decision to stay on the main road, which was hardly moving, or take the E-ZPass Express Lanes to the end in Stafford County, just before the Rappahannock River, where I-17 crosses I-95. The toll at the time was $19.

I continued on the regular lanes of 1-95 to Richmond, where I had to take an exit to I-64/I-15, to the exit to I-85 S diagonally to Durham, N. C. There was another $1.70 toll on that road as it passed through the Richmond downtown area. The traffic was extremely heavy all the way from McLean to Richmond. Once I got to I-85 the traffic was relatively light, but I had to drive another 100 miles to arrive at my destination. After delivering my passengers, I had to turn back and drive again from about 10:00 p.m. till 2:30 a.m. when I finally arrived home, about 12 blocks from where I had started this odyssey.

So what? The next epic I had to endure was having to explain the trajectory of my trip and the tolls to people employed at the Uber call center in India. They are very nice polite people, but they have a heavy accent in English, have never visited the USA, and do not have the foggiest notion of what I was trying to explain in order to recover the tolls I had to pay. The compensation fluctuated from $304 minutes after the trip, to $368, down to $358, and down again to $295. The more I tried to explain the worse things got. I finally had to visit an Uber "Green Point," located in Minnesota Avenue, N. E. in Washington, D.C. I never received proper compensation for the tolls, and the long trip back.

Vignette #7
Multiple pickups at 1680 Capital One Dr., McLean, VA 2210
Capital One Corporate Office Headquarters HQ

CapitalOne prides itself of having an open culture and harnessing collective wisdom of associates with diverse ideas, perspectives, and backgrounds. The problem is that management needs to work harder at harnessing the power of collective wisdom – particularly about educating employees to keep their trap shut when they go into a situation where outsiders are present. This happens to be a critical professional ability... control comments about internal affairs of the company when they are in front of outsiders. Chief Executive Officer Richard Fairbank, without a doubt, has no idea of how important it is to protect company information. In this case, in front of a peer-to-peer ridesharing company or taxi drivers.

The name Uber is linked to "talented," "skilled," "bad-ass," "really bad," "wicked," and other slang and more vulgar terms. It is important for all employees to have an understanding and an incentive to understand what private property ownership is all about, and that it has to be safeguarded. They should not go out as a group to take an Uber and continue in front of the driver a conversation about internal company intellectual property as they are taken to their destination (s). Due to relative proximity to my home, I often hang around McLean, VA, and the Tysons Corner area, right in the area where Capital One built its new headquarters. As a result, I have made over thirty pickups at this location.

A large number of employees are Indian nationals, without a doubt, IT professionals using their skills in the banking sector. They tend to be quiet and very well-behaved. However, there are other young employees that apparently visit corporate headquarters for training sessions or important corporate discussions. They often travel in groups to and from nearby hotels, or transportation points, such as Union Station, Reagan National or Dulles Airports.

They are not alone. Employees of such companies as SAIC, Booze Allen and Hamilton, and Northrop Grumman, to mention only a few, with large employee presence in buildings within a mile of Capital One, and make similar mistakes, including conversations related to bidding on government contracts, including U.S. Department of Defense requests for proposals (RFPs). A lot of the information, without a doubt, is company classified, and possibly government classified at lower classifications, such as "Unclassified//For Official Use Only."

So what? Bottom line, all employees, need to be trained to understand what "situational awareness" is all about:

- Situational awareness is an important skillset associated with personal safety...
- Situational awareness involves watching people – body language may tell what their mouths do not tell...
- Situational awareness involves assessing things or situations that are irregular, and may set off alarm bells...
- Situational awareness involves the work of our subconscious picking up what we don't "see" – intuition...
- Situational awareness involves the ability to conduct normal activities, but paying attention to surroundings, perhaps while not appearing to be paying attention...
- Situational awareness is picking up on levels of noise that suddenly spike... from a normal baseline...
- Situational awareness involves paying attention to the presence of potential predators...
- Situational awareness may mean not being hostage to electronic devices, particularly cell phones...

China's schoolchildren are now the smartest in the world.[295]

---

[295] China's schoolchildren are now the smartest in the world. 3 December 2019. https://www.thestar.com.my/news/regional/2019/12/03/china039s-schoolchildren-are-now-the-smartest-in-the-world (Last accessed on 3 December 2019)

Vignette #8
Chinese passengers in the DC Metro Area

There is a huge number of students from China going to school in the United States, and the chances that they may have some affiliation with Chinese intelligence services is significant. During the school year 2016/17, there were as many as 351,000 Chinese nationals in American schools.[296] They produce an income estimated at about $14 billion for the U.S. economy. It constitutes a noteworthy category of "export" of services. Considering the huge trade deficit with China in goods, income from education services constitutes an important "export" for the American economy.

However, the large number of Chinese students is starting to concern Members of Congress, as well as the intelligence services. The risk of spying and stealing American intellectual property is considerable. Before a Chinese student is given government approval to go overseas for schooling, they are required to go through a Communist Party consent process. For American authorities the process to grant student visas suffers from a lack of access to sources of background information, which makes it more important to crack down on students that show evidence that they may have perverse activities in mind, which may or may not have a direct link to their field of study.[297] Government authorities need to establish new rules for closer scrutiny of Chinese student

---

[296] Statista. Number of college and university students from China in the United States between 2006/07 and 2016/17.
NBC. Cynthia McFadden, Aliza Nadi and Courtney McGee. Education or espionage? A Chinese student takes his homework home to China. NBC. 24 July 2018.
[297] NBC. Cynthia McFadden, Aliza Nadi and Courtney McGee. Education or espionage? A Chinese student takes his homework home to China. *NBC*. 24 July 2018.

activities in an attempt to figure out if there is any suspected activity not associated with normal student behavior. In other words, are some Chinese students "non-traditional collectors" of intelligence? [298] [299] [300] [301] [302]

On the other hand, the Chinese intelligence agencies are concerned that their students in American universities could be targeted for recruitment by the U.S. intelligence community.[303] This is all part of a high stakes dangerous game involving numerous entities and experts on both sides. Espionage is the second oldest profession.

As a percentage of Chinese society, the number of families that can afford to send their offspring to study in the United States is small. However, in a country with a population of an estimated 1.389 billion, even a relatively small percentage represents millions of families with the purchasing power to send their kids to study overseas.[304] The number of Chinese students has been increasing year after year for the past thirty years. As of 2018, China dominates with the largest number of international students for the eighth consecutive year. The increase is reflected in ever-increasing tuition costs, as American educational institutions have created a dependency on international students, particularly to operate

---

[298] Reuters. Patricia Zengerle and Matt Spetalnick. Exclusive: Fearing espionage, US weighs tighter rules on Chinese students. *Reuters*. 29 November 2018.

[299] Dan Golden. Spy Schools: How the CIA, FBI and Foreign Intelligence Secretly Exploit America's Universities. NY: Henry Holt and Company

[300] Nick Roll. The CIA Within Academe. HigherEd. 3 October 2017.

[301] Elizabeth Redden. The Chinese Student Threat? *Higher Ed*. 15 February 2018.

[302] The Washington Post. Why China is so afraid of Chinese students in the United States. *The Washington Post*. 25 May 2017.

[303] The Washington Post. Why China is so afraid of Chinese students in the United States. *The Washington Post*. 25 May 2017.

[304] Population of the World. Population of China (2018). https://www.livepopulation.com/country/china.html.

graduate schools. For money's sake, we seem to be willing to compromise national security.

Well... not really. At the end of the battle, the ground is not covered with the rotting carcasses of hundreds of casualties. In many ways, the espionage and intelligence community has developed acceptable and not acceptable practices and there are numerous similarities in the way the game is played. The PRC sends students to America to learn about our technology, and figure out ways to steal what they can in one way or the other, and to penetrate American society at all levels. Every Chinese student is a potential spy. The American intelligence community is well aware of what is going on, and no opportunity is lost to recruit Chinese to defect and become spies for the United States. This is a serious and dangerous game, with its own set of rules of what is acceptable and not. Both sides understand that it is vital, for verification purposes to achieve some balance in this game to avoid surprises that can lead to war.

***

Ubering a Chinese Student in the D.C Metro Area

On a Friday in September, 2019, I answered a ping from the Uber app and went to the campus of American University, in N.W. Washington, D.C. The passenger was a Chinese High School student attending a private school in Tennessee. He was visiting several universities in Washington as part of a selection process to pick a school for his Bachelor's degree, starting in September, 2020. He was very fluent in English, without any hint of an accent when he spoke. He was clean cut, well dressed, and exhibited excellent manners.

We started a conversation. He told me what he was doing in town, and politely asked me if I could offer some hints about the benefits of going to school in Washington. I told him that there had been very significant changes since I entered college in 1964. Back then, going to school with the Library of Congress, the National Archives, and other resource libraries, was a great advantage. When writing term papers, I could go to the Library of Congress and have access to the largest collection of books and other materials in the world. I could do primary research with access to key documents at the National archives. I did not have to depend on a university library, even though schools like Harvard, Yale, University of Texas at Austin, and University of North Carolina at Chapel Hill, to mention only a few, had very impressive collections in their libraries. To pay high tuition and attend one of the universities in the Capital, one had to take full advantage of all that the city has to offer, or otherwise it would be a complete waste of money.

I acknowledged that my experiences in college took place many years before the computer age and the advent of Internet. Right now, there are many resources available that were not around back in the 1960's, and perhaps location is not as important as it once was. He followed up with some well-thought-out questions, which most high school students would not have asked. The more we talked, the more impressive this young fellow was. He was going to a house off Old Georgetown Pike, in Langley, very close to CIA headquarters, and the rush hour traffic was horrible, so we had almost an hour to talk.

I asked him what he was planning to study, mentioning that other Chinese students I had met seemed to concentrate in high tech areas, including IT. Depending on the major, an education in Washington would have to be looked at from a different angle. His answer was fascinating. He wants to work for the Chinese diplomatic service. I told him that I was retired from the U.S. Foreign Service, and that about 20,000 people take the Foreign Service Entrance Exam annually and only about 300 of them actually are hired after a very strict selection system. In China, with a population of over one billion people, without a doubt the selection process was bound to be just as strict, and with some additional requirements that we do not have in the United States. For example, probably only members off the Communist Party in good standing would have a change to become diplomats, after passing strict exams.

My passenger thought about it, and told me that he did not have a problem with that. He emphasized that he has been a good student for many years, and had excellent foreign language skills that set him apart. I asked him about his family. What did his father do? Was he a high-level government official, or a businessman, or what? He told me that his father has his own business and does quite well, but he could not describe the specifics because his father did not talk much about it. He told me that he has an older half-brother, who did not speak English.

I dropped him off at a home where he was apparently staying, in one off the most elite neighborhoods in the D.C. Metro Area. The house could easily be worth between two and three million dollars, and even the public schools, including Langley H.S., is one of the best public schools in the entire country. He did not disclose anything about who was hosting him during his visit to check schools in the Capital. I have taught college students part time for several years in the Washington Metro Area, as well as in Europe. When I was posted in Spain, I taught courses on Practical Diplomacy, and the Economics of the European Union. I had students from 21 countries, including Russia, Finland, France, Germany, Canada, Spain, Morocco, and the United States. This Chinese H.S. student was well above average. Very impressive young man.

So what? How is all of this relevant to a book about Uber? Nothing. However, Uber drivers have hundreds of opportunities to interact with Chinese nationals, and possibly pick up information that may be relevant to ascertain if they are legitimate students or not. In China that is not how the game is played. The intelligence services most definitely have assets everywhere, typical of dictatorships. *Is that how we want to operate in the United States?* No. But we are not as stupid as we may look... I have transported a large number of Chinese students over a three-year period. Generally, they were polite, clean cut, spoke English well, and clearly showed they were serious about their studies. When compared with American students, they did not have visible tattoos, no long unkempt hair, and dressed conventionally... We are in serious need to reassess how we are training the next generation of Americans, so we do not end up with a large-scale freak show. Note that the OECD triennial study of 15 year-old-students conducted in 79 countries and involving 600,000 students found that Chinese students in Beijing, Shanghai, Jiangsu and Zhejiang outperformed the average students in mathematics and science.[305]

---

[305] https://www.thestar.com.my/news/regional/2019/12/03/china039s-schoolchildren-are-now-the-smartest-in-the-world

Vignette #9
The American Melting Pot

I turned on my Uber App about 2:00 PM on a weekday in Alexandria, VA, and within a couple of minutes, I answered my first ping for a ride from a nearby townhouse. The passenger was a frequent customer, who normally seems to be going somewhere as I complete my normal work schedule as a government contractor. My passenger is a former military officer from a West African country, who is a legal immigrant, and extremely happy to be in the U.S. He normally goes to a Walmart store at a shopping mall in Springfield, Va. This time, however, he was going to an African food store off U.S. 395, near the Seminary Road exit. Along the way I answered another ping, and picked up my second rider for the pool. D.C. She was a young lady from Ethiopia, who was going to downtown D.C. I answered a third ping, and the passenger turned out to be another young lady from India, going to Union Station, near the Capitol, in downtown, D.C.

I commented to my passengers, *"We have the United Nations represented here!"* They all laughed. The older man commented: *"this is what makes America great... people from all over the world come here, and everybody gets along well, work, go to school, and are able to function without fear of government intrusion... as long as one respects the rule of law..."* At that point, the Ethiopian lady's cell phone rang, and she engaged in a conversation in Amharic, which is the official language of her country. Almost immediately, the Indian lady's cell phone rang, and she engaged in her own conversation in what may have been Hindi, Deccani-Urdu, or Telugu. I had no way to know. She had told me that she was from Hyderabad, a city of about 7.7 million people, where all three languages are used, in addition to English, which is the language of business in India. Most Hyderabadis speak or understand all three native languages, as well as some other regional dialects, in addition to English.

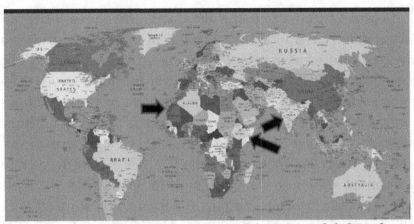

One Uber "pool" trip from Alexandria, Va. – vicinity of Ft. Belvoir to downtown Washington, D.C. with riders from West Africa, Ethiopia, and India. Feb 2019.

The sound level in the car would have driven nuts any American who has not ever been overseas. As a retired American diplomat, I found the experience fascinating, although at the same time, the experience illustrated the rapid change that has taken place in the D.C. Metro Area since the early 1960's. The character of the area has changed dramatically, to the point that the scenes of a Saturday evening in the food courts of some of the large shopping malls resembles some strange foreign scene, with multiple displays of clothing. Veiled women from Muslim countries in particular stand out, and with all due respect, they definitely stand out as alien to American culture, particularly because of the unwillingness to assimilate and give up their religious and cultural convictions and practices, which tend to be oppressive to women.

So what? Driving a share-drive vehicle one gets unusual understanding of what is going on. Diversity can enhance the country's ability to defend itself. Diversity provides all type of potential assets to protect national security. The trick is to revive the old Americanization programs that existed until at least the mid-1960's, to ensure that immigrants understand American culture and assimilate without giving up their own culture. Immigrants can learn English, without having to give up their own native languages. I am all for reopening the old Americanization schools. I attended one in D.C. back in 1962, and I did not suffer any negative consequences from the experience. We would not stand a chance in the multiple conflicts in which the country is involved overseas without people who are fluent in foreign languages and understand local cultures.

Vignette # 10
Ubering to the Katsucon Annual Convention 2017
Gaylord National Resort & Convention Center
National Harbor, MD

Katsucon is an annual 3-day convention dedicated to informing American enthusiasts about Japanese animation and traditional popular culture. Writers, actors, voice actors, comedians, webcomic creators, singers, and other creative people and their followers attend. The event has been held in the D.C. area since 1995, usually over the President's Day weekend. Attendees arrive from all over the world to participate in this popular convention of passionate fans.

I answered a ping to pick up passengers at a hotel in Alexandria, Va., across from National Harbor. I was not prepared for what I encountered when I arrived to pick up my four passengers. I had never heard of Katsucon, but was eager to learn what it was all about as soon as I met my young passengers wearing costumes. They were really nice, lots of fun, and willing to explain what Katsucon was all about, as we crossed the Potomac River over the Woodrow Wilson bridge. The weather was great, considering the time of year. Attendees spilled all over the National Harbor neighborhood enjoying the sunny day. The only drawback was that there was a lot of trash scattered all over the area, which is normally very clean, but the convention goers did not seem responsible for the mess.

I asked my costumed passengers about what they were wearing, and where they were from. They told me that they were from Atlanta, Ga. Computer gaming, according to what they told me, is one of the principal drivers of the convention. However, the principal driver is an interest on Japanese folklore, and a good number of the attendees are taking Japanese studies and learning the Japanese language.

So what? One thing is for sure... An Uber driver never knows what they will come across in a normal day. It is without a doubt a learning experience.

Young Uber riders from Georgia, going to the Katsucon convention in 2018, an annual 3-day anime convention held in the D.C. Metro area for multicultural enthusiasts and entertainment. In 2018 the convention was held at the Gaylord National Resort & Convention Center in Oxon Hill, MD (National Harbor). *Anime* is a style of Japanese film and television animation, typically aimed at adults, as well as children. This type of animation features action-filled plots with futuristic and fantastic themes.

Vignette #11
The bad, the ugly – and the spoiled brats...

On Saturday 23 March 2019, I answered a ping and went to make a pick up at an address in McClean, Virginia, one of the wealthiest neighborhoods in the D.C. Metro Area. Five female teenagers came out of a mansion easily worth at least $3 million, wearing fake green glasses, green plastic crowns, and other items normally associated with St. Patrick's Day festivities. They were between 15 and 17 years old, based on the conversation, as I drove them to an address in another upscale neighborhood in Montgomery County, Maryland. They were all students at private Catholic schools. I happen to live relatively close to where I picked up the girls, and I admit that I paid for my youngest daughter to attend one of those schools. I graduated from High school at one of those schools, St. John's College H.S., a Catholic military academy which is now co-ed.

The girl's ultimate destination was the Shamrock Fest at RFK Stadium from 2 to 7 PM, featuring several bands, including The Mahones, The Mighty Mighty Bosstones, Ballyhoo! Flatfoot 56, The Fighting Jamesons, Icewagon Flu, the Bastard Bearded Irishmen, Gaelic Mishap, Barleyjuice, Bryen O'Boyle, and other performers. It was about a 20-minute ride (about 12 miles) listening to loud music on the Beltway (495 N.). Four of the riders crammed into the backseat and the apparent leader-of-the-pack sat next to me. First question out of her mouth was *"Do you have a cable to connect my Apple iPhone to your radio?"* I told her that I was driving in an eight-lane highway and could not be playing around with my radio, but she could link her phone and play her music, or use my satellite radio, which has over 250 stations to choose from.

She managed to hook up her phone, and she played her music about as loud as possible, and the gals in the backseat sang alone... *It was just wild!* It did not take long to figure out they may have been drinking. I was able to lower the sound using the controls located on my stirring wheel, without having to reach for the radio bottoms, which had been taken over by my passenger sitting next to me. I do not recall any of my own children ever doing anything like it, and I never did anything like it either.

Finally, what I thought was "the ride from hell" came to an end at their destination, which was another multi-million-dollar mansion. As we arrived, and as they were getting out of my car, the Uber App beeped again. I accepted the ride, and to my surprise, another group of teenagers similarly dressed came out of the house where I had delivered the girls. The second group consisted of one teenage boy and three teenage gals. They were my new set of passengers... dressed in similar St. Patrick's Day regalia.

Trip miles from Kensington, MD to RFK Stadium- 22.8 miles via I-495 E (Beltway) and MD-295 S (Baltimore-Washington Parkway). (UberX $30 to $38.

Their destination, the Shamrock Fest. I figure that the teens did not have a good plan for getting to RFK, as the first group asked me if I could take them again. I had to tell them that I had already answered another Uber call, and they would have to call Uber again for another vehicle to take them to their destination. Apparently, a fairly large group of teens had made a plan to gather at the home of one of the members, from where they would ride to RFK stadium. The two groups passed each other without much interaction.

My new group was to constitute the "real ride from hell." The ride would take us on the Washington Beltway I-495, for about a half hour for the approximately 14-mile ride to N.E. Washington where the stadium is located. The young man sat next to me... and before long, he pulled out of his jacket a beer can. He was just about totally incoherent- and drunk.

Just like the previous rider, he took over my car radio and started playing even more incoherent "music" super loud, which' using my controls, on the steering wheel, I managed to periodically lower the volume... which he turned back up using the controls on the dashboard.

Again, references were made to private schools in the area. The young man apparently either attended school at Landon, or went to school at Landon and was kicked out.[306] I told them that I went to St. John's, back when dinosaurs roamed the area. They brought up Gonzaga, the school's nemesis. Other schools mentioned in the generally incoherent conversation were Stone Ridge, Georgetown Visitation, Bishop O'Connell, and Holly Cross. Between the loud music and paying attention to extremely heavy traffic, I did not notice that the girls in the backseat were drinking beer surreptitiously.

I did hear frequent references to their need to pee and that they were about to blowup. However, there is no place to stop along the Beltway. However, once I exited the highway at the Baltimore-Washington Parkway (Route 50), on my way to RFK stadium, I started to look for a gas station or some other place to stop for them to go to the bathroom. Finally, I found a gas station in an area that appeared to be safe. That part of the D.C. Metro Area is not one of the best to allow a bunch of wealthy white girls to get out of the car for a few minutes to go to the bathroom. All four passengers got out to pee, and

---

[306] Located at Wilson Lane, in Bethesda, Maryland, Landon is an elite school was founded in 1929, and is known as one of the top schools in the D.C. Metro for boys from 3-12 grade, with a dynamic academic program that prepares boys for the finest colleges and universities in the country. Tuition for grades third through twelve grades runs $40,000, and for 6 to 12 grades, $43,560. Tuition does not include books, supplies, or athletic equipment. Students who study a music instrument are required to take private lessons after school at an additional cost. Although the school has a financial aid program, only the wealthiest parents can afford to send their children there.

returned to the car. After they returned, we were only about five minutes away from the Shamrock Fest.

After dropping the group off at RFK stadium, I found that the young man had left a half-empty beer can in the area between the two front seats, and the girls had left two empty beer cans on the floor in the back of the car. I had to stop to throw them out in a trash can near the stadium, before I could go on to accept another ride. I had to mentally review my experience with the two last rides.

First, these were obviously wealthy white teenagers, going to excellent private schools, but they did not seem to have much parental supervision, and based on the drinking in the car, and their references to getting high, were probably using marijuana, and God knows what else. Their manners left a lot to be desired, and obviously they were in dire need of a life coach. Comparing the experience to taking very polite Black teenage boys in other Uber rides, their parents were obviously doing a much better job of raising their children.

So what? According to Uber and Lyft rules, anybody under 18 years of age, should not be given a ride without parental presence. However, for all practical purposes it happens all the time. Are riders supposed to be carding anyone who looks below 18 years of age? Are drivers expected to ask for information on whose credit card is being charged for the ride? At one point is a driver possibly engaging in a discriminatory practice? What about compliance with local legislation regarding underage drinking? What about compliance with legislation against drug use? What about picking a possible confrontation with wealthy parents who are paying for their children to take a ride-sharing vehicle to some destination? There are more questions than answers! The only good thing was that these teenagers were not driving a car and were instead taking a rideshare vehicle. Uber saves lives!

Without a doubt the teens in the second ride to the Shamrock festival had been partying and drinking and possibly using some illegal substances before they got into my car. I did not have any way to know that. Police in Montgomery County have been investigating cases involving underage drinking with the knowledge of their parents, after some tragedies caused by drinking and driving. Technically, anyone under the legal age of 21, can consume alcohol in a private residence, as long as the person is under the consent and supervision of family members, normally a parent, who is over the age of 21. Illegal possession of alcohol in Maryland triggers a citation, but not an arrest, as long as they are not driving or violating any other law. DWI violations in Maryland can result in a loss of the driver's license and other serious punishment.

What about potential liabilities for both, the driver, and Uber? The legal implications are huge. If something happened, would there be insurance coverage? Whose insurance? The driver's, or Uber's insurance? What would be the limits of coverage? If service is denied by a driver, would there be any possible liability? There are more questions than answers.

To put it in perspective, these were two rides, out of over 8,000. They represented much less than one percent! The situation was highly unusual. Yet, it happened. It was part of the total experience driving a rideshare vehicle. In hindsight, I should have turned down both trips. This is something called "experience." In one of my other incarnations, I would have been trying to figure out who provided the alcohol, if they were using drugs and/or marijuana, and who was pushing that stuff on them. I am sorry to say that our law enforcement entities are more interested in smoking out potential terrorists than drug enforcement. I personally support strict counternarcotics enforcement.

But what are rules for, if there are no consequences if they are violated? Either there is something wrong with the rules, or there is no enforcement. They need to be enforced or revised. These violations are endemic. They are violated constantly. Yet, nothing happens.

The rideshare companies are losing money, including Uber and Lyft. The drivers are receiving very low compensation, which may not even reach minimum wage levels... The drivers do not initiate the transactions, they answer a ping from the rideshare company! There is joint responsibility. Neither party is apparently unwilling to pass up earning some money, as they are both already under water. Pound wise and penny foolish... The future of rideshare and reaching profitability seems to be impossible under current circumstances. All the fancy financial analysis fails to consider these very real facts about inexistent enforcement of the rules.

Vignette #12
Inauguration Day – 20 January 2017
Driving in Downtown D.C.

On 20 January 2017, several thousand protestors took to the streets of the Capital, and engaged in multiple forms of vandalism. About 200 protesters were arrested after they smashed store windows, set trashcans on fire, fought with police, attacked President Trump supporters, blocked traffic by moving trashcans and other items to the streets. They were dressed in black and other dark colors, with their faces covered. I was driving Uber, and saw firsthand what was going on, and took pictures. Who were these troublemakers? Antifa members, behaving themselves like fascist agitators and violating the law without consequences. Anarchists and fellow travelers should be smashed before they can procreate and endanger the civil liberties granted by the American Constitution.

A good number of people were injured right in front of me, despite my efforts to stay away from the affected areas. The attached pictures were taken on K and 14th Streets, N.W., a key intersection in downtown D.C., as the troublemakers were moving from the area closer to the parade route and the White House, towards Dupont Circle, a traditional gathering point for violent demonstrators. Traditionally, they break away in small groups from large leftist demonstrations of one kind or another, and scatter round the downtown area in guerrilla bands to engage in violent acts.[307] [308] I have witnessed these tactics since the 1960's.

---

[307] Corky Siemaszko, Phil McCausland, Alexandra Jaffee, and Emmanuelle Saliba. EURONEWS. Dozens Arrested in Anti-Trump Protests Around Inauguration. *NBC News*. 20 January 2017.

[308] Oliver Laughland, Sabrina Siddiqui, and Lauren Gambino. Inauguration protests: more than 200 demonstrators arrested in Washington. *The Guardian*. 20 January 2017.

Police broke up the violent demonstrations using pepper spray, and countered violence with violence. As they got pelted with all kinds of projectiles, from bricks to bottles, they used force to try to capture the perpetrators. At least one black limousine was set on fire, and stores were trashed before the police could do anything about it. The masked Anarchist protestors claimed that they suffered emotional and physical abuse by law enforcement officers, when, in fact, they were the ones engaging in violent acts. Several police officers were hurt after being struck by projectiles. When police officers are restrained by their superiors, eventually a police riot ensues after one of them gets hurt... I can recall D.C. cops giving the finger to their superiors and charging the crowds of troublemakers, who, in my experience, tended to be white suburbanites, while D.C. police officers had a large presence of Black members.

Press coverage accurately depicted how Anarchists armed with crowbars and hammers marched through the downtown area topping over trashcans, vandalizing bus stop glass enclosures, spray-painting vehicles and smashing store windows. [309] The sound of sirens, firecrackers, smoke and pepper police grenades, and loud chanting made the area feel as if a civil war was underway.

Does it make sense to be driving Uber in the middle of violent protests? No. However, if one is trolling for a trip in D.C. and a call for a ride comes in, there is no reasonable way to tell if there are any dangers in the pickup or destination areas. It is the luck-of-the-draw!

So what? Most people have never witnessed these types of violent demonstrators, but they do happen. The Constitution grants American citizens the right to assemble and present

---

[309] John Woodrow Cox, Peter Jamison, Aaron C. Davis, and Tara Bahrampour. Inauguration Day 2017: Pomp and chaos collide as Trump becomes president. *The Washington Post*, 20 January 2017.

their grievances... However, when they become violent an endanger lives and destroy property, calling for revolution and the overthrow of the government, they violate the same laws that allow for peaceful assembly and protests. By playing around with *political correctness*, class warfare, and redistribution of wealth, they only waste time that should be spent in a bipartisan effort to deal with the real problems of the economy. These troublemakers are enemies of the system, and should be dealt with by law enforcement, without tying their hands by stupid politicians.

On Inauguration day 20 January 2017, groups of violent demonstrators spread in mobs around downtown Washington, D.C. brake store plate-glass windows, breaking windows and otherwise trashing cars, and setting trashcans on fire. In this picture the mob of Anarchists and associated leftists is shown crossing in a northerly direction at the corner of 14th and K Streets, N. W. Most of these people had their faces covered and used the heavy sticks used as flagpoles to smash property.

Vignette #13
The Day of the Strike (And the IPO...)
8 May 2019

As Uber and Lyft drivers staged a "strike" on 8 May 2019, I turned on my app, as usual, when I completed my regular work schedule at a U.S. Army facility. The Uber app directed me to pick up a passenger off the George Washington Parkway, near Mount Vernon. The rider turned out to be a young man at a multimillion-dollar mansion next to the Potomac River. He had his golf clubs and was on his way to the exclusive private Bell Haven Country Club on Fort Hunt Road in Alexandria, Virginia.[310] It was a short ride from his home. My passenger told me that he is a student at the elite St. Stephen's and St. Agnes K-12 Episcopal co-ed college-preparatory school, located about six miles south of Washington, D.C. The annual tuition at this school runs about $40,000, more than many colleges, and is attended by students from Northern Virginia, Washington, D.C. and Maryland. The upper school is located on St. Stephen Road, in Alexandria.

I could not tell if my passenger was 18-years-old already, but he looked to be close to that age, so I decided to pick him up and take him to his near-by destination. I asked him if he had to wait long to get a ride, but he told me that I answered

---

[310] The Bell Haven Country Club was established in the early 1920's, in land with a rich history going back to 1608, when Captain John Smith founded the native *Dogue Tribe* living in the Great Hunting Creek area. The West Grove Plantation was established in land currently occupied by the club. The plantation house was burned by Federal troops during the American Civil War, because the owner's sons joined the Confederacy and became officers serving under General Robert E. Lee. The name of the club is linked to a time in the early 1700's when Scottish pioneers settled along the banks of the Potomac River, and named their settlement after the Earl of Belhaven. The initiation fee to join the club is about $82,000, and monthly fees cost around $600.

the request right away as soon as he requested a ride through the Uber app. He confirmed that he was a high school student at St. Stephen's. I asked him if used Uber frequently, and he answered affirmatively. He had a debit card, and his own Uber account. I questioned him if he was ever asked how old he was, and if he ever had been turned down by a driver. He told me that he uses Uber fairly frequently, and had only been turned down by one driver some time back. I had no reason not to believe him.

If Uber could issue him his own account, I had no reason to question his use of Uber to get from his home to play golf at his private country club. If Uber could issue this young man an account without questioning his age, I had no reason to do so myself. Nevertheless, this experience is an example of the multiple issues associated with rideshare that still need to be settled. Based on a News4 investigation, some minors use Uber gift cards, even after midnight.[311]

So what? According to Uber rules, account holders must be 18, and cannot request a ride for one of their children or anybody else who is under 18 years of age, unless accompanied by the account holder. Lyft clearly states that account holders must be 18 years old, but does not provide instructions about someone underage allowed to take an unaccompanied ride. Both companies seem to be relying on "driver's discretion" about giving rides to minors.[312] There are several companies that are trying to develop a ride-sharing service for minors,

---

[311] Scott MacFarlane, Rick Yarborough, Jeff Piper and Steve Jones. Children use gift cards to take rideshare trips without parents' permission. *News4 I Team*, Washington. 5 November 2018.
[312] Age Limit: Should Uber Drivers Transport Kids & Minors? Therideshar.guy.com. https://theridesharguy.com/are-drivers-allowed-to-transport-minors/. (Last accessed on 9 May 2019)

including HopSkipDrive, Kid Car, Kid's Kruiser, Sheprd, Zem Car, and Zum. At least two other companies, Kid's Lyft and Shuddle, started to serve the need for rides for underage passengers but apparently went out of business.[313] [314]

---

[313] Rideshare services for children and young teenagers (minors). RideGuru. 28 July 2016, updated 15 March 2019. https://ride.guru/content/newsroom/rideshare-services-for-children. (Last accessed on 9 May 2019)

[314] Amy Iverson. Is it safe for kids to use ridesharing services like Uber and Lyft? *Deseret News*. 10 May 2017. https://www.deseretnews.com/article/865679640/Is-it-safe-for-kids-to-use-ridesharing-services-like-Uber-and-Lyft.html. (Last accessed on 9 May 2019)

Vignette #14
Business rules vs. Business Requirements
*Are Uber drivers given the criteria and
conditions for making a decision?*

Business rules outline what can and cannot be done, and what are the consequences if the rules are violated. Are employees allowed to use their own criteria and conditions for making a decision regarding interpreting a business rule? Generally, no.

On Wednesday 10 June 2019, I answered a "ping" on my Uber app. I followed the instructions and found myself entering the campus of a high school in Alexandria, Virginia. There were two female students talking near the school's main door. I waited, and waited... then one of them looked at my car, and apparently figured out that her requested Uber ride had arrived. I could not tell if she was 15 or 18 years old. I decided to test several Uber rules to get a better sense of reality in rideshare.

I asked my passenger if she was the person listed as the *"requester."* According to Uber rules the requester for a ride has to be one of the passengers. She said that she was the requester. I asked her if she had her own credit card. She replied that she had a "student account," whatever that means. I asked her if she was aware that the person riding as a passenger in an Uber car had to be the same person that requested the ride. She did not provide a conclusive answer initially, but then she told me again that she was the person that requested the ride. The business rule was tested and met!

I followed up with another question- *Do you know if any of your classmates or friends have been questioned by Uber drivers about their age, or if they were questioned about who had ordered the Uber?* - My passenger told me that she was not aware of any such incidents. Again, I asked her if other Uber drivers had ever questioned her about any of these issues. She said that I was the first driver to ask any questions. I asked my passenger if she was ever asked by an Uber rider if she was 18 years old, or older. She answered that she had never been asked such a question.

By asking questions I was bound to get a nasty rating by my passenger, which would have a negative effect in my overall rating as a driver. In my case, not being dependent on Uber to make a living, I could afford to be inquisitive. Other drivers would not take the chance of getting a bad rating by questioning a rider about her age.

So what? Drivers use their own criteria for making a decision to ask or not ask a question about the age of passengers that appear to be minors. How much leeway do drivers have to interpret the rules and the information provided by the passengers? Drivers are acting based on their own interpretation of the rules, and, without a doubt, they will act on the basis of their own financial interests, without considering all the potential consequences if an accident were to happen.

> *"It is time to drain the swamp in Washington, D.C."*

> *Donald J. Trump*
> *17 October 2016*

☰ Online

📍 Find trips toward destination ✕

ACHIEVEMENT ⟩

You've completed 3000 5-star trips, Rafael

That makes you kind of a big deal around here. Celebrate your new record!

CELEBRATE AND SHARE

As of July 24, 2017, trip booking fee is increasing by $0.25 for Uber X

Rider appreciation

You were tipped

 35 times

You were complimented

5 times

Your top compliment was **Great Conversation**.

Feedback from your riders

If a rider rates a trip 4 stars or below, they're required to pick a reason from a list. Thanks to Ratings Protection, the rating will not count against you if the reason is out of your control (traffic, payment issues, or problems with UberPool, for example).

Top issues riders reported:

1	Driving
1	Conversation

If you want to learn more about customer feedback or how to improve your rating, this blog post has you covered.

Take a look →

Other stats

Your acceptance rate

 91%

Your cancellation rate

0%

You had 17 5-star days last month

This means all your trips received 5-star ratings

Index

This Index was generated by software. It is created based on the way names appear on the manuscript in alpha-numerical order. Thus, people are listed as they appear in the text by their first name instead of their last name.

C

California xiv, 11, 41, 56–57, 83, 91, 153, 181
California's Assembly Bill 5 153
Canada xiii, 24, 86, 91, 98, 205
Canadians 22
CapitalOne 237
Capitol Police 26
Casey Xavier Robinson 83
Caterpillar 100
Catholic schools 84, 251
Cherry Blossom Festival 50, 202
Cherry Blossoms 60
Chesapeake Bay 201
Cheyenne, Wyoming 82
Chicago 77, 79, 206
China 17, 24, 61, 97, 203, 239–240, 244
Chinatown 229
Chinese 22
Chrysler 95, 97–98
Civil Libertarians 39
Civil Rights Act of 1964 128
civil society 125, 127
CNBC 33, 170, 180, 185
CNN 82, 85–86, 89, 106
Code of Federal Regulations 194
Code of Hammurabi 27
Code of the District of Columbia 204
Colombia 24
Communist Party 239
Congo 24
Congress xvii, 94, 202, 207, 239
Connecticut 41, 152
Conservatives 10, 13
Constitution 126–127
Crimea 230
Crystal City 222
Cuba 94, 205, 212
Cuban 4, 215

D

Daimler Benz 102
Dale Carnegie xiii
Dallas 182

Dara Khosrowshahi xi, xiv, 16, 154, 160, 162, 186
David Rosenthal 82
Dayton, Ohio 38
D.C. City Council 207
DC Metro 5, 23, 45, 50, 83, 231
D.C. Metropolitan Police 26
D.C. Police 83
Defense Advanced Research 100
Democrats 10
Denver 74, 182
Department of Justice 229
de Tocqueville 126
Detroit 98
DIA 225
Diagnostic and Statistical Manual of Mental Disorders 72, 131
District of Columbia 4, 13, 36–37, 43, 67, 114, 201, 203–205
Diversity 246
Dolly Madison Blvd 235
Donald J. Trump 11, 202, 266
Draining the Swamp 2
Duke Medical Center 235
Dupont Circle 105, 230, 257
Durham 235
DWI violations 255
Dynamex 56, 154
Dynamex v. Superior Court 56, 154

E

Economic Policy Institute 52
Egypt 24
Elk Grove 91
El Salvador 24, 82
Emily Post 203
Employment Appeal Tribunal 58
Employment Tribunal 58
Enterprise 102
eponym xii, 189
Espionage 210, 240
Executive Office of the President 225
Exodus 27, 217
Expedia xiv, 16
Exxon 35–36
EZPass 5

270

F

Fairfax 30, 35, 216, 225
Fairfax City 216
Fair Labor Standards Act 66
FBI 26, 75, 83, 240
FBI, 83
Federalist Papers 126
Federal Trade Commission 150
Fidelity Investments 14
FIFA 231
firearms 13, 71, 74–75, 83, 88
FISA 40
Flexcar 102
Ford 94–95, 98, 100
Foreign Intelligence Surveillance
    Court 40
Forest Heights 4–5
Fort Belvoir 261
Fourth Amendment 39–40
France 24, 80–81, 126, 203
free markets 126
French 23
French Revolution xiv
Frigidaire xii
FUTA 52

G

Ganiou Gandonou 82
Garret Camp xi, xiii,
Gazprom 229
General Motors 95, 97
Gentrification 127, 181
George Danton xiv
George Mason University v
Georgetown 30, 230, 253
George Washington 28, 127, 201,
    222–223, 261
Georgia 98
German 4, 23, 97
Germany 4, 24, 81, 97, 203
gig economy 11, 55
GM 12, 33, 95–96, 98, 100, 102
GoGet 102
Gonzaga, 253
Governor Andrew Cuomo 11

GPS xv, xvi, 25, 30–31, 102, 138,
    196, 215, 233
Greeks 193

H

happenstance 8, 88
Harbir Parmar, 90
Harvard 96
Hellenistic Age 210
Hellenistic Age, the Roman
    Empire 210
Hillary Clinton 11, 128
hippie movement 129
Hispanics 4
Hollywood 127
home-grown extremists 75
Honda 36, 49, 59–62, 64, 98
Honda Civic 36, 49, 59, 62, 64, 99
Honda Insight Touring 59
House of Representatives 40
Houston 182
Howard Beach 90
Hungarian 4

I

Icewagon Flu 251
Illinois 98
Illinois, 98
India xvi, 24, 90, 203, 217, 221,
    236, 245
Indian Head Highway 83
Intelligence 22, 40, 210, 240
Intelligence Community (IC) 22
Inter-American Defense Board 22
Inter-American Development Bank
    (IDB) 22
Internal Revenue Service (IRS) 65
International Monetary Fund
    (IMF) 22
IPO 16–18, 28, 32–33, 156, 167–168,
    170, 173, 189, 261
Iran 11, 24
Iraq 11, 225
Ireland 24
Irish 4–5

Israel 24, 96
Italian 23
Italy 203
Ivory Coast 24

J

Jamal Khashoggi 163
James Bryce 126
James Madison 126
James River Insurance 141
Japan 24, 95, 97–98, 203, 205
Japanese 90, 96–98, 206, 249
Jason Dalton 76
John Deere 100
John Kasich 10
JUMP 103, 105
JUMP electric scooters 103
J.W. Marriott 92

K

Kalamazoo 76
Kansas 98
Kansas City 9
Katsucon 249
Kazakhstan 24
Keith Avila 91
Kentucky 98
Kid's Kruiser 263
Kid's Lyft 263
Kleenex xii
Korean 97, 206
Kremlin 229
Kuwait 24

L

Labor Department of New Jersey 158
laissez-faire 192
Landon 253
Lao Tzu 189
Las Vegas 42, 45, 74–76, 203, 218
Latin America 95
Laura Loomer 12–13
Liberals 10, 13, 15
Liberty gas station 35
Libya 11

Lincoln Memorial 202, 205
Lisbon 206
Logan Green 154, 196, 198
Logan Square 77
Los Angeles 40–41, 56, 79, 81, 83,
    154, 203–204, 206, 215
Lyft 3, 12–13, 15, 26, 29, 31–33, 41,
    43, 45–46, 54, 56–57, 69, 82,
    102–103, 133, 140, 146, 152–
    154, 196, 198, 228, 254, 256,
    261–263

M

Madrid 80, 206, 209
MAGA hats 13
Manatee County 79
Mandalay Bay Resort and Casino 74
Marjory Stoneman Douglas High
    School 75, 77
MARTA 181
Maryland 3–4, 26, 36, 41, 43, 45, 67,
    83, 251, 253, 255, 261
Massachusetts 39, 41, 57, 229, 231
Massachusetts Avenue 231
Maximillian Robespierre xiv
Mayor Bill de Blasio 11
McClean 251
McDonald's 20
McLean 235–237
MEDICARE 52–53
Medicare taxes 68
mental illness 8, 72–73, 76, 88–89,
    131–132
mentally ill 72–73, 75, 132
Mexicans 22
Mexico xiii, 5, 24, 80, 98, 206–207
Mexico City 80, 206
Miami Metro 9
Michael Brown 40
MicroMobility Robotics 104
Middle East 6
Middle Easterners 5
Mighty Mighty Bosstones 251
Mikhail Yuriyevich Lesin 229
minimum wage 66, 69, 256
Minnesota Avenue 5, 236

If the slogan for Google is 'Don't be evil', then the slogan for Uber is 'Do a little bit of evil & don't get caught.'

Peter Thiel
German-American entrepreneur

As a global disrupter, Uber is no stranger to conflict, and its instinct has always been pugilistic.

James B. Stewart
Lawyer, journalist, author

It is a truth universally acknowledged, in the enlightened Liberal semi-Socialist California circles in which I often move, that Uber is evil.

Jon Evans
CTO. HappyFunCorp

The regulatory systems in place disincentive innovation. It's intense to fight the red tape.

Travis Kalanick

If you get the product and technology right, then the rest usually falls into place.

Dara Khosrowshahi

Printed in the United States
By Bookmasters